Praise for *The All Americans*

"Anderson is a graceful storyteller and his is a compelling, heartfelt drama about the loss of innocence of a generation at war and on the football fields in another time in America. This is a fascinating look at World War II from a completely new point of view."

—Doug Stanton, *The New York Times*
bestselling author of *In Harm's Way*

"A tremendous tale from a fresh new voice."

—W. E. B. Griffin, *The New York Times*
bestselling author of *Retreat, Hell!*

"A gripping story of football and war. The bravery these men show on the battlefield can first be seen in the valor they display on the football field. Lars Anderson gives us a fresh, fascinating look at the Army/Navy rivalry and what the game of football was like in 1941. *The All Americans* reminds us of why, even in times of war, sport matters."

—Peter King, *Sports Illustrated* senior writer
and HBO football analyst

"Anderson has done a marvelous job of intertwining the worlds of history and sports. *The All Americans* uniquely combines the stories of four men, who share the distinction of being stars on the football field and war heroes."

—*Tulsa World*

D0197727

· ALSO BY LARS ANDERSON

The Proving Ground: A Season on the Fringe in NFL Europe

Pickup Artists: Street Basketball in America

The ALL AMERICANS

LARS ANDERSON

St. Martin's Press New York

THE ALL AMERICANS. Copyright © 2004 by Lars Anderson. All rights reserved. Printed in the United States of America. No part of this book may be reproduced in any manner whatsoever without written permission except in the case of brief quotations embodied in critical articles or reviews. For information, address St. Martin's Press, 175 Fifth Avenue, New York, N.Y. 10010.

Design by The Book Design Group

www.stmartins.com

Library of Congress Cataloging-in-Publication Data

Anderson, Lars.
    The all Americans / Lars Anderson.
        p. cm.
    Includes bibliographical references (p. 251)
    ISBN 0-312-30887-6 (hc)
    ISBN 0-312-30888-4 (pbk)
    EAN 978-0-312-30888-9
    1. Kauffman, Hal. 2. Busik, Bill. 3. Romanek, Henry. 4. Olds, Robin. 5. World War, 1939–1945—Biography. 6. United States. Army—Biography. 7. United States. Navy—Biography. 8. United States. Military Academy—Football—History. 9. United States. Naval Academy—Football—History. 10. Football players—United States—Biography. I. Title.

D736.A65 2004
940.54'1273'0922—dc22
[B]

2004050713

First St. Martin's Griffin Edition: November 2005

D 10 9 8 7 6 5 4 3 2

This is for my dad, Commander Robert L. Anderson, JAGC, and all the other Americans who rest in honor at Arlington National Cemetery in Arlington, Virginia

CONTENTS

PART ONE

PART TWO

On November 29, 1941, Army played Navy in front of 98,942 fans. Eight days later, the Japanese attacked Pearl Harbor. This is the story of four players' journey from the football field to the battlefield.

He either fears his fate too much,
  Or his deserts are small,
Who dare not put it to the touch,
  To win or lose it all.

—EARL OF MONTROSE,
a seventeenth-century Scottish commander

The
ALL AMERICANS

PART ONE

I

D-DAY

THE YOUNG MAN STOOD on the deck of the U.S.S. *Garfield*, look-ing across the English Channel, into darkness. It was just after midnight on June 6, 1944, and the defining hour of Henry Romanek's life was at hand. The *Garfield*, a transport ship, had just left the coast of England and was motoring south across the channel, its destination the waters off northern France, about ten miles outside of a quiet, enchanting beach the Allies called Omaha.

As Romanek gazed onto the black horizon, a cold wind dusting his cheeks, beams of moonlight filtered though the clouds to reveal an ar-mada of ships so vast that it took his breath away. Over five thousand ves-sels were plowing through the whitecaps, the column of ships stretching as far as Romanek's eyes could see to the east and the west. The day of reckoning, D-day, had arrived. "Good God," Romanek said softly to himself, "Lord, have mercy on us."

The twenty-four-year-old Romanek was a platoon leader in the 149th Engineer Combat Battalion. Like all the soldiers in his company, he was dressed for battle. He wore a steel combat helmet that was outfit-ted with a fabric interlining. A life belt (a flotation device) was wrapped snugly around his waist. His first layer of clothing was a wool undershirt, wool underwear, and thick wool combat socks. On top of that were protective leggings, wool pants, a flannel shirt, an olive drab jacket, and waterproof jumpshoes. He also carried a field bag on his back that held a pancho, toilet articles, a towel, canned food, and a knife, fork, and spoon. A loaded carbine hung over his shoulder, and his dog tags dangled from his neck. On the ring finger of his left hand was his graduation ring from West Point, his dearest possession.

Romanek had received the ring a year earlier, and now as he looked down on it, the black onyx stone glittered in the moonlight. Romanek was in charge of a platoon of forty-five men, and they were constantly asking him to tell stories from his days at the military academy, especially what it was like to be an Army football player. Romanek had been a two-way standout at the Point in 1941 and '42, playing tackle on both offense and defense. The game he was most often questioned about was the '41 Army-Navy contest, which was played before 98,942 screaming fans at Philadelphia's Municipal Stadium. As Romanek drew closer to what he knew would be the bloodiest fight of his life, that game was still alive in his mind, its details burned into his memory. He must have told his men about that Army-Navy clash a hundred times, maybe more.

Though three and half years had passed since he last donned an Army football uniform, Romanek still looked like the strapping star he was. Barrel-chested and long-armed, Romanek, at 6' 2", 195 pounds, was more toned than muscular. He didn't seem to have an ounce of fat on his tight frame. He had a fair complexion, sleepy blue eyes, caramel-colored hair that was in a crew cut, and a soft, gentle smile that made ladies blush whenever he looked their way. He was, by all accounts, a dashing figure, the kind of clean-cut, riveting young man that people turned to stare at whenever he strolled into a room.

Yet the boys in his platoon—and to Romanek, they were *boys*, as most of them were still teenagers—looked up to Romanek not because of his handsome looks but because he was their leader. Romanek thought of his men as an extension of his own family, and he worried and fretted about them probably more than he should have. He spent every night after training reading all their V-mail letters that they were sending to loved ones back home. Because Romanek was the official censor in charge of screening all outgoing U.S. mail for his platoon, he came to know all of his men's deepest secrets and greatest fears. He talked to the men in his platoon about everything, from how they missed their sweethearts back home to the art of making a proper block on the football field. Even when Romanek was agitated, he rarely raised his voice when speaking with his men. Instead, in a firm and steady tone, he would simply lay out what needed to be done and how it would be accomplished. Then he always ended by saying how much he trusted everyone and how they should treat each other like they were blood brothers.

Romanek's soldiers were from the Midwest, mostly raised on farms and in small towns in Iowa, Missouri, and Nebraska, and they were as gritty as any soldiers Romanek had ever been around. Romanek cared deeply for them, which made him vulnerable on this early morning: Romanek knew that many of them wouldn't survive the coming day. "If all the soldiers on our side are as good as you guys," Romanek told his men a few days before the invasion, "the Germans don't have a chance."

Along with the rest of his battalion, Romanek and his men had sailed out of New York harbor on the early morning of December 29, 1943, and had spent the better part of six months on the south coast of England preparing for the invasion. The 149th practiced everything from landing on beaches to laying live mines to booby-trapping houses with explosives. The combat engineers had perhaps the most complex mission of any on D-day. They would be among the first to hit the beaches, and they were assigned multiple tasks. They were to identify and blow up any beach obstacle—most were large pieces of steel rail—that would interfere with the landing of troops as the tide began to rise. Then, as quickly as possible, they were to set up signs that would act as guideposts for incoming landing craft. Finally, if they were still alive, they were to clear roads from the beach and set up supply dumps.

Romanek had gone over the mission dozens of times with his men. He explained to them that the first assault waves on D-day were going to be DD tanks ("duplex drive" tanks that were modified M4 Sherman tanks, which could travel on water as well as land). These tanks would be rigged with rubber devices so—the hope was—they would float. The tanks would be followed by a wave of infantry and engineers. Romanek's engineering platoon was married to the 116th Infantry Regiment of the 29th Infantry Division. They would ride into Omaha Beach together on landing craft, and they would be among the first of the forty thousand men scheduled to land on Omaha, a beach that was about six miles long and slightly crescent-shaped. Romanek reminded his men over and over that what they really had to focus on was erecting the large marking panels for the D-3 exit so that subsequent landing craft would know where to go.

Now on the *Garfield*, the landings at Omaha just hours away, Romanek told his platoon to gather around him. When Romanek looked at his men, their eyes seemed to glow like full moons—wide-open and bursting with anticipation. "Now is our opportunity to participate in the greatest armada ever launched in history," Romanek said above the drone of the *Garfield*'s engines. "And history will be made by what we do here today. Now let's do our jobs and make our country proud." There were no replies from any of Romanek's men. They merely stared at their leader in silence.

At around two in the morning, when the *Garfield* was about twelve miles off the coast of France, the order was sounded; "Now hear this! All assault troops report to your debarkation areas."

Romanek made his way to the spot where he would descend onto a LCM (Landing Craft, Mechanized) that would ferry half of his platoon—approximately twenty-three men—and about eighty infantry personnel to the beach. Along with the hundred or so men on the LCM, there would also be explosive devices and marking panels on board, which Romanek and his platoon of engineers would erect. The marking panels were stored in twenty-foot-long polelike casings. The markers were large triangles that would be staked into the sand and would signify the D-3 exit at Les Moulins, an area on the beach that included a road that led inland to St. Laurent—a D-day objective for the infantry. Romanek carried one of the cases with him as he walked to the disembarkation point.

Boarding the LCMs was treacherous. The small vessels had already been lowered into the water and they were now bobbing up and down in the ten-foot swells. The men threw a rope net over the side of the *Garfield*. In a firm tone, Romanek told his men to go, to climb down the net and then jump into their LCM. "This won't be easy," Romanek said as men began to descend. "Don't lose your grip." Because the engineers were loaded down with weapons, ammo, rations, and a life preserver, mobility was limited. At the disembarking point, one of the men turned to Romanek. His face was white and he was so cold with fear he could hardly move. "Sir, I'm scared," he told Romanek.

"So am I," said Romanek, trying to calm the boy's spirit with encouraging words. "Listen, we're all apprehensive. But don't worry. I'll be by your side the whole way. Nothing will happen to you."

"But sir . . ."

"Come on, soldier, get in," Romanek said.

"Yes, sir."

As a parting salute before going over the side, Romanek took out an American-made glass bottle of beer from his pack. His wife Betsy had mailed the beer to Romanek while he was in England, and he took a big, hearty swig. He then handed it to his men and they each gulped a swallow and passed it along in silence.

Once everyone was on board, the engineers stood in the back of the LCM, the infantrymen in front. They were packed so tightly there was no room to sit. The LCM then pulled away from the *Garfield* and circled around to get in formation with the other landing craft. The moon had disappeared behind the clouds, and it was nearly as dark as blindness. The LCM continued to pitch sharply in the deep swells. Waves punished the sides of Romanek's LCM, sending sprays of water into the craft, quickly soaking the men. Within minutes, many of the men were vomiting as the LCM rocked up and down, side to side, up and down. Romanek had spent numerous days at sea in his young life, but now, for the first time, even he became seasick. This wasn't promising, this sad start to the invasion.

As Romanek tried his best to inflate the morale of his men, he noticed that one of the 116th infantry division's battalion commanders was in his LCM. Major Sidney V. Bingham Jr., was twenty-nine years old, but to Romanek he seemed like an old man, a savvy veteran. Glancing around at all the men on board, Romanek was struck by how young everyone looked. But not Major Bingham. Confidence seemed to radiate from his eyes, and it relaxed Romanek. He had seen this look before, many times before actually, on Earl "Red" Blaik, his football coach at Army. It was the dead-set-to-win expression that Blaik always wore on his face before a big game.

Raised in Rutherford, New Jersey, Romanek first became interested in West Point during his junior year at Rutherford High. Romanek was on the Rutherford football team that won the 1937 Group Three Northern New Jersey State Championship. Two weeks after capturing the state title, the team held a banquet dinner. The keynote speaker was an assistant coach from Army who delivered a pep talk to the players. He concluded by presenting all of the boys with gold footballs that commemorated their championship season.

Before he stepped down from the dais, the coach asked the players to raise their hands if they were A students. Romanek, along with two of his teammates, lifted his arm. The coach later chatted with Romanek one-on-one for a few minutes, eventually asking Romanek if he'd like to come visit the Point. A junior in high school, Romanek had never given serious consideration to the U.S. Military Academy, but he was possessed with a devouring curiosity—he could suck the information right out of a room—and so he said, "Sure, I'll visit. Why not?"

A few weeks later Romanek rode in a car with his coach, Eddie Tryon, to West Point. Not expecting anything, Romanek was awed by the place. The cadets in their sharp dress uniforms, the granite buildings, the broad green Plain, the granite-cliff shores of the Hudson, the motto of duty, honor, country—all of it stirred feelings inside him that he didn't even know existed. The assistant football coach chaperoned Romanek around campus and took him to the doctor's office for a physical. Romanek passed, and by the time he was shaking hands with the coach and preparing to get back into Tryon's car, both coach and player hoped that they'd meet each other again. Young Henry Romanek had seen his future.

Aside from his grades and athletic ability, what made Romanek such an attractive West Point candidate to the Army coaches was his leadership. His high school coaches marveled at how, when things went bad on the field, Romanek was the player everyone seemed to look to for answers. Even when he was a high school junior, in 1937, Romanek had a reassuring manner. This was evident when Rutherford hosted Passaic High at the end of the season. Rutherford was the state's Group Three champion, Passaic was New Jersey's Group Four champion. Held at Rutherford Senior High School Field on a snowy afternoon, the game was a defensive battle. Romanek, playing the line on both offense and defense with no substitutions, was a terror, ripping opening holes on offense for their star back Jimmy Blumenstock—who would later play for Fordahm and the New York Giants—and leading his team in tackles on defense. Passaic, however, pulled the game out late in the fourth quarter when their kicker drilled a 45-yard field goal in the snow to give his team a 3–0 win.

In the locker room afterwards Romanek walked from player to player, telling each one that he had nothing to be ashamed of, that they all had left their hearts out on the field. Romanek's performance against Passaic caught the attention of college coaches all around the tri-state area. Scholarship offers would soon come, but once he toured the grounds at West Point, his mind was made up: He wanted to go to the U.S. Military Academy.

Now it was 5:30 in the morning on D-day. As Romanek's LCM motored toward the beach, the loud thudding of the engine made it difficult to communicate. Nerves were tense, but the men were optimistic that the heavy naval gunfire of the Allies would destroy the Germans' shore defenses before they arrived at the beach. "That beach is going to be all torn up by the time we get there," said one solider in Romanek's platoon to another. "I bet we won't even see a single bullet!"

The LCM sped closer to the sand. At about 5:45 the first hint of daylight started to sliver across the eastern sky, and the Allied bombers began assaulting the German positions at Normandy. The Germans responded with antiaircraft fire, which from Romanek's position appeared to fill the sky with giant sparks. Here it was, he thought, the start of the D-day battle, two forces going at each other as mightily as angels and demons. Still Romanek and his men pushed forward to the beach.

The German shore batteries started firing on the naval fleet, the shells whizzing over the landing crafts. Seconds later, the fleet responded with a fury. As Romanek stood in the back of his LCM that was about four miles off shore, the air filled with the sound of a thousand thunderclaps bursting at once. Romanek could feel the noise in his chest—*thump, thump, thump*—with every breath. When he looked up into the still-dark sky, there were luminous streaks of flames shooting in every direction. There was no going back now.

Every gun in the Allied fleet was firing on the German shore batteries, pillboxes, fortified housing—anything that could pose a threat to the incoming landing craft. By 5:50 A.M., the first wave of landing crafts was closing in on the five beaches of Normandy. Once the LCTs (Landing Craft Tank) started deploying their DD tanks—the tanks that were designed to "swim" ashore with their rubber devices—the warships would lift their guns and begin shooting at targets inland. The first American troops were about to set foot in France on D-day, and the Allied fleet didn't want to take out any of its own with friendly fire.

Romanek could see the shoreline. But something wasn't right, and the sight made his skin feel numb. The DD tanks, which were supposed to provide cover for Romanek and his engineers, weren't swimming. In fact, they were sinking, dropping into the water like boulders. The swells were so high that the tanks simply disappeared into the water as they rolled off their LCTs. Romanek could see men desperately trying to crawl up through the hatches as the tanks sank, but most didn't make it out. Suddenly on Romanek's LCM, fear crept into everyone's heart.

Just as the first wave of Allied troops was about to hit the beaches, an Army teammate of Romanek's named Robin Olds was in the air above

Normandy, flying in his P-38 and prowling for Germans. Olds' orders were strict: He was only there to blast away at enemy planes should they appear. Olds had been firmly told by his commander that he wasn't to fire on anything on the ground. "We might accidentally take out our own guys," Olds was told in a briefing meeting before the invasion. "We're only there to keep enemy planes from strafing the ground."

As Olds buzzed over Normandy steady at 500 feet, he was overwhelmed by what he saw. It seemed as if every ship ever built was visible in the distance, firing on Normandy. Down below him the sea seemed to be crawling with large dark water bugs, all inching closer to land, every landing craft leaving a white wake in its trail. It would take Olds hours to count the number of vessels that were in his field of view. "Jesus Christ," Olds mumbled to himself. "It looks like the end of world down there."

Olds knew that his good friend Henry Romanek was somewhere below him, preparing to hit the beach. Over the last five years, Olds and Romanek had become the tightest of friends, almost as close as brothers. They attended prep school together in Washington, D.C., in 1939 for one year and they had played football together at West Point for three seasons. Among the Cadet players Romanek was known for his commanding presence and unflappability; Olds, a tackle who played on the line with Romanek, was renowned for being the toughest player on the squad. "If Robin ever wrestled an alligator," Romanek once told a friend, "I'd feel sorry for that alligator."

Olds' father, Major General Robert Olds, was a renowned pilot who had flown in World War I. Robert stayed in the service after the war to end all wars and taught aviation at Langley Airfield in Hampton, Virginia, where Robin grew up. As a boy, planes mesmerized Robin; he loved watching them take off and land at Langley. The sight of so much power always held his eyes, so much so that by age six he was already dreaming of one day flying a plane. "I'm going to become a pilot just like you," he announced to his father at dinner one evening.

"Well, you better be prepared to work for it," Robert Olds replied to his son. "Work hard and never back down to anybody, and you can do anything."

Some afternoons father and son would sit on their porch at their base home and watch the planes land. Little Robin liked to impress his father by identifying the approaching aircraft simply by listening to the distant sound of its engine. By age ten, he had such a discerning ear that he could tell the difference between the roar of the Pratt & Whitney radials in the Keystone bombers, the gentle hum of the Curtiss V-12 in the Curtiss P-6Es, and the loud belching and clacking of older planes, which were usually powered by antiquated Liberty engines.

At night, Robin enjoyed reading pulp magazines about World War I fighter aces, romantic as they were about how a battle unfolded. On these pages there was no mention of blood, or screams of horror, or grown men crying themselves to sleep at night. Inside these magazines were pictures and words that glorified the life and times of the fighter ace. His father tried to tell him what it was really like, that there was more to being a fighter pilot than winning medals and receiving kisses from beautiful blondes with heart-shaped mouths of red lipstick, but Robin had already made up his mind. He was going to follow in the footsteps of his father. This was one dream he wasn't going to let die on his pillow.

Other than flying with his dad, which Robin first did at the age of eight in an open cockpit byplane, Olds' other passion as a young boy was riding horses. Most days after school Robin would head to the stables at the base and tend to the horses that many of the officers rode. By age fifteen Robin had developed into a proficient rider himself, and a few officers at the base suggested that he'd make a fine candidate for the cavalry. But Olds paid no attention to them. Ever since he saw the 1934 movie *Flirtation Walk*, in which actor Dick Powell played a West Point officer, Olds had decided that his life path would lead to West Point. There on the Hudson Highlands he would become an officer, learn to fly and, if he could find the time, he might play football.

Olds reveled in the hand-to-hand combat that took place in the trenches of the football field. In 1937, his junior year at Hampton High and two years before he would go to prep school, Olds helped lead the team to the state title. By then, Olds had already developed a reputation for being the roughest player on the squad. At 6' 2", 190 pounds, Olds played tackle both on offense and defense. He even looked the part of a fierce player. With his short blond crew cut, his coat-hanger shoulders, and hands that were almost as big as catcher's mitts, he looked like he didn't even need to wear pads. His teammates often marveled at the intensity that flickered in his mischievous blue-gray eyes. He treated every play in practice—indeed, every drill in practice—like he was fighting with an enemy in a blood feud. When his temper reared, he had a mean streak that was so wicked even players on his own team feared him. Sometimes, it was as if a dark emotion suddenly sprang from the basement of his soul, and it usually left the person he was battling on the field wishing he'd never met Robin Olds. "Football ain't for sissies," Olds liked to tell his teammates. "You gotta be tough, and you gotta be a man. Don't ever back down, not to anyone."

Romanek looked at his watch. It read 6:30 A.M. Though his LCM was scheduled to land in a few minutes, they were still about six hundred yards from shore. Romanek eyed his men. Almost all of them were seasick, their faces as white as milk. They had been on the landing craft for about four hours and nearly everyone had vomited at least once. By this time Romanek's LCM had taken in so much water from the crashing of the waves that the men had to use their helmets to bail it out. Romanek and his men couldn't wait to get to the beach. Anything, they figured, was better than this.

They pushed closer. Through the black plumes of smoke that rose from the explosions on the beach, Romanek could see that the first wave of LCUPs had hit the beach—to his horror he saw that the infantry were being slaughtered. Entire LCUPs were getting blown to pieces by the German shore batteries, which clearly hadn't been disabled by naval gunfire. In a matter of heartbeats it was clear to Romanek that very little on Omaha Beach was going according to plan. Many of the rockets had fallen short of their targets, while others had simply missed. The Germans were firing artillery and machine guns from the bluff, and the soldiers on the beach were easy, inviting targets. Adding to the confusion were the rough seas and strong wind, which threw the landing crafts off course. Very few of the Allied units were landing where they were supposed to.

Romanek's landing craft continued to breast the waves, moving closer. At a distance of three hundred yards, Romanek could see that all the steel, X-shaped landing obstacles had been exposed because of the ebb tide. He looked up at the beach. The first wave of infantrymen, who had been scheduled to land three minutes ahead of Romanek's LCM, were instructed to gouge the German infantry. But instead, Romanek saw that many of the Americans had turned around and were diving for cover behind the obstacles. But there were few places to hide. They were under heavy machine-gun, mortar, rifle, and artillery fire. One after another, they fell to the sand, face-first.

As the LCM got within a hundred yards of the beach, Romanek noticed many soldiers were floating with the tide toward the beach, dead, their faces turned down to the water. He looked up at the beach and, through the haze of smoke from the grass fires that drifted down from the bluffs, could see that the beach had become a blood-stained killing field. Directly in front of Romanek, up on the cliffs, he saw a cherry red flicker of flame. A moment later there was a loud explosion on the beach, a black burst of smoke, then dozens of soldiers sprawled on the ground, all dead. "Everybody stay focused on what we need to do," Romanek yelled above the battle noise. "Let's just do our jobs and everything else will take care of itself."

Romanek and his men, who were all soaking wet, put on their assault gas masks. They expected a chemical attack, most likely the use of mustard gas, and a sealed mask would offer some protection. The infantrymen in the front of the LCM grabbed their rifles and machine guns and carbines. Romanek could hear the clack of bolts being drawn and rammed as the infantryman prepared to shoot. Incoming enemy fire started hitting the LCM—*ping, ping, ping*. The LCM began to slow.

At about fifty yards out, the LCM came to a stop, causing all the men to lurch forward. Several landing craft to Romanek's right and left were sinking or burning. The Coxswain in Romanek's LCM, a young coast-guardsman, quickly moved from the protected tiller in the back of the LCM to the front to release the security clamps off the ramp. As he returned on the starboard upper walkway, bullets struck his head and chest. He fell, lifelessly, onto the troops in the LCM. He was the first man on Romanek's LCM to die on this day.

The square-faced ramp on the LCM came down. Everyone yelled, "Go, go, go!" But several German machine guns and artillery batteries were concentrating their fire on the ramp exit. Romanek and his men were still in the back of the LCM and now they could see their fellow soldiers being ripped apart by bullets. Blood and limbs and intestines flew through the air, the men falling forward in heaps. "We gotta get out of here," Romanek yelled to his engineers. Yet some of his men were frozen, unable to move. One soldier's head was blown off; another was killed when both of his legs were torn off his torso.

Romanek continued to yell to his men, telling them to push forward, to complete their mission. All the planning, all the months of training, all the miles they had traveled, it had all been done for this moment. But now? Now, even before Romanek had gotten off his LCM, more than half of his engineers and more than half of the infantrymen he'd been riding with were dead. Order was slipping away.

Still Romanek pushed forward. He could hear one bullet after the next clank off the metal sheeting of the LCM. "Get the hell out of here!" Romanek yelled again at his men. Many soldiers who'd been hit had fallen and were slumped over, draped in blankets of blood, impeding the path of Romanek and his engineers who were still alive. Finally, Romanek made it to the exit ramp. He was pulling several of the cases that stored the beach panel markers. He tossed them to a few of his men who'd made it to the water. Then Romanek, who was weighed down with about forty pounds of equipment and gear, jumped as fast and as far as he could into five feet of water.

In the closed cockpit of his P-38 Lightning, Olds couldn't stop looking down at the battle, his eyes drawn to the carnage taking place below. Flying low at about 500 feet, Olds and the other pilots from the 434th Fighter Squadron of the 479th Fighter Group buzzed over Omaha to protect the Allies in the sea and on the beach from attacks from the Luftwaffe, the German Air Force. But the Luftwaffe never appeared. "We're not doing anything up here," Olds said to another pilot over his radio. "Our boys are getting killed down there. God damn it, we've got to do something!"

"Remember our orders," Lt. Harold "Bud" Grenning, Olds' wingman, replied. "We're only here to take out the Luftwaffe. That's it."

"I know," said Olds, "but those are our boys down there."

Olds continued to roar over Normandy, flying through the clouds of smoke that billowed up from the battle. He itched to pull the trigger in his P-38, which was powered by two liquid-cooled engines, had a top speed of about 400 mph, and carried a 20 mm cannon and four machine guns in its nose. But Olds knew better than to disobey a direct order, so with an aching heart he just watched the destruction and deadly chaos unfold on Omaha beach. His frustration grew by the moment, knowing that guys like Henry Romanek, his friend and teammate, were down there dying.

The bullet pierced the left side of Romanek's chest even before he hit the water. It momentarily paralyzed him and robbed him of breath. It was as if a burning rod had just been shoved through his lungs. The gas mask container Romanek was wearing kept his head above the water, the air in it keeping his head afloat. He was in a daze. He couldn't focus on time, place, or purpose. His thoughts drifted through years of memories, with no order, like random dreams.

He knew that today was June 6, 1944. If there hadn't been a war— and if his course load hadn't been cut from four years to three at the U.S.

Military Academy—he knew that today would have been his graduation day from the Point. How he wished he could be back there right now, living in those crowded hours of happiness when he was a cadet and an Army football player. It seemed so long ago that he was lining up alongside Robin Olds in their leather helmets and crouching in a three-point stance. That was a different world and a different time when Romanek and Olds took on Navy and their star tailback Bill Busik in front of almost a hundred thousand fans in Philadelphia on an autumn afternoon in 1941. For a little more than two hours, Romanek and Olds were the biggest sports stars in America, as most of the nation had tuned their radios to the game and listened to the crackling account. Thinking about West Point caused Romanek to realize that he didn't want to lose his class ring, not here, not in five feet of freezing-cold water off the coast of France. His ring was as important to him as oxygen. He looked at his left hand in the water, saw the gleam of the thick gold band around his finger, and clenched his fist. "I can't lose my ring," he thought to himself. "I can't lose it. And I don't want to die here today."

After a few moments, Romanek began to regain his senses. He popped off his life belt so his feet could touch the sandy bottom of the water. He pulled off his gas mask container, stripped off his backpack and dropped most of his gear. He knew he had to get out of the water, but still felt sluggish, as if he could only move in slow motion. He could hear bullets hitting the water—*plop, plop, plop*—all around him. Every sound, every scent, seemed magnified. Romanek wanted to get to his men, his soldiers. He felt responsible for them; he could see many of them being cut down right before his eyes. Romanek had spent months talking to his platoon about the brotherhood of soldiering, about the kinship that bound all of them together, about the obligation each one had to look out for everyone in their band, but now Romanek was helpless to do that. "What's going to happen?" Romanek kept thinking to himself. "Who's going to show them where to go? Who's going to help them survive?"

Slowly, the fog lifted from his mind. Romanek marshalled his thoughts. He knew he had good sergeants; he trusted them, and he realized that they would take his place if he were to die here in the water now. That was the order of things. Ever since he first arrived at West Point, both in the classroom and on the football field, Romanek had been taught about the need for order, for preparedness. But now he was trapped in a situation that had no order, a situation that no man could really be prepared for.

Romanek tried to move his arms and legs and make his way to shore, but his strength had left him; it had leaked out through the holes in his chest and back. Still he tried to inch his way forward, but his body wouldn't respond to what his brain was telling it to do. He could now see blood—his own blood—rising up from the steel-gray water. "Oh God," he thought, "I *am* going to die here."

As Romanek wearily stood in five feet of water, running out of breath, a navy corpsman spotted him. Wearing a navy medic helmet that had a small red cross inside a white circle and a Red Cross armband, the corpsman came running from the beach and plowed into the water. There were numerous men floating in the sea who were already dead—too numerous to count—but there was Romanek, his head above water, gasping for air, still alive. The corpsman grabbed Romanek and, without a word, he put an arm around him and dragged him ashore. When they got to the beach, they lay huddled behind a metal beach obstacle as bullets continued to perforate the air around them. Romanek looked up at the corpsman, saw that his big eyes were wide with fear. He was a just a boy really, and even in Romanek's addled state he could tell that the young man was scared as all hell, as frightened as anyone Romanek had ever seen. "Let's head for cover," the corpsman yelled.

He grabbed Romanek's right hand and began to pull him across the gold, wet sand. Romanek tried to push with his legs as he was being dragged, but all of his strength was gone. They were trying to make it to the shingle, which was about two hundred yards away and would put them out of the line of machine-gun and mortar fire coming from the bluff, where the Germans had dug trenches. The shingle, named for the small stones that washed up there, was the first rise in the terrain. Located at the high water mark, the shingle on the western edge of Omaha Beach piled against a roadway that ranged in height up to five feet.

As the navy corpsman dragged Romanek across the open beach, they moved from beach obstacle to beach obstacle, ducking behind the steel rails to avoid being hit. Whenever they rested, both Romanek and the corpsman could hear the ping of slugs bouncing off the metal structures. They also heard the cries of the mortally wounded; some shrieked in pain, others pleaded for help. Body parts were scattered everywhere; arms, legs, and feet were lying in the sand.

While being pulled, all Romanek could do was watch the men behind him. Another wave of landing craft had just hit the beach, and, in some instances, not a single soldier had made it out of his boat. Men would fall as if they'd been hit by lightning as soon as their ramp came down; others would get blown into dozens of blood-splattering pieces. Romanek couldn't tell how many of his boys were now dead on the beach.

Supreme Allied Commander Dwight Eisenhower and his planners didn't know it, but the night before the attack, the Germans had reinforced the area with an extra division. On the night of June 5 the German 352nd Infantry Division had performed a training exercise at this precise location and were still there when the Allied troops invaded. Now death was everywhere; Romanek could even feel it tugging on his own soul. With every passing second he was losing more blood, and it was getting harder to breathe, harder to focus on anything but how badly he wanted to close his eyes and sleep.

The corpsman and Romanek finally reached the shingle. The corpsman laid Romanek down on the small rocks that had washed up there. Romanek, still struggling to take in air, again looked up at the corpsman's childish face and uttered his first words since being shot. "I played football at Army," Romanek said in a voice barely louder than a whisper. "I played in two Army-Navy games, and I never knew navy guys could be as nice as you. Thanks. The navy should be proud that they have a guy like you."

Moments later, Romanek was silent. He went into full-blown shock. He was swallowing his tongue and shaking violently, his body rattling with twitches. The corpsman, realizing what was happening, put a finger into Romanek's mouth, and pulled his tongue back. He then wrapped his arms tightly around him hoping to warm Romanek and save his life. This was all the corpsman could do, so he hugged Romanek as hard as he could. Still, Romanek stayed silent.

2

THE ARMY BOYS

FOUR YEARS EARLIER . . .

Carrying nothing but a wallet in his back pocket, the young man strode purposefully through the grimy catacombs of Penn Station in New York City. He had just stepped off the local train from Washington, D.C., and as he climbed the stairs that rose from the tracks below, he walked with the earnestness of someone who knew exactly where he was going—both in the next few minutes and in life. High above him, gold chandeliers hung from the vaulted ceiling. The morning sunshine rinsed through the station's towering arched windows, setting the station aglow in an almost heavenly light. Men in red caps flitted about the concourse, pushing carts of luggage past the Roman columns and the marble sculptures. Businessmen dressed in bowler hats and wing tips clawed their way through the rush-hour crush, many carrying a copy of the *New York Times*, whose front-page, triple-decker headline blared: RUSSIANS BATTLE RETIRING RUMANIANS; LAND TANKS FROM AIR IN OCCUPATION; CHAMBERLAIN DENOUNCES PEACE TALK. It was July 1, 1940, and on this Monday morning eighteen-year-old Robin Olds felt like he was about to step into a dream. The place he'd fantasized about ever since he was a little boy was just another fifty miles up the Hudson River Valley. He could hardly believe it: West Point was near.

As Olds wove his way toward the uptown subway train that would carry him toward a ferry that would take him across the Hudson River and drop him off at a train reserved for new cadets bound for West Point, Henry Romanek sat on the front steps at a friend's house in Fort Totten, Queens. For the past month Romanek, like Olds, had been counting down the days on the calendar, anticipating the arrival of this life-altering morning. The nineteen-year-old Romanek was waiting for his friend's father to come out of the house and drive him and his buddy to the Point.

"It's finally here," Romanek told his friend, Oliver Bucher, as they prepared to climb into the '38 Ford four door owned by Colonel Bucher. "I've got butterflies in my stomach."

Romanek and Olds both looked forward to renewing their friendship once they arrived at the Point. For six months of the previous year they had lived and studied together at Millard Prep in Washington, D.C., a school established to ready students for the entrance exams at the U.S. Military and Naval Academies. Founded by Homer B. Millard, a West Point graduate who fought in World War I, Millard Prep was an intense institution, a place that was as serious as a court room. Though the students didn't march and they weren't trained in firearms, they were given a taste of the disciplined lifestyle the service academies would demand. The days revolved around academic tutoring and studying; at night the lights went out in the dorms at precisely 10:00 P.M. The one reprieve came on Saturday evenings, when the school gates were opened and the students were free to leave campus. No student liked to skylark on Saturdays more than Olds, and when he and Romanek ventured off the campus and into the night, Olds often told his friend, "Let's see what kind of trouble we can rustle up."

Romanek and Olds both enrolled at Millard after graduating from high school, and they quickly bonded. They both loved sports—football in particular—and they both could talk for days about their hatred of Hitler. Their personalities, though opposite, meshed well: Romanek was steady and calm, and Olds was tempestuous and emotional. Eventually they started double-dating on the weekends, escorting their ladies to dances on the roof of the Army Navy Club in Arlington, Virginia. When they returned to campus, they'd invariably wind up wrestling in the hallway until someone—usually an irate teacher—told them to stop. Sometimes a whole group of boys would tussle, and more often than not, Olds and Romanek would be the last two standing. Their friendship never wavered, even as Olds and Romanek went after each other as if they were fighting a steel-cage match and the loser would be tossed to the lions.

When they got caught their punishment would be to do as many pushups as they could, right there on the spot. But neither minded this late-night exercise, because both Olds and Romanek enjoyed testing the limits of their physical strength the same way most people enjoyed a trip to the soda fountain. This was why they could raise so much hell on the football field, as the nation would soon find out.

Robin Olds was a hard-core, never-quit perfectionist, a trait he acquired from his father. Robin's mother died when he was four years old. As a single parent, Robert Olds taught his boy two lessons with drill-Sergeant intensity: always be tough and, no matter what the circumstances, always mind your manners. An imposing figure with big shoulders and a military-style crew cut, Colonel Olds' words were law, so Robin obeyed his father's demands without question. Consequently, around the airbase at Langley, young Robin had a reputation of being a courteous kid.

In his senior year of high school, Olds received a football scholarship offer from the Virginia Military Institute. Dartmouth also offered Olds a financial aid package if he would play football for them, but he turned both of them down to attend Millard and get ready for the West Point entrance exam. In his free time at Millard, Olds often listened to radio broadcasts of Hitler's speeches. He couldn't understand a lick of what he was saying, but the way he ranted and raved, Olds was convinced that Hitler was a madman.

One afternoon shortly after Germany invaded Poland in 1939, Olds got an idea. He was sitting in a classroom when the brainstorm came to him, and as soon as the bell rang he tore out of his seat and left the Millard campus with a wild hope in his heart: He wanted to become a pilot for the RCAF, the Royal Canadian Air Force. Olds figured this was the quickest way he could get overseas and join the fight. He walked into the recruiting office with a confident smile on his face and boldly asked where someone signed if he wanted to kill some Germans. He was handed an application, but as Olds filled it out an officer grew suspicious. Though Olds had a mature, developed physique, he still had a boyish face.

"How old are you, son?" asked the officer.

"Um, I'm twenty," he replied, even though he was actually eighteen.

"Sorry, son, you have to have a parent sign this consent form," Olds was told as the officer handed him the consent form. "Come back after you have a signature."

When Robin took the form to his father, the colonel hit the roof. "You're going to prep school and then the military academy," he told Robin. "End of discussion." Olds wanted to explain it all to his dad, how he had a plan, how he longed to fly in the war that raged in Europe, but instead he bit his lip and said nothing. It was no use trying to argue with his father. He'd have to wait until the United States got dragged into the conflict before he could begin his own personal battle with the Nazis. The only question was, how long would it be before that happened?

To make sure his boy won an appointment to the academy, Colonel Olds made several calls to congressmen asking them to support Robin's candidacy. (To gain entrance to both the U.S. Military and Naval Academies in the late 1930s, a prospective cadet or midshipman had to be appointed by a congressman—the same process that is still required today.) He finally found a representative from the state of Pennsylvania who agreed to make Robin his first alternate on the condition that Robin spend time living in his district. So after Olds graduated from Millard in the spring of 1940, he packed his bags and traveled alone to the southwestern corner of Pennsylvania, the heart of coal country, to a small burg called Uniontown, a place that to Olds seemed as remote as the dark side of the moon.

"It's awful," Olds told his dad over the phone after he arrived. "My God, it's the pits. It's going to be tough just to last a few weeks out here. There's nothing to do."

Olds lived in a tiny room at the YMCA and worked for an army recruiter. To earn extra money, he swept floors at various grocery stores. Sometimes on his way to work Olds saw miners who had just come up from the Pennsylvania earth, their faces plastered with dirt, their eyes devoid of hope. The place depressed Olds, and just when he thought he couldn't stand it one more day, he received a call from his father on the first of June. He had good news: Congressman Daniel Flood had decided to give Robin an appointment. His dad also said that he'd passed his entrance exam. "So it's official, son," Colonel Olds said, "You're going to West Point. You've been accepted."

Exactly one month after learning of his acceptance to the academy, Olds was making his way to West Point. After arriving in Penn Station, he took a subway uptown, then caught a ferry that took him across the Hudson River and dropped him off at the train station in Weehawken,

New Jersey. Because he'd grown up in a military family and because he knew as much about West Point as an outsider could, Olds didn't bother bringing any clothes or toiletries with him. The academy, he knew, would take care of all that.

In Weehawken, he boarded a reserved train for the last leg of his trip. As he took his seat, he noticed that one of his childhood friends, Gordon Steele, was sitting a few seats in front of him. Olds plopped down next to Steele, and the two of them talked excitedly of how these next four years would be the best of their lives. As the train rolled up the Hudson River Valley, past Bear Mountain, Olds knew West Point was close. In a matter of minutes he would become a Beast (meaning a new cadet) and he knew he'd be hazed by the upperclassmen. Some extremely difficult times awaited him, he understood that, but he was also sure of one other thing: He'd eat dirt before he would quit.

The four-door '38 Ford wove in and out of the midday traffic, motoring north up the Hudson River Valley along the Storm King Highway. It was approaching noon on a July afternoon that felt as hot as a kiln. As Henry Romanek sat in the backseat of the car, he looked out at the lush valley and silently wondered, "Will I ever go home again?" All Romanek had with him was a shaving kit in his right back pocket and a wallet in his left back pocket. Like Olds, he understood that once you stepped onto the grounds of the military academy, your civilian life was over. There was no point in packing a suitcase and bringing personal items. At the fighting factory of West Point, you were a body being molded into a solider. Period.

Romanek had been gearing up for this day ever since he first walked on the West Point grounds. A few months after that memorable stroll, Romanek joined the New Jersey National Guard at the age of eighteen during his senior year of high school, hoping it would make him a more attractive candidate. He was a whiz at math—it was as if numbers spoke secrets to him—so Romanek was assigned to an engineering regiment. He then began studying for the exam that would determine who would win the one appointment that the New Jersey National Guard could give out. Romanek hit the books for several weeks, but he didn't feel adequately prepared for the test, which would be administered at the beginning of the summer. But as he fretted, he was given some advice that would change the direction of his life: An officer at the national guard told Romanek that he should attend prep school at Millard in Washington. "It will help you win an appointment," the officer said. "They'll teach you everything you need to know to pass the entrance exam."

Romanek took his word. After he graduated from high school in June, Romanek rode a train to Washington and enrolled at Millard. One of the first students he met there was Robin Olds, who lived just down the hall in the same dorm.

As is the case with most kids, leaving home wasn't easy for Romanek. Carl Romanek, his father, immigrated to the United States from the Austrian Empire prior to World War I. When Henry was two, his father moved his family out of their home in Brooklyn to build a house in Rutherford, New Jersey, and a new life. It was a three-story home in which three families lived; the Romaneks (Henry, his father, mother, and three younger brothers) occupied the top floor. The three families—all Polish—had a business together building and selling wicker furniture. They didn't make great money during the Depression, but they got by better than most.

One day, when Henry was seventeen and hoping to attend the Military Academy, his mother Marianne asked him why he wanted to be a solider. "There's a war coming, Mom," he said. "I'd much rather be an officer than a private." This made sense to Romanek's mother, because she knew that there was trouble brewing with the Germans in her homeland. Born on a farm outside of Posnan, Poland, Marianne came to the United States at the age of fifteen to escape an arranged marriage. Her father died young, and Marianne was the oldest of six children. Because Marianne's family needed a man to work their farmland, the community leaders arranged for Marianne to marry a young Polish man who lived down the road. When Marianne's mother got wind of this plan, she was irate and quickly fired off a letter to her relatives in Brooklyn, begging them to take care of her oldest daughter. About a month later, Marianne was on a boat steaming for Ellis Island. She moved into her aunt's home in Brooklyn, which served as a boarding house for Italian, Polish, and German laborers. Most of these men, who were recruited to come to the States by the U.S. government, were paid a dollar a day. Some of the more naïve believed they were digging for gold under the streets of New York City; in reality, they were carving out space for New York's subway system.

Marianne's job at the boarding house was to make the beds and prepare the food. She kept in touch with her family that she'd left behind, occasionally sending money and bundles of goods to her mother and siblings. When the letters she received from home started detailing the German's aggression—in 1939, Hitler's army marched right over her family's farmland on its way to Warsaw—she knew that world stability was crumbling. She felt certain that one day the United States, and her boy, would be forced into action. So when she heard young Henry say that he wanted to be an officer rather than an enlisted man, she didn't argue with him. It made perfect sense.

All throughout high school, Romanek, like most kids in his neighborhood, held a few jobs to help his family make ends meet. He cleaned city rest rooms, painted lines on city tennis courts, and pumped gas for 16 cents an hour—which is exactly what a gallon of gas went for in 1937. Romanek's favorite job in high school was folding newspapers. Though the task was as exciting as watching paint dry, it was special to Romanek for one reason: He performed it with fifteen other members of the Rutherford High football team, his band of brothers.

Romanek hoped to play football at the U.S. Military Academy—and that goal suddenly seemed possible when, one afternoon in May 1940, Romanek received a letter from Senator William Barbour of New Jersey. Romanek had graduated from Millard just weeks earlier, and now, as he opened the letter, his hands were shaking visibly. "This is it," Romanek thought to himself. He then read the news: Senator Barbour was awarding his second appointment to Romanek. The letter also told him that he had passed the entrance exam and that his application had been accepted by the admissions office at the Point. Romanek had never felt so happy; he ran outside shouting to his neighbors that he was West Point bound. (Senator Barbour's first appointment, Romanek later found out, went to a young man named Ernie Barker, who in 1942 would become the first of Romanek's friends to be killed during pilot training.)

About a month after learning that he would become a cadet, Romanek sat in the back seat of his friend's car on his way to West Point. The car sped north along the Storm King Highway, winding along the Hudson River. The water sparkled and glistened in the summer sun. As he gazed out the window, Romanek's heart raced with anticipation. His boyhood was over, Romanek knew that, but now his life was teeming with possibility. The place that would transform him into a man was just a few odometer clicks away. The Point was close.

3

THE NAVY BOYS

AT THE CROWDED TRAIN depot in Pasadena, California, two young men gathered with their families. It was the morning of June 27, 1939, a morning fraught with beginnings and endings for Bill Busik and Hal Kauffman. In a few minutes the two nineteen-year-olds would step onto a train and leave their hometown, riding the rails across the country to the U.S. Naval Academy in Annapolis, Maryland. It seemed a universe away, which was why twenty friends and family members of Busik and Kauffman turned out to bid them farewell on this golden California morning. Their mothers, wearing their fanciest Sunday dresses and hats, were overwhelmed with sadness. Both holding Brownie cameras, which were made of molded plastic and were one of the first simplified cameras ever invented, they snapped one picture after the next of their young boys as they stood on the wooden platform, trying to freeze this moment in time.

As Busik and Kauffman waited at the whistle stop for the steam-engine train to push into town, each took comfort in the fact that they wouldn't be alone on their odyssey. They had met a year earlier at Meade Prep in San Marino, California. During their six months of intensive studying at Meade, a school much like Millard Prep in Washington, D.C., which was established to prepare students for the U.S. Military and Naval Academies, Busik and Kauffman became good friends. On the weekends they'd double date, escorting their ladies to movies like *You Can't Take it With You*, starring James Stewart, and *The Adventures of Robin Hood*, featuring Errol Flynn as the Prince of Thieves. Or they'd hop into Kauffman's '28 Ford convertible and take their dates on lazy moonlight drives down Pasadena's stately Orange Grove Boulevard, where some of the grandest hotels and mansions in all of America stood—the Wrigley Mansion, the Gamble House, and other breathtaking homes on Millionaires' Row. This majestic boulevard was a playground for the wealthy, a strip of asphalt that Busik and Kauffman liked to visit on Friday nights to see how the rich and powerful kicked back.

Bill Busik grew up in a working-class neighborhood in Pasadena on Atchison Street. His father, Jack, was a line-type operator for the *Pasadena Star News*. Jack had been an editor at a paper in Minnesota in his younger years, but when he and his wife, Lillian, honeymooned in Pasadena in 1909, they liked it so much they decided to stay. Pasadena in the early 1900's could do that to you. Once a farming community, Pasadena had plenty of wide-open spaces—and plenty of sunshine—for Midwesterners looking to escape a cold climate. Jack Busik was a farmer by nature and spoke as softly as a summer breeze, but he was also as tough as rawhide. He taught his four boys the lesson of responsibility at a young age by buying them a thousand fertilized chicken eggs and storing them in four large incubators down in their basement. It was up to Busik and his three brothers to handle the eggs and to turn them at the appropriate times. As soon as the eggs hatched, Busik and his brothers would move the chickadees to a barn across the street and care for them. When the chickens were old enough, the brothers Busik sold each one for a dime. They also hawked golden bantam corn that they raised in a field behind the barn. A dozen ears went for two bits, or 25 cents. At the end of one summer, young Bill had sold enough chickens and corn to have $5 worth of coins clanking in his pockets, which to him felt like more money than was possible to spend.

But around the neighborhood, Busik was known more for his love of sport than his salesmanship. By the time he was in high school, he had all the characteristics of a commanding athlete, even down to the way he walked. In the school hallways and on the sidelines of a football field, Busik moved along with the cool strut of a mountain lion, each step more effortless than the last. At 5' 11" and 185 pounds, Busik had the sturdy build of a blacksmith, and he was endowed with easy, graceful strength. Like most boys his age in California, Busik parted his dark brown hair to the side and slicked it back with pomade. He had big, shiny brown eyes. But the one thing that everyone noticed about Busik was that, no matter what the circumstances, he always seemed to be smiling, and his perfect white teeth had a way of catching the sun and reflecting his happiness. It was a wonderful smile—all of his classmates agreed—and when it flared it made girls weak in the knees.

One of Busik's best friends growing up was a skinny kid who lived a few blocks over named Jackie, who was black. Bill and Jackie first met when they were in kindergarten. At recess the two would often shoot marbles or kick around the soccer ball together. They were as inseparable as shadows. Pasadena in the 1920s had no segregation laws on the books, but the separation of races was still strict. The public swimming pool in Brookside Park, for example, was only open to blacks one day a week, and movie theaters had separate sections for blacks and whites. But the public schools weren't segregated, and as young boys Bill and Jackie simply saw each as that: young boys. Even though their families lived in segregated neighborhoods, young Bill and Jackie never once talked to each other about the color of their skin. To them, it simply wasn't an issue.

In their junior year at Pasadena Junior College, which was the equivalent of a four-year high school, Bill and Jackie tried out for the football team together. In preseason camp Jackie quickly emerged as the star of the squad. He had astonishing quickness; if you hesitated just for a moment as a defender, he'd cruise right by you. Playing tailback in the single wing, Jackie ran and juked like a cornered rabbit, and that's what they started calling him: Jack the Rabbit. But a week before Pasadena's first game in 1936, the Rabbit broke his ankle in a scrimmage. Bill, playing the same position as the Rabbit, had struggled during camp and was buried on the B squad. But when Jackie went down with his injury, Bill was elevated to the traveling squad. Still, he didn't expect to play in Pasadena's first game at Compton Junior College, a team that was the defending state champions.

When the first-string tailback failed to consistently move the ball on offense against Compton, the Pasadena coach benched him. Same thing happened to the second-stringer—and the third. All the while on this hot afternoon, Busik sat on the bench chewing orange slices and sucking on sugar cubes, typical energy food at the time which the trainer supplied the players on the sidelines. Finally, late in the second quarter, the coach told

Busik to stop eating and get in the game and return a punt. He grabbed his leather helmet, snapped his chinstrap, and excitedly ran onto the field. On the first play of his high school football career, Busik caught the punt cleanly at his own 1 yard line—he should have let it roll into the end zone—and returned the ball 10 yards. When he was tackled, one defender hit him high and one hit him low. The defender who dove at his feet had broken one of Busik's toes on his right foot. In spite of the pain, Busik stayed in the game at tailback and proceeded to astonish his coaches.

The tailback called the plays in Pasadena's version of the single wing, the prevailing offensive alignment in the late '30s and '40s that featured four backs—a tailback, fullback, quarterback, and wingback. The tailback lined up about 4 yards behind the center. The quarterback positioned himself a yard behind the tackle on the strong side. The fullback stood next to the tailback about 2 yards away; he could line up on either side of the tailback depending on the play call. All three backs crouched with their hands on their knees. The remaining back, the lone wingback, who gave the formation its name, set up in a three-point stance just off the tight end's outside foot. There were no wide receivers.

On his first play, Busik, now in at tailback, called his own number on an off-tackle run. He scampered for 20 yards—Pasadena's longest play of the day. Ten plays later Pasadena scored a touchdown. For the rest of the afternoon, Busik seemed to scorch the earth as he ran, sprinting around and through the Compton defense. With his running and passing, he went on to lead Pasadena to victory over the defending state champs.

When Jackie returned to the team at midseason, he and Bill were interchangeable at tailback and fullback. They were an unstoppable duo, tossing passes to each other and blocking for each other. At the end of the season, after Pasadena had been upset in the state playoffs, the team voted for its MVP. It wasn't even close: Bill won it over Jackie in a landslide.

After football season ended, Bill and Jackie often played baseball together, just the two of them. After school they'd head out to one of the many ballfields in the area and at first they'd just play catch. Though they received many quizzical looks as the two of them, each carrying a bucket of baseballs, walked side-by-side on the sidewalk—as in most parts of the country, blacks and whites didn't interact frequently in Pasadena—Bill and Jackie would just smile at whoever was making odd faces in their direction. The bond of their friendship, which was forged on the fields of sport, ran deeper than skin color, and they never allowed any of their friends or anyone else to undermine their special relationship.

Once they'd finally reached the ballfield, Bill would usually pitch to Jackie at bat. Bill loved pitching to Jackie; it was one of his favorite things to do when he was in high school. It wasn't that Bill enjoyed the fact that Jackie usually crushed the ball. It was that Bill knew he was witnessing something rare and he took pains to make sure that these images of Jackie hitting the horsehide became etched in his mind. It was as if Jackie was swinging a knight's sword, the way he wielded that baseball bat. And even after the sun had gone down, Bill and Jackie would stay on the field together, as Jackie would send one moonshot hissing into the dark after the next, no matter how fast, low, or high Bill pitched.

"You're one of the swellest guys I know," Jackie told Bill one day at Pasadena Junior College in 1938. "You're going to do terrific things in your life, Bill. I know you will."

"So will you, Jackie," Bill replied. "I believe in you. Just don't take any guff from anybody. Be yourself and everything will turn out fine for you."

Bill was right. Nine years later, in 1947, Bill's good friend Jackie Robinson would become the first black player in Major League Baseball history.

Ever since junior high, Busik had been interested in the U.S. Naval Academy. He often listened to their football games on the radio in his living room in Pasadena. Lying on the floor, Busik would close his eyes and imagine he was there in the stadium, watching the action, joining in with the roar of the crowd, seeing all the midshipmen in the stands in their dress whites. Just the name of the naval academy sounded glamorous to him; it conveyed some magical faraway place where everyone was smart and strong. Busik, like most boys in California his age, never considered the implications of combat. Unlike Robin Olds and Henry Romanek and other boys who lived on the East Coast, Busik and his buddies rarely talked about Hitler. There were fewer new European immigrants living in California in 1938, and so to Busik the rumblings being generated by Hitler seemed a distant thunder—a storm cloud that Busik and his family couldn't yet see on the horizon. When Busik was being recruited by Navy assistant coach Edgar "Rip" Miller to come to the academy and play football and basketball, war was the last thing on Busik's mind.

Busik knew all about Rip Miller. Every football fan in the country did. On October 18, 1924, Miller played on the offensive line for Notre Dame as the Irish faced Army at the Polo Grounds in Manhattan. Up in the press box that day was a newspaper writer for the *New York Herald Tribune* named Grantland Rice. After the game, which Notre Dame won 13–7, Rice penned what would become the most famous lead in the history of sportswriting. "Outlined against a blue-gray October sky, the Four Horsemen rode again," Rice wrote. "In dramatic lore they are known as Famine, Pestilence, Destruction and Death. These are only aliases. Their real names are Stuhldreher, Miller, Crowley and Layden."

The Four Horsemen were halfbacks Don Miller and Jim Crowley, quarterback Harry Stuhldreher, and fullback Elmer Layden. Rice also dubbed Notre Dame's offensive line as the "Seven Mules," which included Rip Miller at right tackle. Being a "mule" made Miller as recognizable as any college offensive lineman had ever been, and he liked to joke that the eleven starters on offense had repeatedly voted that the "Seven Mules" were more important than the "Four Horseman." "It's funny how that vote of those eleven guys turned out," Miller often said. "The Seven Mules always won over the Four Horsemen, by a count of roughly seven to four."

Miller graduated from Notre Dame in 1925 and spent the next season as an assistant coach at Indiana. The following year he joined the football staff at Annapolis. When he began recruiting Busik, he served as the team's offensive line coach. Miller didn't travel by rail to Pasadena to woo Busik; instead they corresponded by mail. "We think you would be a great addition to the naval academy," Miller wrote in one letter to Busik. "You're the kind of outstanding young man that, one day, will be a leader in our country."

Miller was a pigskin revolutionary, as he developed the first sophisticated recruiting operation in college football history. Called the Bird-Dog System, Miller relied on graduates of the U.S. Naval Academy, former sailors, and friends of his to act as his eyes and ears all over the nation. These scouts lived on the East Coast, the West Coast, the plains, the deep South, the Southwest—they were, simply, everywhere. If there was a good high school football player in their area who had the grades to get into the academy, Miller knew about him.

Most of Miller's scouts made their living in the sales business, including Abe Stacey. A 1922 graduate of the U.S. Naval Academy who worked for Wilson Sporting Goods in Pasadena, Stacey attended football games all over southern California. He carried a little black notebook in his back pocket and scribbled notes on the players he saw. Sometimes, when he saw a player who really impressed him, he'd write so feverishly that his hand would cramp. One such player who had him writing excitedly was Busik.

After watching a game at Pasadena Junior College, Stacey approached Busik, intrigued by his rugged running ability.

"What do you know about the naval academy?" Stacey asked Busik.

"I know a lot about the Army-Navy football game," replied Busik. "To me it's always the biggest game of the year."

"Let me tell you something," Stacey said. "If you want to go to the academy, and I think you're a good candidate, you need to study the right subjects and get yourself to prep school. Do that and you'll pass the entrance exam, and we'll help you get an appointment."

Busik was almost speechless. Hearing these words was like finding out he had a chance to guarantee his slot in heaven. Stacey also discussed the naval academy with Busik's family. Sitting in their living room, Stacey explained what the academy looked like, detailing its vast and beautiful lawns on the banks of the Severn River. He also assured the Busiks that the government would pay for the tuition. No one in the Busik clan had ever attended college before, so this sounded like a deal of a lifetime to Busik's parents. In fact, as John Busik sat there listening to Stacey with rapt attention, he smiled as broadly and as proudly as he ever had before. That his boy might be able to get a free college education made him feel as lucky as a man who just got dealt four aces in a game of poker.

In the late 1930s, there were two ways to gain admission to the U.S. Naval Academy after passing the entrance exam: A candidate could either be appointed by a congressman, or he could join the navy and try to win an appointment out of the fleet by taking a series of competitive examinations. Following Stacey's advice, Busik enrolled at Meade Prep after graduating from Pasadena Junior College and started taking his studies more seriously.

After Busik's father dropped him off at Meade, one of the first people he met was Hal Kauffman, who was assigned to the same dormitory as Busik. The two hit it off immediately. Kauffman, who was from Glendale, California, had read about Busik's exploits on the football field in the newspaper. "You and Robinson were a great one-two punch for Pasadena," Kauffman told Busik. "I'm surprised you guys didn't win the state championship. Maybe someday you and I will be playing together at Navy—if we can get in."

For six months, Busik and Kauffman prepared for the three-day entrance exam. Information tended to stick in Busik's mind like glue, and when he finally took the test at Los Angeles City Hall, it was a breeze. He passed, no problem. Busik had joined the marine reserve a year earlier, and soon after aceing the exam, he was awarded a fleet appointment. Finally, it became official: Bill Busik was going to the U.S. Naval Academy.

Hal Kauffman could be a tornado of a boy. Nearly every day after high school, at the urging of his father Vern, Hal would walk to the orange orchard located down the street and fight one of his classmates. Though Hal was as gentle and sweet as any boy in his eighth grade class, he raised his fists because his dad demanded that he go to the orchard and "toughen up." Hal got his share of black eyes and cracked ribs, but in the process he learned what it meant to be a man—just as his father had hoped.

Little Hal always had a strong will; if he hadn't, he would have died years earlier. When he was born in West Portal, Colorado, in 1920, baby Hal refused to drink the breast milk from his mother Rose. When she tried to give him cow's milk, he refused that as well. As he lay in his crib near death, his father Vern purchased a goat as a last resort. He milked the goat in his backyard, put it in a bottle, and then gave it to his baby son. Little Hal drank it, and for the first few months of his life, all Hal consumed was the milk of the goat that lived in his backyard.

Vern Kauffman was one of the preeminent engineers of his day. In the early 1920s he helped oversee the construction of the Moffat Tunnel in Colorado, which, when it opened in 1928, became the longest railroad tunnel in the western hemisphere. In 1927 the Kauffmans moved to Glendale, California, in a home that was a few miles away from the L.A. Coliseum, which had been built only four years earlier. Vern had been transferred to Los Angeles to help design the Pacific Coast Highway. It was an important job, but Vern considered his real calling to be raising his son. Whenever Hal came home bloodied from a fight in the orange orchard—Hal never would have raised his fists if his father hadn't told him to—his father would take him in the backyard and the two would box a few rounds in their bare knuckles. If my boy is going to get his ass kicked once today, the father told the son, then he may as well get a whuppin' twice. Vern was a small man, only 5' 5" and 160 pounds, but he could be as ornery as an aroused python when he fought his son. Soon, Hal quit losing fights in the orange orchard.

Unlike Busik, Kauffman was not a natural athlete. He ran track and played football at Glendale High, but he was an overachiever who got by on courage and determination rather than on inherited talent. At 5' 9" and 160 pounds, he had a thin frame. His brown eyes were the size of bullets and he had chubby cheeks, which gave him the appearance of someone who hadn't yet shed all of his baby fat. Though he didn't have movie-star good looks, Kauffman intrigued many girls—mostly because he had a tenor voice that the gentler sex loved to listen to.

On weekends during high school Kauffman's mother would drive him to downtown Los Angeles where he'd sing at different social events for teenagers. Kauffman was usually quiet, sensitive, and introspective, but once he stepped on stage all of his shyness left him. By the time he was a junior in high school, in 1937, he was performing songs that were popular on the radio, hits like "Pennies from Heaven," by Bing Crosby. Kauffman's sweet voice tugged on the heartstrings, and he glowed every time he stepped on the stage; people could see the happiness welling up and shining inside of him. He thought someday that he might become a professional singer, but that idea was quashed the moment his father found out about it. No son of his, he made quite clear to Hal, was going to be a sissy and sing for a living. And with that one pronouncement, Kauffman's hopes of a singing career came to an abrupt end.

What made Kauffman a special singer was the fact that he put his heart into every performance. Kauffman prided himself, in fact, on being big-hearted. In the summer of 1936, when he was fifteen years old, Kauffman's caring nature was put to the test. Always a determined young man, Kauffman had won a trip to Yosemite National Park by selling more *Saturday Evening Posts*, *Country Gentlemans*, and *Ladies Home Journals* than any other kid in the Los Angeles area. On the second day at the park, Kauffman was walking along the Merced River, enjoying the scenery and the serenity of the morning, when he heard a scream for help. Kauffman looked into the river, and what he saw caused his pulse to quicken: A little boy was bobbing up and down in the water, struggling to breathe. It was clear that the boy, who looked to be five or six, was drowning.

Kauffman tore off his shirt and darted into the cold water, sprinting as fast as he could. "Hang on, I'll get you!" Kauffman yelled to the boy. Kauffman quickly swam to the boy. The water wasn't very deep—it was only about six feet—but it was flowing rapidly. The boy was in the current and drifting downstream, struggling to keep his head above the water.

"Help me!" the boy screamed as he flailed his arms. "Mommy, help me!"

Kauffman kicked his legs furiously and plowed his arms through the water, performing the breaststroke. Just before Kauffman reached the boy, he went under again, this time sinking to the river bottom. Kauffman took a deep breath and dove, keeping his eyes open. Frantically, he looked all around where he thought the boy had gone down, but Kauffman was running out of air. He didn't want to pop back up for another gulp of oxygen—he feared that he'd never find the boy if he did that—so he continued his underwater search. Just as Kauffman was about to give up and surface, he saw the boy's body, limp and lifeless, on the river bottom. Kauffman quickly grabbed him and shot up to the surface.

"Come on, you're going to make it!" yelled Kauffman.

Moments later, while they were still in the water, the boy coughed, water squirting from his mouth. Kauffman put the boy on his back, told him to hang on tight, and towed him to the shore. Just as they crawled out of the water, the boy's parents came running up to Kauffman, concern etched on their faces. Kauffman explained what had happened, how he'd just plucked the boy from the wild river. But before he could finish, the parents hugged the breathless Kauffman.

After resting by the water for a long spell, Kauffman continued his walk, feeling like a new person. The experience of saving a life had given him a rush, almost like he'd taken a drug. It also made him respect the absolute power of water. When he returned home after his trip, he started spending more time at the beach, surfing or just sitting on the sand and staring out into the ocean, the crashing and receding of the tide as soothing to him as a lullaby. "Maybe I should join the navy," Kauffman often thought as he sat on the beach. "Or maybe I should go to the naval academy."

Two months after saving the boy, Kauffman was in his tenth grade English class on a Friday afternoon when he noticed a girl named Lois Bradburg sitting in a desk by the window. Bradburg was new to the school and Kauffman had never seen her before. As he looked at her, the sun bounced off her long blond hair, giving the appearance of an angelic light framing her flowing tresses. From his seat Kauffman could also see her eyes. They were the color of the bluest ocean, and right away Kauffman was bewitched. After class he convinced a friend to introduce him to Lois. For years after, Kauffman would swear it was the best day of his life.

In 1937, Kauffman, now a junior in high school, began visiting naval ships that were moored close to his home, trying to learn as much about life in the navy as possible. On these ships, he finally arrived at a decision about his future: He was going to apply to the naval academy. "I want to be an officer in the navy," Kauffman told his father. "I know it's a long way from home, but the naval academy just seems right for me." His dad told him he thought it was a fine idea.

To make himself an attractive candidate, he ran for senior class president of Glendale High in 1938—and won. He succeeded Frankie Albert, a star quarterback at Glendale who would later become an All-Pro with the San Francisco 49ers. An overwhelming majority of classmates voted for Kauffman because he had the reputation of being authentic. He had no enemies. Though he liked to keep to himself, it seemed as if everyone considered him a friend. Maybe this was because there was a sweetness to his character that was rare among the boys in his high school. At heart, he was still a singer who liked to croon about emotions. He figured he'd always be this way.

After graduating from Glendale High, Kauffman enrolled at Meade Prep to study for the Naval Academy entrance exam. While at Meade, Kauffman had only one regret. One evening, as he was taking a break from studying, Kauffman felt like he needed to burn some energy. He was feeling frisky and figured that a friendly sparring match with his buddy Bill Busik was just what he needed. So Kauffman ran up and down the halls yelling that he was challenging Busik to a boxing match, and if anyone cared to make a wager on the bout, well, he wouldn't stop him. This was all news to Busik, but never being one to shy away from some friendly competition, he met Kauffman later that night in the gymnasium, a night that neither of them would ever forget.

At first, both Kauffman and Busik thought they would just hit each other lightly, nothing serious. But moments after they raised their bare fists, with the adrenaline and testosterone flowing, things got serious. First Kauffman hit Busik with a light punch. Then Busik smacked Kauffman on the chin with a swing that nobody in attendance would have described as soft. The two traded a few more blows, hard punches all of them. The boys who were watching yelled in approval, prodding Busik and Kauffman to tear each other apart. But then, after just a minute or so of sparring, Busik landed a right on Kauffman's jaw that seemed to pack the power of a thunderbolt, knocking Kauffman out cold. Busik stood over his friend, blood dripping from nose, looking very much like a seasoned prizefighter.

"We're going to have a rematch when we get to the naval academy," Kauffman joked to Busik after coming to his senses. "How come I never saw that punch coming?"

Four months later, after they had both passed their entrance exams and won their appointments, the friends readied to board the train that would ferry them eastward. When the train finally arrived at the Pasadena depot, the conductor yelled, "All Aboard!" The boys smiled for a few more photos, hugged their mothers one last time, then stepped into their car. Sticking their heads out the windows, they waved good-bye to their friends and families who stood on the platform. Their mothers each waved white handkerchiefs above their heads and, with tears dripping from their eyes like candle wax, shook them frenetically. The train started pulling away. Busik and Kauffman kept waving. But soon their mothers were specks in the distance. Soon they could no longer see home.

When Pasadena finally faded from view, Busik and Kauffman took a long look at each other. They didn't have to say a word: The journey of their lives had begun.

4

ARRIVAL IN ANNAPOLIS

FOR FIVE DAYS and four nights, Bill Busik and Hal Kauffman rode an iron horse across the belly of the nation. Sitting next to each other in their crowded rail car, they broached almost every subject imaginable. They talked of how they both enjoyed the movie *Wuthering Heights*, which had hit theaters six weeks earlier. They chatted about how they each wished to visit the World's Fair going on in New York, to see a vision of the future that included nationwide television broadcasts, suburban homes built with plywood, and a transcontinental highway system. They also debated whether or not gangster Al Capone, who was up for parole in a few months but was now ill with third-stage syphilis, should be let out of the pokey. Yet no matter what twists and turns their conversations took, the stream of their thoughts always seemed to veer back to one topic: what the next few years would be like at the academy.

When they weren't talking they'd look out the window and watch the land flow by. On their first night they saw, there in the pale moonlight, the Western hills, which seemed to stretch all the way up to the North Pole. When they rolled across the prairie of Nebraska they spied farm houses with sagging porches, all looking as if an overweight farmer had spent too much time sitting on his rocker in the middle of the wooden planks. As they neared the Mississippi River, they saw what they swore was the greenest grass on earth, framed by a bright blue sky. And as the train crossed into western Virginia, they passed into the teeth of a summer storm, which sent sprays of lightning crackling to the ground all around the hurtling locomotive.

The train stopped every few hours at small towns and big cities alike to pick up and drop off passengers, which only made the cross-country journey seem longer than it really was. And it didn't speed up at night when both Busik and Kauffman struggled to fall asleep; their minds just wouldn't shut off. Though the train made a lulling sound as it swayed and chugged eastward on the slender iron lines, Busik and Kauffman were preoccupied with the fact that they had left the familiarity of home. No longer could they predict what the next day would bring, a realization that was as troubling as it was exciting. So at night, while the train clickety-clacked along the rails, they let their imaginations run wild, daydreaming about their new lives at the naval academy and how they'd fit in. In these quiet moments, as both Busik and Kauffman laid in a bunk in their sleeper car, they both made a promise to themselves: No matter what hardships the future threw at them, they wouldn't quit the academy. They both knew that in the U.S. Naval Academy Class of '39, which had graduated one month earlier, only two-thirds of its original members had made it through the rigors of the academy and received their officer's bars; the others either quit or were kicked out.

"I'd rather shoot myself than be forced to leave the academy," Busik said to Kauffman one evening. "I'll do whatever it takes." For the rest of that night Busik and Kauffman looked out the window, gazing at the clusters of stars that looked like a cooling fire against the dark sky.

Finally, on the afternoon of July 1, 1939, the train pulled into the station at Baltimore, Maryland. Busik and Kauffman both grabbed their small suitcases—unlike Olds and Romanek, they needed a few changes of clothes for the train ride—and then hopped on the Toonerville Trolley for the last leg of their journey. The trolley carried them out of Baltimore, across eastern Maryland, across the Severn River, down Main Street in Annapolis, and right into the Yard at the naval academy. This was the first time that either Busik or Kauffman had ever seen the academy in person, and the sight of the place made them go bug-eyed. As they panned the two hundred acres—about seventy city blocks—on the southern bank of the Severn River, they saw old stone buildings and sprawling lawns that were

studded with oaks, maples, and walnut trees. To them, the academy represented greatness—and more important, the chance to achieve greatness. Maybe they were getting ahead of themselves, but at this moment,
at this juncture in their young lives, if felt right to dream big about all
they could someday do.

When they stepped off the trolley, Busik and Kauffman were greeted
with a vigorous handshake extending from the arm of Rip Miller, the
Navy assistant coach who had recruited Busik and who had told Kauffman
he should try out for the team. Miller arranged for them to stay together
in a local boarding house while they took their three-day physical exam.
Busik and Kauffman had passed rigorous physicals before they had left
California to make sure that the doctors at the naval academy wouldn't
find anything that could lose them their appointment. So that night neither fretted about passing the exam as they were fed their first home-
cooked meal in what felt like weeks. It was made by the head of the
boarding house, a woman who was married to a former Annapolis graduate who had died in World War I. After their chicken and potatoes dinner,
Busik and Kauffman retreated to separate bedrooms and had their first
good night of sleep since leaving home.

The next morning the heat index in Annapolis rose rapidly. By the
time Busik was walking over to Bancroft Hall for his physical, the blinding midday sun was cooking the academy's grounds. A California boy,
Busik was accustomed to warm weather, but he wasn't used to the kind of
heat that sticks to you. His physical was scheduled on the fourth floor of
Bancroft, and by the time he climbed all those stairs, his shirt was soaked
with sweat. Not only that, his heart rate was accelerated. When the doctor measured Busik's temperature, he looked at Busik as if he was in the
wrong place, because no potential midshipman could have a temperature
and blood pressure that high and hope to gain admittance. "I'm just ner-
vous," Busik told the doctor. "And I've never felt heat like this."

The doctor then noticed that Busik had a deviated septum. Because
the leather football helmet that he wore in high school didn't have a facemask or any bars that protected his face, Busik had broken his nose at
least three times in games during his high school days. "Sorry son, but
you won't be attending the naval academy with that nose," the doctor told
Busik. "If you have a deviated septum, you can't pass this physical."

Terrified at the prospect of failing before he even started his naval
career, Busik asked the doctor if he could use his phone. He called Rip
Miller and, with his heart jackhammering, told him that he'd flunked his

physical. "Don't worry," Miller said into the phone. "Go down to Franklin Street. It's a short walk. There's a doctor down there who's my friend. He'll check you over to see if you really have problems with your nose and your temperature."

Busik beat it down to Franklin Street. All kinds of terrible thoughts floated through his mind. "What if I have to get back on the train and go home? What will I tell my parents? What will my dad say? What will Jackie think?" When Busik finally walked through the door of the doctor's office, he'd convinced himself that his naval career was over. In the examination room the doctor told Busik to calm down and take some deep breaths. "Everything will be okay," the doctor told Busik in a parental voice. "I've got some advice for you. When you go back to Bancroft Hall, you'll get to the first deck and there's a scuttlebutt there. Use it."

"What's a deck and a scuttlebutt?" asked Busik, genuinely confused.

"The deck is the navy term for the floor you're on and a scuttlebutt is a drinking fountain," replied the doctor. "On the first deck drink that nice cold water from the scuttlebutt and rest. Then go up the ladder . . . er, the stairs, and on the second deck use the scuttlebutt there. Keep doing that until you get to the fourth deck."

Still feeling an anxious knot in his stomach, Busik followed the doctor's advice and returned to Bancroft Hall. He took sips from the water fountain on each level of the hall and by the time he reached the fourth floor his temperature and blood pressure were normal. But there was still the matter of the deviated septum. "I'm telling you son, this is a real problem," the naval academy doctor forcefully told Busik. "There's nothing I can do about this. My hands are tied by the regulations."

Nearly despondent, Busik once again called Miller. Just by Busik's quivering voice, Miller could tell that his young recruit was frightened. "Let me speak to the damn doctor," Miller said to Busik, who then handed the phone to the doctor.

"Hello, Rip," said the doctor, "how can I help you?"

"God damn it doc! I thought you *had* to have a deviated septum to get into the naval academy!" screamed Miller at the doctor, who was holding the phone six inches from his ear, allowing Busik to hear Miller's raised voice. "You should pass this boy, and you should pass him now!"

Minutes later, Busik walked out of the doctor's office and into the scorching summer afternoon. He had full clearance to be sworn into the naval academy in two days. As he strolled back to the boardinghouse, he felt energized, like an electrical current was passing through him.

"What a welcome to the naval academy," he thought to himself. At the very least, Busik took comfort knowing that Rip Miller was on his side. Now he knew that he had a friend in his corner, a friend he could stand shoulder-to-shoulder with for the next four years.

On the morning of July 3, 1939, under the blue-and-white flag of the U.S.S. *Chesapeake* in Memorial Hall, Busik, Kauffman and a room full of other first year students (called plebes) took an oath of allegiance to the United States and formally became midshipmen in the United States Navy. This was a take-your-breath-away moment for all of these young men, but especially so for Busik and Kauffman. Not only had they been preparing to take this oath for more than two years, but they also were two of just a handful of plebes from the West Coast. This meant they would not see their friends and family back home for at least a year—perhaps longer. But right now they didn't care about that. Right now they stood as straight as they could and, with their right hand raised, wedded their future to the United States Navy.

And with that, the hazing began. Suddenly the upperclassmen, who had moments ago seemed so friendly, now all treated the plebes as if they'd just personally insulted their mothers. As the plebes sat in a sweltering room in Memorial Hall and stenciled their names onto the uniforms and whiteworks they had been issued at the midshipmen's store, the upperclassmen showed no mercy. They employed two tactics of intimidation: verbal insults and physical punishment for inadequate responses to questions. The U.S. Naval Academy student handbook gave the upperclassmen permission to haze; it was all in writing.

"It is the duty of the upperclassman to impress upon the plebe that there is nothing that walks or crawls the earth that is lower than he," it was stated in the handbook. "He learns that as a plebe, he has no name, that he is 'Mister' to the members of every class but his own, and that 'Sir' is the word he will use most frequently. After a while, he becomes used to it, and learns one of his most valuable lessons—that to be able to command, one must know how to obey." It was, of course, the getting-used-to-it part that was so difficult for the plebes; some were so terrified of the upperclassmen that they feared getting out of bed each morning.

After receiving their gear and stenciling their names on every item, the plebes were assigned a roommate and led to their rooms. All the rooms in Bancroft Hall were identical. The spartan furnishings consisted of a rough wooden table with a reading lamp, two unpainted wooden chairs, two iron single beds, a radiator, a washbasin, and two lockers. A plebe was allowed to keep a photograph of his sweetheart pasted on the inside of his locker, and he could have a few books on his bookshelf other than textbooks, but all other personal items from home were prohibited.

After the plebes unpacked, they marched to the mess hall in Bankcroft for lunch. Once they came to a halt in the center of the vast room, the order of "Seats" was given and the plebes sat down, twenty to a table. Already, Busik had become friends with a fellow plebe named Gus Brady, his roommate. As they sat next to each other for their first meal at the academy, a midshipman officer sat at the head of the table. Midway through lunch, the officer, an upperclassman, looked at the plebe sitting directly to his right and yelled the question, "Mister, what are you famous for?"

Sitting on the other end of the table, Busik had no idea how to answer that query. Unlike most of his classmates, Busik hadn't memorized a book of sayings that had been sent to him months earlier in which all the answers to such questions had been given. Anxiously, he nudged his new roommate, asking him what he should say. The plebes were going around the table clockwise and attempting to answer the question. Most were failing and had to do forty-three pushups—because they were the '43 class—while the midshipman officer told them how pathetic they were. Others who answered incorrectly had their seats taken away, and were forced to endure the pain of assuming a seated position without the support of a stool.

As his turn got closer, Busik again asked his roommate for help. Busik figured that Brady—a boy from nearby Baltimore, who just had to be wise to the traditions of the naval academy—knew plenty of right answers.

"Just tell him that you're famous for tearing sheets of toilet paper in half," Brady whispered to Busik.

"Are you crazy?" replied Busik, a timber of fear in his voice.

"Just say it!" replied Brady.

Finally, it was Busik's turn. "Mister, why are you famous?" demanded the officer.

"Sir, I'm famous for tearing sheets of toilet paper in half, sir," Busik said with a straight face, though on the inside he was cringing and expecting the worst. The officer looked at Busik as if he had three eyes. He studied Busik carefully, slowly, looking at him up and down. He acted as though he was going to say something, to scream something, but then he just moved on to the next plebe, who happened to be Brady. When Brady got the question, he knew he couldn't say the same thing as Busik and so he answered, "Sir, I'm sorry, but I don't know." He then had his chair removed and was forced to squat in pain. For the rest of the meal, Brady shot dirty glances at Busik.

"What in the heck happened in there," Busik asked Brady after the two of them were back in their room.

"What happened is, thanks to me, you son of a gun, you outsmarted the officer," Brady replied.

"How?" asked Busik honestly.

"The officer knew that if he had asked, 'Why?' to your response, you could have nailed him," said Brady. "You could have said, 'Sir, I'm famous for tearing sheets of toilet paper in half for half-assed bastards like you."

Brilliant, Busik thought as he broke out in a fit of laughter. That night Busik started studying the thin handbook that had been issued to him earlier that summer. Even though all of his classmates that afternoon thought he was the sharpest guy around because of his ability to bewilder the class officer in the mess hall—all of them, that is, except Brady—Busik knew it was time to get serious about hitting the books. Next time a smart-ass reply might not be sitting right next to him.

For the remainder of July and August, Busik, Kauffman, and the rest of the plebes were worked to the bone. They went almost nonstop from the time that reveille sounded at 6:30 A.M. until taps was played at 10:05 P.M. Because Busik and Kauffman had matriculated at Meade Prep and had more experience in fundamental military drills than most of their classmates, they were frequently put in charge of squads. This elevated status meant that they weren't hazed as intensely as their classmates. This was a break, because both Busik and Kauffman saw some of their friends wilt in the summer heat, as one officer after the next jawed at them and had them do pushups until they vomited. For all of July and most of August, Busik and Kauffman were merely spectators to the hazing rituals. But all that changed in late August. That's when plebe football began.

At first, Busik wasn't going to play. Even though he'd had success in high school and had been named his team's MVP over Jackie Robinson, Busik decided to concentrate on his first love: basketball. Plebe summer had been so demanding that it sucked his passion for the sport right out of him; the idea of putting on pads and practicing in the scorching August heat was as appealing to Busik as doing more pushups just for the fun of it. Besides, Rip Miller had told Busik that as long as he played either football or basketball, he'd support him.

Two days before the tryouts for plebe football began, however, Busik changed his mind. Walking across campus, Busik and a classmate discussed football. The classmate told Busik that his older brother, who had graduated from the naval academy the previous June, was exactly Busik's size and that he hadn't been big enough to make the Navy plebe football team. "Are you kidding me?" replied Busik, adamantly. "Size doesn't make a difference. If you've ever played football, you know that there's a lot more to the game than bulk. There's quickness. Toughness. Intelligence. Desire. That's what makes a good football player."

"No way," replied the classmate, "size is the most important thing."

For the next fifteen minutes, the two argued, Busik's blood boiling. Finally, they made a bet. If Busik, who stood 5' 11" and weighed 185 pounds, made the plebe traveling squad—which consisted of the top four strings on the depth chart—then he'd win $2. If he didn't make it, he'd pay his classmate the same. To Busik, this was more about proving a point than making a team. But, goddamn it, he was going to win the bet and be a member of the traveling team. Suddenly, Busik had found his engine—the engine that would power his competitiveness for the next three years.

The tryouts began the afternoon of August 20. Football was the most popular sport at the U.S. Naval Academy, and almost half of the 833 plebes from the class of '43 appeared in the wrestling loft for the introductory meeting with head football coach Emery "Swede" Larson, who was set to begin his first season at Navy. At 6' 0" and 190 pounds, Larson seemed bigger and heavier than he actually was. That's because he had a presence, an air, that you could feel when he walked into a room, as if it brushed up against your body even if you were twenty feet away. Though he didn't have a booming voice or a heavy-set build, Larson commanded attention with his magnetizing persona. It was a trait he inherited from his father.

Back in 1895, Swede's father, A. T. Larson, had been the captain and guard on the University of Minnesota football team, an interior lineman who was as unrelenting as a crowbar. He had a bottomless passion for the game and he passed it on to his oldest boy, Emery, whom everyone called Swede because his father had emigrated from Sweden. A promising collegiate prospect in 1917, Swede played first string at West High School in Minneapolis, alternating between center and tackle. Largely because he understood the game more thoroughly than most coaches, Swede outwitted his opponents as much as he outmuscled them. His cerebral play earned him the admiration of his teammates, who voted him team captain his senior year. When it came time for Swede to decide where to go to college, his father figured that his son would follow his footsteps and play ball at Minnesota. But soon after high school graduation, Swede announced he was joining the marines and heading off to war.

"What's a marine?" his father asked.

"Well," Swede said, "it's something like a—"

"Soldier or sailor?" his father asked.

"Both," replied Swede.

"Don't make jokes," his father sternly replied. "No one can be both."

Though his father wasn't familiar with this relatively new branch of service called the marines, Swede enlisted anyway on May 18, 1917. Once he finished boot camp he was eager to get to France and join his American brothers in World War I, but instead he was assigned a Stateside post at Bear Mountain Station near West Point. Frustrated and disappointed, Larson especially missed football. Some friends of his in the Marine Corps mentioned that he'd be a great candidate for the naval academy, a place where he could pursue his twin dreams of national service and football. After writing several letters and taking a test, Larson was discharged from the Marine Corps on June 28, 1918, when Congressman Harold Knutson of Minnesota awarded him an appointment as a midshipman to the naval academy.

Right away, Larson went out for the football team. At the time plebes were eligible to play varsity and Larson, displaying the same kind of skill that made him the captain of his high school team, quickly worked his way up the depth chart. He was the second-string center by the time Navy took on its arch-rival, the Great Lakes Naval Training Station. Early in the game Navy's first-string center struggled, fumbling the ball twice. Gil Dobie, the Midshipmen's legendary coach, told Larson to start warming up, so Swede began running up and down the sideline. Problem was, Dobie quickly forgot about Swede and never put him in the game.

But that Great Lakes game in 1918 was a memorable one for Larson. From his spot on the sideline, he saw one of the most bizarre plays in college football history. Late in the fourth quarter, Navy led 6–0 when a Great Lakes running back broke free. He had outrun the Navy squad and, as he sprinted down the sideline, nothing stood between him and the goalline. Halfway to the endzone, however, a Navy player hopped off the bench and sprinted onto the field. Before anyone could stop him, he dove and tackled the Great Lakes runner at about the Navy 30-yard line.

The referees didn't know what to call, because such a play wasn't covered in the rulebook. The Great Lakes coaches thought they should be awarded a touchdown. The Navy coaches argued that the rules called for a penalty against the Midshipmen for illegal interference, but nothing more. The argument quickly heated up, as coaches and players on the field started shoving one another. That's when Admiral Eberle, the U.S. Naval Academy superintendent, intervened. He proclaimed that a touchdown be awarded to Great Lakes. After kicking the extra point, Great Lakes won the game, 7–6.

Larson went on to have a spectacular playing career at Navy, one that would glow in the consciousness of Navy football followers for a generation. In 1920, he was named on Walter Camp's second All-America team. He again made Camp's second team the following year in '21, while he was also serving as the lone team captain. The following spring he was named a first-team All-American in lacrosse. Because he was a standout in two sports, Larson won the Thompson Trophy Cup as Navy's outstanding athlete in '22. But his proudest moment came in his final football game as a Navy Midshipman. Facing Army at the sold-out Polo Grounds in New York, Swede helped Navy to a 7–0 victory in '21. Late in the game Swede was taken out so that his backup, Zeke Sanborn, could see some action. As Swede jogged to the bench he saw his father standing on the sideline. It was the only time his father had made the trip from Minneapolis to see him play. As he held a blanket for his son, his eyes flashed. "Boy," he told Swede as he wrapped the blanket around him, "this is the happiest day of my life."

After graduating and accepting a commission in the Marine Corps, Swede was stationed at Quantico, Virginia, for three years. There he coached and played on the Marine team. Like at the Naval Academy, Swede stood out. In December of 1922, playing against the 3rd Corps Area Army team in front of fifty thousand people at Baltimore's Municipal Stadium, Larson led his Marine team to a 13–12 victory. Swede's rival coach that afternoon was an aggressive young man named Dwight D. Eisenhower, and nine out of ten people who were there swore that Swede outcoached the future president.

During his itinerant career as a marine, Swede always found a way to teach football. In 1937, for example, he was assigned to the 2nd Marine Brigade in Shanghai, China. The Sino-Japanese conflict had just gotten off to a bloody start, but that didn't stop Swede from imparting some pigskin wisdom to the team of the 6th Marines that he coached. One afternoon, while practicing in Shanghai's City Park, a battle erupted all around them. With gunfire whistling directly over the park, Swede continued to work out his players, oblivious to the danger that was enveloping them. One player finally yelled to Swede, "Coach, all we want to hear you say is, 'No more workout today!'" Before Swede could respond, the entire team started running for cover. Swede quickly followed and no Americans were hurt.

The next year, in 1938, Larson was named the commanding officer of the Marine Detachment at the U.S. Naval Academy. He didn't have any official coaching duties, but he still kept his hands in the game. After working hours he'd head to a back lot where he'd give pointers to officers' kids who were playing sandlot football. While the kids played, Swede would stroll up and down the sideline, a slow, preoccupied walk that suggested a philosopher in deep thought. One afternoon in the spring of 1939, while Larson was at the lot, Navy's director of athletics approached. He had a broad smile on his face. "Larson, how would you like to coach Navy?" he asked.

Larson, who had always considered coaching Navy as the ultimate job, nearly fell over. He felt as if he'd been preparing for this position all of his life, and he immediately replied yes, he'd like to coach Navy. Now, three months later, he stood before the plebes, who had quieted down the moment Larson walked in. With his long, skinny face, his dark hair that was flecked with gray, his high cheek bones, and tan, weathered skin, he looked a bit like Abraham Lincoln without the beard. Some of the players even took to calling him Honest Abe, and honesty was what he started to talk about as he preached to his players. Swede told the young men in the wrestling loft that the tryouts would be fair and that he really liked kids who hustled and played with a mean streak. Larson spoke for twenty minutes, detailing his goals for Navy football, how he was going to build this team into a national power, and the plebes hung on his every word.

Larson spoke in a low and smooth voice—the kind of voice you didn't question. "You are the future of the varsity team," Swede told his players. "You are the guys who will someday lead this program to greatness. It will be a lot of work, I'm not gonna lie to you. In fact, we are going to work you harder than you have ever been worked before. But that's why, when it really matters, we'll be victorious. It all starts out there on the practice field. That's where we'll win games. Now let's get to work and do this together."

. . .

The first few days of the tryouts did not go well for Busik or Kauffman. Neither felt entirely comfortable in their new surroundings yet—they felt a twinge of homesickness—and it showed on the field. They made uncharacteristic mistakes, like missing tackles on defense and missing blocking assignments on offense, that dropped them both down to the fifth team after two weeks of practice. Busik figured he'd lose his bet. To make matters worse for Busik, he'd had an encounter with an upperclassman that had left him shaken. After all the upperclassmen had returned from their summer cruise in late August, Busik was walking into the academy rotunda one afternoon when a big, burly officer—who Busik assumed was a football player—saw Busik out of the corner of his eye. "Mister, into the room," said the officer to Busik, pointing to a broom closet. "Get that broom out of the closet and give it to me. Then, mister, assume the angle."

Following orders but very much wanting to punch the officer, Busik went into the closet and handed him the broom. He then bent over. The broomstick thwacked his behind. Again and again. In minutes Busik's buttocks started to bleed. As he was getting pummeled, Busik looked back and saw, on his aggressor's lapel, a nametag. It read: A. Bergner. That name seems familiar, Busik thought. After the hazing incident was over, as Busik gingerly walked out of the broom closet, Busik remembered that Allen Bergner was the captain of the football team. It was a name he wouldn't soon forget.

"He's mine on the football field," Busik thought to himself. "I'll make that bastard regret what he just did."

On the day before the annual plebe-varsity football game, played on August 30, all the plebes received shots. They were inoculated for influenza, small pox, and malaria, among other potential diseases they could contract while serving in the navy. The next afternoon, when Busik and Kauffman showed up at the practice field to prepare to play the varsity, they thought the game had been postponed, because only a few of their plebe teammates were on the field.

"Where is everybody?" Kauffman asked Busik.

"This place is a ghost town," replied Busik.

Most of the plebe players, it turned out, were sick in bed. Nearly half of the plebe team suffered a reaction to the shots and were in no condition to play football. But neither Busik nor Kauffman experienced the same negative reaction that many of their teammates had. Busik, who had been the sixth team tailback, suddenly was elevated to the first string. Out of nowhere, he had an opportunity thrust upon him—an opportunity to impress his coaches and, more important, a chance to get on the same playing field as A. Bergner.

The plebes had been training for two months, so they were in fine shape. The varsity players, because they had returned from their summer cruise just a week ago, weren't yet in football condition. This disparity showed right away. Operating out of the single wing with Busik calling the plays from his tailback position, the plebes moved the ball up and down the field. They stormed to a 12–0 lead early in the second quarter. That's when Busik noticed A. Bergner enter the game. Bergner played defensive tackle and his name was written on a piece of tape that was spread across the front of his leather helmet. Busik's eyes blazed with excitement. He had just spotted a bullseye.

"Okay gents, here's what we're gonna do," Busik told his team in the huddle. "We're going to run our 42 play over and over right at our friend, A. Bergner. Everyone hit him hard. We're going to do this until they haul his ass off the field."

Forty-two meant that the four-back (the tailback) ran the ball into the two-hole (the gap between the left guard and the left tackle). With offensive linemen Vito Vitucci, Gene Flathman, Moose McTighe, and Jake Laboon serving as Busik's front wall, the plebe team hammered away at Bergner, play after play. Whenever Bergner had a chance to make a tackle, Busik didn't elude him. He simply lowered his head like a bull and charged straight into Bergner, trying to inflict as much pain as possible. On a few occasions Busik sent Bergner flying into the air; he'd land on the ground with a thud. Watching this from the sideline, coach Larson started asking his assistants where this Busik kid had come from. He ran with a fury, a sense of purpose, that was as rare as dinosaur bones. After one particularly devastating collision with Bergner in the fourth quarter, Busik hopped up. Bergner didn't. He lay on the ground, motionless and unconsciousness, with Busik standing over him and smiling like a farm boy. Just as Busik had prophesied, Bergner was eventually taken off the field on a stretcher.

Midway through the fourth quarter, plebe coach Johnny Wilson benched all of the plebe starters. The plebe team held an 18–14 lead, and neither Wilson nor Larson wanted to demoralize his varsity players with a loss. The varsity wound up beating the plebes 21–18, but the fact that the first-year players had fared so well against the older, stronger players bode well for Navy's future. In fact, after the game, Larson privately admitted to friends that he thought these plebes, given time to grow and mature, could be a dominating group. Maybe he was being premature, but even before he coached his first game at Navy, Larson was already constructing a road map in his mind, a map that he believed would lead to the sweetest of destinations: the national championship.

5

WEST POINT 1940

AS SOON AS ROBIN OLDS stepped off the train at the small West Point depot, his welcome to the U.S. Military Academy rushed at him like a bucket of ice water to the face. Olds and the other young passengers were met by several cadet officers, who proceeded to vociferously herd them into groups. As they were being organized, the fresh-faced young men were reminded, in less-than-pleasant language, that their mommies were no longer around to care for them, and their daddies couldn't protect them any more. The words were hurled like sharpened spears, but Olds was unfazed. Frankly, he'd expected the torment to be much worse than this, but some of the kids who had no military background were in a near state of shock. Just wait until the Beast Detail gets ahold of them, Olds thought to himself as he glanced at a few of the future cadets who were already trembling with fear.

It was now approaching noon on July 1, 1940. All that was left in Olds' journey, which began in the predawn darkness at Washington's Union Station, was a four-hundred-yard walk up the Hudson Highlands. For weeks Olds had imagined himself joining the long gray line, and now as he left the train depot on the west bank of the river, he was minutes away from realizing a dream. He gazed up the hill and saw, outlined against the azure sky in front of him, the gray stone of the administration building, also known as base headquarters. To him, the building looked like a monstrous, impenetrable castle on a bluff, its massive stones glistening in the sunshine. The sight was awe-inspiring. There was an air of solidness, of importance to the place. Right then Olds thought the Point was the perfect place for him.

As the group continued to walk upward, they could see the tops of the trees on campus. No one talked. Olds could sense the anxiety level rising with each step. The group passed through the stone portal that led to the Plain. Still no one talked; all Olds could hear were the footfalls of all the young men who were now walking toward their futures. This was the same path that Douglas MacArthur had walked in 1899 after he arrived at the Point via the West Shore Railroad. Many of the young men were aware that General MacArthur, a former superintendent of the school, had once been here, and to them it was almost as if they could see MacArthur's image as they climbed the steep hill, step by agonizing step.

When the group finally reached the Plain, which from the river bluff stretched west for half a mile and housed all the academic buildings, barracks, and the parade ground, they were guided into the open quadrangle of the cadet barracks. Then they were handed over to the Beast Detail— cadets who were in charge of indoctrinating the new plebes into what were gently called the "traditions" of the academy. And that was when all hell broke out. If any of the young men had any romantic notions about life at West Point, they were about to be dashed.

"Pull in that chin, mister!"

"Stand up straight, mister!"

"You have no chance of surviving here! You will not make it, mister!"

"You think you're tough? We'll show you tough, mister!"

"You are a disgrace, mister!"

And on and on it went for most of the afternoon, the white-gloved upperclassman acting like wolves chasing sheep. After their initial berating, the young men were issued uniforms, and then they were taken to the campus barber to have their hair shaved to a quarter inch from the scalp. While waiting in line to have his trim, Olds locked eyes with Henry Romanek, his old friend from Millard Prep in D.C., who was also waiting in line. Romanek had arrived an hour or so before Olds and had been dropped off by his father's friend. All morning Romanek had been screamed at and told how pathetic he was, and now seeing the familiar face of Olds brought a smile to his face.

"I didn't know if you'd actually show up," Romanek joked to Olds. "But it's good to see you."

"You never need to worry about me, Henry, I can take care of myself just fine," Olds replied with a smile. "You're the one who's going to be hauled out of here on a stretcher."

Around 5:00 P.M., the Beasts were shepherded out to a place called Trophy Point, which overlooked a bend in the dark, glittering river, and they were asked to raise their right hand. There's no going back now, Olds thought to himself as he lifted his right hand skyward. Amid the lengthening afternoon shadows, the Beasts swore allegiance to the United States. It had been a long day, but finally Robin Olds and Henry Romanek were Army cadets.

Every Beast knew war was coming. President Roosevelt was already warning the American people that there would be no compromise with Germany and Italy, which he called "the new corporate governments" of the world. "The new governments generally destroy the legislative and judicial branches and delegate all powers to an executive or dictator, thus striking at the heart of fundamental liberties by which men should and must live," the President told reporters at a press conference on the same afternoon that Olds and Romanek arrived at West Point.

Days earlier, France had surrendered to Germany. General Charles Huntziger had signed away France's freedom in the same railway car in Versailles in which the Germans were forced to sign the surrender at the end of World War I. The terms of the capitulation were mild but troubling: Any German national was to be handed over to the German authorities on demand; and any French national caught fighting for the British was to be treated as an insurgent. A day after the surrender was signed, a picture of Hitler standing in front of the Eiffel Tower ran in newspapers around the world, and accompanying stories discussed Hitler's likely next move: the invasion of England.

The dominoes were beginning to fall. Romanek and Olds both understood that. Days after France had lost her freedom President Roosevelt asked Congress for the largest defense budget in U.S. history. Roosevelt needed the money for two main reasons: to fund a 1.2 million man army and to build fifteen thousand new planes.

. . .

In spite of the school's rich football tradition, Army was not considered a powerhouse in the summer of 1940. The previous season, 1939, had been catastrophic. The Cadets stumbled to a 3–4–2 record with a squad coached by William Wood, Army's first losing season since 1906. Worse, the Cadets had been shut out in three of their last four games of the '39 season. The team's sagging football fortunes put an intense amount of pressure on Wood, a 1925 graduate who had collected twelve varsity letters. He knew the future success of Army football would be tied to this freshman (plebe) class—he planned on playing many of them once they became eligible the next season—and so when the tryouts for plebe football commenced in mid-August of 1940, he watched all of his young players with careful, critical eyes.

The practices were unlike anything Olds and Romanek had ever experienced. They weren't overly long—they started at 3:15 and lasted until 5:30—but the players weren't allowed to take a single break. Before and after each practice, the team trainer, Beaver Beaven, weighed each team member. It wasn't unusual for some of the bigger players (such as Olds) to sweat off eight to fifteen pounds during their 2 hour and 15 minute sessions. Coach Wood wanted his team to be as physically fit as any in the nation, and he wanted his players to dominate in the fourth quarter, so he tried to make his practices more difficult, more demanding, than anything his players would face all season. The downside to this approach was that after a few weeks, the players were worn down and physically deflated. Olds played offensive and defensive tackle, and by the end of most practices he'd feel as if he'd just pushed a boulder up a mountain. Once the whistle blew and practices were over, Olds would spend at least 30 minutes in the whirlpool, trying to soothe his aching muscles. A few times, Romanek, who played next to Olds on the line, jumped into the swimming pool to cool down with his pads still on after practice, too exhausted to peel them off.

Once the plebe season started, the team was predictably flat, as the players had no freshness in their legs. After losing their first three games, the Army plebes hosted Fordham's freshman squad on a cold, rainy afternoon at West Point. Against the Rams, Olds and Romanek played both ways on the mud-drenched field for the full 60 minutes. By the time the game was over—final score: 0–0—Romanek was so sore he was hobbling like an eighty-year-old man. After a hot shower in the locker room, he headed straight for bed, skipping dinner.

The next morning the pain and stiffness still had a grip on him—head to toe. When Romanek awoke, it hurt just to get out of bed. But Romanek grabbed his gray overcoat and staggered out to ranks. He made it there by first call, which was 5 minutes before assembly. As he stood there in a cold, driving rain, his squad leader strolled up. He was a varsity football player and he took it personally that the plebes hadn't defeated Fordham. The squad leader figured Romanek, like all the plebe players, needed some toughening up.

"Pull in your crock right now," he yelled as he put his face within a few inches of Romanek's.

"Yes, sir," Romanek replied.

"More!" screamed the squad leader.

"Yes, sir," said Romanek.

"More, god damn it!" again yelled the squad leader.

Romanek pulled in his chin as tightly as he'd ever done before. He stood ramrod straight, but then, seconds later, he fell to the ground. Passed out cold.

"Get a medic!" yelled one plebe that had seen Romanek tumble to the earth. No one was terribly worried about Romanek's condition because several plebes had passed out during Beast Barracks. In Romanek's case, tucking his chin tightly into his chest cut off the blood flow to his brain—an all too common occurrence among the Beasts. After a few moments, he opened his eyes and asked what had happened. When he figured it out, he silently wished for the same thing that Bill Busik had when he got hazed at Navy: an opportunity to go one-on-one on the football field with his aggressor.

The plebe football players who had seen this incident were irate. "You're a mean bastard," one yelled at the squad leader as Romanek awoke.

"You'll get it for this," shouted another plebe player.

As Romanek struggled to his feet, he was comforted by the fact that his young teammates were sticking up for him. Maybe, he thought to himself, there was hope for this team after all.

The 1940 season was one long, waking nightmare for varsity coach William Wood. Though he was pleased with his plebe team in spite of their slow start—his young boys, led by Olds and Romanek, had gotten progressively stronger throughout the season and finished with a record of 3–4–1—his varsity squad limped to a 1–7–1 record. It was the worst season in the fifty-one years that Army had been playing football. The low-point came on November 16 at Franklin Field in Philadelphia against the University of Pennsylvania. One of the spectators in attendance that afternoon was General Robert L. Eichelberger, who had just been named to succeed General Jay Benedict as superintendent of the U.S. Military Academy. Eichelberger would officially assume the position on the following Monday, and he wanted to get a first-hand look at the state of the school's football team. What he saw was the worst defeat in Army history, as Penn routed the Academy, 48–0. Eichelberger knew that something drastic had to be done to revive the flagging program, and he had a bold idea.

On the following Monday, in his first official act as superintendent, Eichelberger called a meeting of the athletic board. "I was impressed Saturday by the way the cadets cheered our team right to the end," he told the board. "It looks as if we are developing the finest bunch of losers in the world. By the gods, I believe the cadets deserve a football team which will teach them how to be good winners. Our graduate officer–head coach system has long been outmoded. I propose to ditch it, and, if I can, get Red Blaik back here from Dartmouth."

Dating back to 1890, Army always had a graduate officer serve as its head football coach. Eichelberger believed that this was the reason why the program had fallen into decay, and he made it his top priority as superintendent to rescind this unwritten policy and hire a coach with an off-the-charts football IQ. After his meeting with the board, he went to his office and personally typed a letter to Blaik, who was the head coach at Dartmouth and a 1919 West Point graduate. No longer in the army, Blaik was in the process of leading the Big Green to a 5–4 record in 1940. "If you have not signed a new contract," Eichelberger wrote, "don't sign any until you have talked to me first."

Once he received the missive, Blaik quickly replied with his own telegram. "I understand what you mean," Blaik wrote. "I will see you next week at the Army–Navy game."

So on the eve of the 1940 Army–Navy contest, Eichelberger and Blaik met in the general's suite in Philadelphia's Benjamin Franklin Hotel. For more than two hours, Eichelberger explained how the U.S. Military Academy needed Blaik to restore luster to its football team. Eichelberger said he would abolish the graduate officer rule and that he'd give Blaik all the resources he needed to turn around the football team. Blaik asked for time to weigh the offer.

"Take all the time you want, Earl," said Eichelberger. "But just remember one thing: West Point needs you."

For nearly a month, those last four words echoed in Blaik's mind. The colors had called him. He knew, deep inside, he couldn't turn that down.

Born to Scottish parents in Detroit, Michigan, in 1897, little Earl Blaik had a mop of copper-colored hair—everyone called him "Red"—and he played the role of the rambunctious redhead to a T. In school he sassed his teachers, telling them how things ought to be. He often got the paddle after class, but that did little to calm this tempest of a boy. He found that the best place to channel his energy was on the athletic fields, where he could dominate boys nearly twice his size simply because they couldn't match his intensity.

When he was ten years old in 1907, Blaik formed a neighborhood football team and appointed himself coach. He named the team the "Riverdale Rovers," after the *Rover Boys* books he liked to read at night before bed. The Rovers played with a round, black ball that more closely resembled a soccer ball than a football, which made it almost impossible to pass. Even though the forward pass had been legalized in 1906, Blaik as a young boy didn't care much for an air attack. He never would, in fact, mainly because of what he learned on the sandlots while playing with the Rovers. He found that the ground game was much more reliable than the pass, and that if you could dominate your opponent running the ball, you could break his spirit as easily as a carrot stick.

The Riverdale Rovers played other neighborhood teams after school, and the games more often than not devolved into rock fights. One Thanksgiving, young Red showed up for dinner two hours late and was in no condition to sit down at the table with his family. His face was scratched, his clothes were torn, and dirt covered a good portion of the clothes that weren't ripped. His father William, who saw no future in football, was about to ban his son from ever playing the sport again when one of Red's friends spoke up. "But Mr. Blaik," the young voice said. "He won the game!"

Blaik was never one of the biggest boys around—by age eighteen he was 5' 9" and 135 pounds—but from his father he inherited the gift of raw strength. William Blaik came to the United States from Glasgow, Scotland, in 1883. Three years later he opened a blacksmith and carriage shop on Twelfth Street in Detroit, and he quickly acquired a reputation as being one of the most reliable blacksmiths in town. William was a considerate man, but the one thing that really upset him was when Henry

Ford came around. The elder Blaik could always hear Ford before he saw him, because Ford was experimenting with a horseless carriage, and when he ran his "contraption" down Twelfth Street it made such a racket that it riled the horses. In some cases, it caused them to bolt out of their stalls, agitated, and sprint down the dusty streets. When Ford's cart broke down—as it often did—the blacksmiths along Twelfth Street all whooped and hollered in approval right in front of Ford's face. Yet when Ford went to William Blaik and asked to borrow some tools for repairs, Blaik never once refused. Even though he didn't like what Ford's cart potentially could mean to his future livelihood, William Blaik never hesitated in opening his shop up to Ford. Like most immigrants, Blaik had an appreciation for what it meant to lend—and to receive—a helping hand.

In 1901 William Blaik sold his business to become the Ohio and Kentucky sales representative for the Capwell Horseshoe Company. He moved his family to Dayton, Ohio, and it was there that young Red experienced the defining event of his childhood. On March 25, 1913, when Red was sixteen, one of the most disastrous floods in the history of the United States swallowed a good portion of Dayton. On the morning of the catastrophe, police and fire alarms awoke Red at 4:00 A.M. Five days of constant rain had swollen the Great Miami River, and now the threat of a massive flood was high. At 7:30 the levees above the Herman Avenue Bridge broke and water rushed down the streets. By 8:30 the raging channels reached the front steps of the Blaik household. Minutes later the Blaiks—father, mother, Red and his brother and sister—linked hands and waded into the rising, rapid waters. After two horrifying hours, they made it to higher ground at the Forest Avenue Presbyterian Church, which is where they stayed for the next few days.

Others weren't as lucky. Because several bridges had been washed out and the lines of communication were dead, many people were stranded on their rooftops, paralyzed with fear. Entire houses were being swept away and, from his spot at the church, Red Blaik could hear the screams of people struggling to stay afloat in the rapid waters. At the flood's crest, Dayton lay under fourteen feet of muddy water. Young Red saw it all, and couldn't help but wonder: Why wasn't the city prepared for this? Why didn't the city have a plan? When nightfall came, Blaik and his family saw a fire break out in a downtown office building. The fire soon engulfed an entire block. When it reached a paint company, explosions shot high into the sky. In the afterglow of the blasts, Blaik could see people stranded on their rooftops, frantically trying to find help.

After four days, the water began to recede. Red was one of the first people to get to the downtown area and what he saw left him speechless. It looked as if the apocalypse had dawned. Many buildings were burned out; others had been completely washed away. An eight-inch layer of mud covered everything. Bloated carcasses of hundreds of dead horses were strewn in the streets, reeking of decomposing flesh. Again Red thought to himself: Why wasn't the town ready for this? Over one thousand homes and buildings had been demolished and more than three hundred people had died in the disaster. To Red, it seemed an utter waste. A lack of coordination and foresight had made the flood worse that it should have been, and Blaik would never forget this. This partly explained why, years later, he would become the most meticulous, organized, detail-oriented coach of his time—a coach who would revolutionize the sport of football with his approach to the game.

Blaik attended the University of Miami at Oxford, Ohio, where he starred at end for three seasons. Like some other college football players of his time, Blaik got to start his college football career over again when he was accepted to West Point after graduating from Miami. Army didn't recognize the three-year eligibility rule until 1930—an intercollege athletic rule that stated, in effect, that a player only had a total of three years of varsity eligibility—so when Blaik arrived at the Point in the summer of 1918, he joined the plebe squad. The next year, when he was elevated to the varsity, Blaik became a favorite of General Douglas MacArthur, who at the time was superintendent at the school. MacArthur so enjoyed watching the football team play that on many autumn afternoons he put aside his responsibilities and attended football practice. There he would stomp up and down the sidelines, his riding crop stuck under his arm, and encourage the young cadets to play stronger, to run faster, to hit harder. MacArthur always believed that there was a strong correlation between sports and war, and before he left his post as superintendent for the Philippine Islands in 1922, his thoughts on the subject were inscribed over the entrance to the Physical Education office in the South Gym:

UPON THE FIELDS OF FRIENDLY STRIFE
ARE SOWN THE SEEDS THAT,
UPON OTHER FIELDS, ON OTHER DAYS
WILL BEAR THE FRUITS OF VICTORY

MacArthur had always dreamed of playing football for Army, but when he arrived at the academy in 1899, he was just 5' 11" and 133 pounds. He was also something of a mama's boy, and Mary MacArthur didn't want her son getting hurt playing football. For four years Mary MacArthur lived in the West Point Hotel. From her vantage point in the hotel, she had an unobstructed view of Room 1123 in the barracks. At night if she didn't see young Doug with his head buried in a circle of lamplight, she'd talk to him the following day about why he wasn't studying. Finally, in his first class year (his senior year), MacArthur found a way to accommodate both his mother's desire that he not play football and his desire to be connected to the football team: He became the equipment manager.

When MacArthur was superintendent in 1919, no cadet impressed him more than Blaik. Playing end, Blaik was named to Walter Camp's third string All-America team and won the saber as the best athlete in his class. After graduation in 1920 Blaik hoped to be stationed in Europe, but instead he was sent to the Mexican border with the 8th Cavalry. Three years later, with World War I over and the Army poised to reduce its number of troops, Blaik resigned his commission to join his father's real estate and contracting business in Dayton. He felt ready to begin a normal life.

Blaik married a local Dayton girl and for the next few years he led a perfectly ordinary life. He worked nine to five, mowed his lawn on the weekend, and started a family. In 1922 he received a surprise letter from MacArthur, who had just been given a new command in the Philippines. MacArthur invited Blaik to become his aide-de-camp. But MacArthur didn't know that Blaik had already resigned his commission, so the offer was moot. Later MacArthur took to Manila another former West Point football player, Dwight Eisenhower.

Working with his father in Dayton, Blaik was content except for one thing: He missed football terribly. It wasn't that he didn't like his job at the firm of W. E. & E. H. Blaik, but he thought of football as his first love, and he couldn't get his strong feelings for the sport out of his heart. So he started looking for ways to get back into the game—just on a part-time basis. In 1926 he landed a coaching job as an unpaid assistant at Wisconsin. The next season he traveled to West Point to help out with the team, still as an unpaid assistant. He always returned to his job in Dayton after the season ended, but for seven straight years he coached at West Point in the fall, learning as much as he could and quietly formulating his own strategy that he would one day implement when he became a head coach. That day came in 1934. Blaik announced that he was leaving his father's business for good in order to seek a job as a head coach of a college team.

Army couldn't hire him because of the regulation barring civilians from being its head coach, but Blaik got an offer from Dartmouth. He then led the Big Green to it first-ever victory over Yale in 1935 and to Ivy League titles in 1936 and 1937. Blaik had his players run the single-wing almost to perfection, and his reputation grew by the year. When Eichelberger offered him the Army job the night before the Army-Navy game in 1940, Blaik said he would only consider leaving Dartmouth if two conditions were met: He wanted to bring all of his assistants to West Point and he wanted Army to abolish its weight and height restrictions. The restrictions were implemented in 1931, when the Surgeon General issued a directive stating that overweight candidates would not get a waiver to attend the U.S. Military Academy. Based on the theory that slimmer men have a greater life expectancy, the Surgeon General instructed the examining boards to strictly adhere to an age-height-weight chart. According to the chart, a candidate who was 6' 4", for example, could weigh no more than 198 pounds. Blaik, like many at West Point, believed these restrictions were undercutting any chance that Army had to be competitive in football, and he told Eichelberger that he wouldn't coach the team unless Eichelberger did something about it. Eichelberger said he'd look into it after the game.

About 265 miles to the southwest of West Point, the state of affairs at the naval academy were much more settled in the autumn of 1940—thanks in large part to a young player named Bill Busik. Just as Navy coach Swede Larson had hoped, his 1940 varsity squad was bolstered by the additions of several players who had shined on the '39 plebe team. The biggest surprise was Busik. In the first scrimmage held in September 1940, Busik lead the team in rushing and passing. Whenever Busik busted into the open field, he ran like a man who was bolting from a jailhouse, leaving defenders in a swirl of dust. His strong performance prompted Larson to breathlessly compare Busik to Buzz Borries, a bowlegged running back who had been an All-American for Navy in 1934.

Larson knew Borries's skills well. In 1936 Larson coached the football team aboard the U.S.S. *Pennsylvania*. Their chief rival was the team on the U.S.S. *Arizona*. In November of '36, after the *Arizona* and *Pennsylvania* had been out at sea for a few months, both ships came to port in San Pedro, California, which was where one of the American fleet's bases was located in the mid-1930s. By the time each ship had docked, the football players had enough pent-up testosterone to raise the dead. The *Arizona* and *Pennsylvania* teams, which had been practicing aboard ship for months, faced off in a dilapidated, rickety baseball stadium in San Pedro. A football field was marked off with paint and a few thousand fans showed up and watched Borries put on a show. Operating out of *Arizona*'s single wing, Borries ran both inside and out, with quickness, power, and guile. Even though Borries rushed for nearly 100 yards, the *Pennsylvania* squad won the game—and the fleet championship—because Larson had them playing disciplined, smart, savvy football. Yet Borries's performance left a lasting impression on Larson, who often said that Borries was the best back he'd ever faced. So when Larson compared Busik to Borries, it was the highest of praise.

The fastest player on the Navy team and also one of its strongest, Busik in the preseason of 1940 had worked his way up from sixth-string to first by the time the Midshipmen opened the season against William and Mary. He quickly developed into a triple threat in Navy's single-wing of-fense. Not only did he call the plays, but he also was charged with being the team's primary runner, passer, and punter, and he led the Midshipmen to a 5–3 record in their first eight games of the '40 season. Their season finale came against Army on November 29, 1940, the fiftieth anniversary of the first Army-Navy rivalry, a game that Romanek and Olds—both Cadet plebes—would have to watch from the stands.

"Number 63 (Busik) is the guy that makes their entire team go," coach Wood told his players at Army's final practice before they boarded a train and traveled to Philadelphia for the Navy game. "Busik is the guy we always need to be aware of. He's the guy we're going to have to stop."

Midway through that '40 season, as it became increasingly clear that Busik was the team's top player, sportswriters started calling him "Barnacle Bill." The nickname stemmed from a popular Betty Boop black-and-white cartoon in 1930 named *Barnacle Bill*, which was based on the song "Barnacle Bill the Sailor." In one version of the song—and there were several—the first two verses went:

> *It's only me from over the sea,*
> *Said Barnacle Bill the Sailor,*
> *I'm all lit up like a Christmas tree,*
> *Said Barnacle Bill the Sailor.*

I'll sail the sea until I croak,
Drink my whiskey, swear, and smoke,
But I can't swim a bloody stroke,
Said Barnacle Bill the Sailor.

Though Busik had little in common with the Barnacle Bill in the song—Busik never drank or smoked, and he could swim like a fish—Busik didn't mind the nickname. He figured he must have been doing something right to have earned the admiration of the press. And the sobriquet made him think of the Rabbit, Jackie Robinson. Ever since Busik had left southern California, he and Robinson corresponded through letters. Robinson was now at UCLA and, like Busik, he was rapidly developing into a star football player. The two followed each other's success on the field as closely as they could, writing about once every two months, keeping each other up to date with how the plot of their young lives was evolving.

Thirty minutes before the kickoff of the Golden Anniversary game between the U.S. Naval and Military Academies, Robin Olds and Henry Romanek walked onto the field at Philadelphia's Municipal Stadium. Wearing their dress uniforms, they marched in formation through the field gates with the rest of the plebes and nonvarsity football players. The crowd greeted the Cadets with a mighty roar. As Olds and Romanek looked up into the sold-out stands, the 102,311 fans seemed to stretch from sideline to skyline, all their hands vigorously clapping. Neither of them had ever heard such a booming noise at a football stadium before.

The Army and Navy regimental commanders then met at midfield and shook hands. A crackling voice came over the public address system. "This shaking of hands symbolizes the unity of Army and Navy in the common cause of national defense." Again the crowd belched a roar, cheering so loudly that it seemed to Romanek and Olds as if everyone in the stands was screaming at the top of his or her lungs. After the game Philadelphia's *Evening Public Ledger* noted, "The spirit of unity that is massing a nation . . . electrified the crowd today."

Navy was the three-to-one favorite over Army. The Midshipmen's record stood at 5–3; Army was 1–6–1, its lone highlight holding Notre Dame to one touchdown in a 7–0 loss to the Irish on November 7. Most everyone expected a blowout. On the eve of the game, one reporter in the *Baltimore Sun* joked in print, "If Navy doesn't beat the Army decisively, it means it has gone backward faster through November than any good football team in history and there should be a congressional investigation."

Red Blaik sat behind the Army bench with Eichelberger. Blaik was eager to see the talent level of the Cadets, to gauge whether or not he could cobble together a winning team in just one season—if he decided to take the job. Army received the opening kickoff, but was forced to punt after three plays. Busik returned the punt from his own 36 to the Cadet's 42. On Navy's first offensive play, Busik floated a pass to Everett Malcom, who was pushed out of bounds at Army's 18-yard line. Three plays later Busik scored on a 2-yard plunge into the endzone. After the extra point, Navy led 7–0 just 6 minutes into the game. Busik, the Cadets quickly found out, was as good as all the sportswriters were saying.

It was right about this time that President Roosevelt, who was listening to the game on a radio in the Oval Office, phoned Secretary of War Henry Stimson, who was sitting in a box on the Army side of the field. Roosevelt not only wanted an eyewitness account of what was transpiring at the stadium, but he also wanted to keep Stimson informed of the latest developments in Europe. Earlier that morning the Associated Press, citing an unnamed source, reported that Hitler's Germany was planning to invade Great Britain within the next three weeks. Roosevelt discussed this report with Stimson. But when the two weren't talking about foreign affairs, they chatted about the game. Roosevelt, a former assistant secretary of the navy, was no doubt thrilled that Busik and the Midshipmen had taken the early lead.

One person who wasn't pleased with the events on the field was Olds. "I wish I was out there to stop Busik," Olds told his plebe teammates as they watched the action from the stands. "I think I could make a difference. I think quite of few of us could make a difference." Seated a few feet away from Olds, Romanek felt the same way. "Next year, boys," he said over and over to his teammates. "Next year."

The Cadets, who were outweighed and outmanned, lost 14–0. In the closing minutes of the game, as the Midshipmen were trying to run out the clock, the school bands assembled behind the north goal. As soon as the final gun sounded, the bands started to belt out the first strains of the "Star Spangled Banner." The music echoed throughout the hushed stadium, as everyone in attendance stood and sang in unison. But a few excited Midshipmen had already run onto the field and were tearing down the wooden goalpost in the south endzone. Once they realized that everyone was singing the "Star Spangled Banner," they stopped. A few Middies sat on the crossbar as they saluted the flag, all of them unable to conceal their canary-swallowing grins. As soon as the music was over, the goalpost came tumbling down.

"This is obviously the highlight of my season," Busik told reporters after Navy's victory. "There was just so much excitement in the stadium today. Running out onto the field and seeing all those people was just incredible, something I'll never forget. I've never experienced anything like it. I can't wait to play Army again next year."

As soon as Busik was done talking to the reporters, one of the first players to congratulate him on his stellar performance was Hal Kauffman, who had suited up for the game but didn't see any action. Yet even though he hadn't stepped onto the playing field, Kauffman, who was buried on the depth chart, felt like he was a big part of the victory. He'd played on the scout team in practice and, on the sideline, provided constant encouragement. Unlike some young men, Kauffman understood that not every player is destined to be a football star—he certainly wasn't—but that didn't diminish the joy of the moment for him.

"You were terrific, Bill," Kauffman said after the game. "But all of us knew you would be. Good golly, you looked like a pro out there." With that, the two friends from Pasadena shook hands. A few years later, half a world away and under dramatically different circumstances, they'd recall this moment, and how simple and sweet their lives had been when all that mattered was beating Army.

After watching the Cadets fall to the Midshipmen, General Eichelberger became even more determined to get Red Blaik to coach at the Point. Shortly after the game Eichelberger contacted the surgeon general and asked him to ease the age-height-weight restrictions. Eichelberger wanted the chart to be more of a suggestion than a strict rule. After all, Eichelberger noted, sometimes the chart said a man was obese when, in reality, he simply had a stout, athletic build. Eichelberger also convinced General Edwin Watson, President Roosevelt's aide-de-camp and a West Point grad, to lobby the surgeon general. Watson was more than happy to put a call into the surgeon general. Watson, like many high-powered West Point graduates in Washington, was tired of losing bets on Army-Navy games to high-ranking navy officials. Finally the surgeon general, after much verbal sparring with Eichelberger and Watson, relented and loosened the restrictions.

A month after the Army-Navy game, Blaik still hadn't made up his mind. His biggest reservation was that he didn't know how he'd be received being the first graduate head coach not in the service. In mid-December Blaik traveled to West Point and articulated this feeling to Eichelberger, who in turn had a strange request for Blaik. "Go over to the Officer's Club," Eichelberger said, "and get your hair cut by Tom Impel. When you get back, let me know how long it took."

Blaik did as he was told. Impel was known around West Point to dole out conversation in direct proportion to the importance of the customer in his chair. When Blaik sat down and introduced himself, Impel let the words fly. He slathered Blaik's face with shaving cream and fired one question at him after the next. About 45 minutes later, Blaik returned to Eichelberger's office, his hair freshly shorn and his face as smooth as the skin of an apple. "How long did Tom have you in his chair?" asked Eichelberger.

"About forty-five minutes," Blaik answered.

"A shave and haircut for a second lieutenant takes Tom about five minutes," Eichelberger replied. "The superintendent usually gets forty-five minutes of cutting and conversation. Right now you're the second ranking person on the post. You'd better take the job, Red."

On December 22, 1940, Blaik did. He met General Eichelberger at a hotel in midtown Manhattan and told him he accepted the offer. Blaik's orders were to come up with a "crash" program to restore Army football. He was bestowed the rank of full colonel and appointed athletic director. The program was completely his. Change—badly needed change—had arrived at the Point, and football at the Military Academy would never be the same.

6

PRESEASON 1941

THREE WEEKS AFTER ACCEPTING THE head coaching position at Army, Blaik summoned Ray Murphy to his office. Blaik had not yet spoken to any of his players and he figured that Murphy was the logical player to call in first. Two months earlier, Murphy, an interior lineman who played both ways, had been one of a handful of players nominated to be team captain of the '41 squad. The vote took place the evening after Army's loss to Navy. Just outside of Newark, New Jersey, as the team's locomotive chugged north through the autumn twilight, the three candidates stood in the front of a rail car. An assistant coach then asked everyone on the team to raise his hand if he wanted the first candidate, Murphy, to be captain. With Manhattan glowing outside the windows like a giant orange torch, about 90 percent of the players raised their arms. Murphy, it was quickly decided, would be the team's lone captain for the 1941 season.

Murphy was from Anaconda, Montana, a gritty mining town located in the foothills of the Rocky Mountains. At Anaconda High Murphy was a bear of a lineman, and when he played he had an air of ruthlessness about him. He was so talented that he became the rare Montana high school player who got recruited by several Division I schools. What helped make him such a menacing interior player, according to his coaches, was that he worked year-round as a logger. On the weekends and after school he'd cut down trees, haul timber, and occasionally help build log cabins. The labor was strenuous, but because Murphy had fore-arms as thick as fence-posts, he often did the work of two men. Murphy would have been perfectly content spending his entire life chopping wood and breathing the cool Montana air that was tinged with the scent of pine needles and wood smoke, but then he started listening to Army football games on the radio and his ambition got redirected, as if a giant hand had swooped down from the sky, tapped him on the shoulder, and pointed to West Point. In the late '30s, this was happening to boys all over the nation, especially to country boys like Murphy.

By the time he was fourteen, Murphy would come home from work on fall weekends and sit in the living room with his father. Together they would listen to play-by-play radio broadcasts of Army football games. Murphy had to adjust the directional antenna every few minutes because the reception failed, but that never stopped him from being captivated by the static-filled accounts. Before long, those faraway Cadet players became Murphy's gridiron heroes. As the games played out in the world of his imagination, Murphy believed that the players must surely have glowed in the dark each time they donned the black and gold Army uniform. They were America's heroes. How he wished to be one of them.

Five years later, he *was* one of them. Yet there was nothing epic or lyrical about going 1–7–1. Murphy had heard from teammates that Blaik had turned around the program at Dartmouth, so he was optimistic that Blaik could work that same magic at the military academy. But in just one season? Murphy's eligibility would be over at the end of the '41 season, and he wanted to be on at least one Army team that had a winning season. "Things are going to be completely different from now on," Blaik told Murphy in their initial meeting. "We are going to work like you've never worked before. No team in the United States will be as fit as us. That's why we'll win games next year. In fact, we'll win a lot of games."

Blaik continued. "I don't care what you did last year, every position is up for grabs," he said. "You'll have to earn the right to start. I'll give everyone a fair chance, but just know that what you did last year or two years ago no longer matters. All that matters is what you do from right now until the first kickoff of the season."

Instead of waiting until March to begin spring practice—which is what virtually every other team in the nation did—Blaik told his players to meet him in the fieldhouse on a late afternoon at the end of January. Snow swirled on the plain in the winter winds as the Cadet football players, all wearing their long gray coats, trudged through the blistering dusk to meet their new coach. Once they opened the fieldhouse doors, there stood Blaik in the entry. He cut an imposing figure. At 6' 2", 190 pounds, he was in excellent shape. He had bronze hair and piercing pale blue eyes—eyes that seemed to indicate that he was all business, all the time. He always stood perfectly straight—it was as if the man had steel in his spine—and now he wore a serious look on his face. The coach knew that the air had leaked out of his players' football dreams, and he understood that it was his job to inflate those dreams once again. That process was about to begin.

Once the entire team was present, Blaik began speaking. "Gentlemen, we have a lot of work to do in the next few months," he said. "We are going to master the fundamentals of this game before we move on to anything else. I believe we can have a winning team this year if we work harder than any other team in the nation." Blaik continued speaking for about another 30 minutes, emphasizing to his players that the only way they were going to get better was to trust each other and the coaches. At the end of his talk, Blaik had a surprise for the players. Though none of them had brought their cleats to the meeting—they expected this to be nothing more than a get-to-know-you session with their new coach— Blaik ended his remarks by telling the squad, "Practice starts right now. Everyone out to the field." In the early '40s there were no rules restricting the number of practices a team could hold in the winter and spring, so Blaik, being the impatient man that he was, put his boys to work even though snow and ice covered the ground.

In reviewing film from the '40 season, Blaik determined that Army's biggest weaknesses were blocking and tackling, the two most fundamental skills in football. Starting at the end of January and continuing until the beginning of June, Blaik had his players work on blocking and tackling almost every day from 3:45 to 5:15. Only occasionally during these eighteen weeks of practice did Army work on actual plays. Instead, Blaik drilled his players in rudiments of the game. The typical drill pitted two players against one. A coach would toss the ball to an offensive player, who was given a simple command: He was to try to push forward and gain as many yards as possible against the two defenders, both of whom were in three-point stances directly in front of him. With the coaches watching closely, the two defenders had to display perfect technique in making the tackle before they'd be given a breather.

Of course, these sessions were particularly brutal for the backs and receivers. Archie Hill, a back out of New Mexico, had his appendix removed two weeks before Blaik had started "spring" practice. Wanting to impress the coaches, Hill didn't tell the coaches about his surgery and began practicing with his teammates. But after three days of nonstop pummelings, Hill was taken to the hospital because of internal bleeding. When Blaik discovered that Hill was still recuperating from an appendectomy, he couldn't help but be impressed. Hill was his kind of player: tough, relentless, and willing to play with pain. If he had a team full of Archie Hills, Blaik commented to several players, then he was sure that Army would win the national championship. Not in three seasons. Not in two. But next season, with most of the same players who couldn't even win two games in 1940.

Blaik also believed that changing the mindset of his players was just as important as improving their fundamentals. This became clear to Blaik during one of his first meetings with the entire team. Standing in front of a chalkboard in a classroom, Blaik diagrammed a running play and then turned to his players, who were seated at desks. "Boys, the most important part of football is line play," Blaik said. "Football games are lost because of poor line play and . . ." Just then, Blaik noticed a player in the back of the room who was dozing off.

"Mister," Blaik yelled, "where are most games lost?"

Startled, the player opened his eyes and saw Blaik, red with anger, staring at him. "Uh," the player stammered, "right here at West Point?"

The players in the field house wanted to laugh, but they kept their feelings muted for fear of further upsetting Blaik. There was nothing funny about that comment, Blaik told his team. He went on to deliver a sermon about what it takes to win—not only on the field of football, but also on the field of combat. "There's a bigger battle going on in the world right now, and everything we do here as a team will help you get ready for the obstacles that you'll be facing once you leave the academy," Blaik told his players that day. "Let's never lose our focus and try to get better each and every day. This will make you a better player and a better soldier."

During these four months of "spring" practice, Blaik usually arrived at the south gym by 8:00 A.M. He'd ride an elevator to the top floor and then walk up another flight of stairs to his office in the tower. Blaik's office was his second home, as he spent more time in there than he did under the roof that he shared with his wife. On one wall hung a West Point coat of arms. Behind Blaik's mahogany desk was a framed photograph of a saluting MacArthur, his hero and role model. Every morning, in the soft, amber light of his office, Blaik would plan in painstaking detail every minute of practice. From the moment that the players left the dressing room at 3:45 until the final whistle sounded at 5:15, Blaik scripted everything. He set times for all the drills and for learning new plays. Blaik memorized every practice schedule and all the players' assignments in every play so he wouldn't need to bring notes to practice; he expected his assistants to do the same, because he believed it sent a good message to the players. Indeed, coaches all across the nation talked about the importance of preparation, but Blaik took it to another level. Years later one of Blaik's assistants, a young coach named Vince Lombardi, would be so impressed with Blaik's preparedness and attention to detail that Lombardi would copy Blaik's approach to the game when, at the age of forty-five, he became the head coach of the Green Bay Packers in late 1958.

Blaik held a daily staff meeting that usually began at nine and lasted until two in the afternoon, with a brief break for lunch. After practice the staff would reconvene and often the meetings would go deep into the night. The most time-consuming aspect of the staff's job was watching film. Blaik, without question, watched more film than any coach in the country. He had a projector in his office and it ran continually, spitting out grainy, black-and-white images of upcoming opponents. Blaik charted opposing team's tendencies based on the down, distance, and field position, and he was one of the first coaches to grade his own players on their effectiveness on each play. By the time he'd be done watching a film, Blaik would have a mountain of notes. But part of Blaik's genius as a football coach was that, after film study, he'd distill those notes into a simple, well-crafted, well-oiled game plan that was easy for his players to digest and comprehend.

Coaches all across the country watched film, but no staff in America took film study as seriously as Blaik's. Even as early as January 1941, Blaik was watching the films of the teams Army would be facing nine months later once the '41 season kicked off. He paid particularly close attention to the games that featured the naval academy. Blaik knew that, even if Army lost every game but managed to defeat the Midshipmen, the year would be judged as a success by his superiors. So Blaik and his assistants all studied film—both of Army's practices and of past games of their upcoming opponents—as if their jobs depended on it, which, in a way, they did.

Blaik got so caught up in viewing film, in fact, that it made a dent in his social life. A few times during these four months of practice, Blaik's wife, Merle, hosted cocktail parties on Friday evenings. Much to his wife's displeasure, Blaik often showed up late because he got bogged down viewing film. One time when he arrived mid-party he didn't understand why so many people were in his house. He'd forgotten all about the party his wife had been planning for weeks. Not only was football the man's livelihood, it was also his life.

For the players, it was hard to concentrate on football, with all that was going on in the world. In late 1940, Franklin Roosevelt became the first man in the history of the United States to be elected president for a third time. Roosevelt defeated Republican Wendell Wilkie in a landslide, and the consequences of Roosevelt's victory were significant. Roosevelt had spent months warning the American public about the evils of fascism. FDR believed that the United States couldn't remain isolationist forever, but he always chose his words carefully because he didn't want to alienate the "America Firsters," those voters who were passionate in wanting the United States to remain a bystander in the growing global conflict. But with Roosevelt securely in office for a third term, he almost immediately strengthened the United States' ties with England. "We should do everything to help the British Empire defend itself," Roosevelt said after the election.

By early 1941, the attitude of the American public toward the possibility of entering the war was beginning to change. A poll in *Fortune* magazine showed that a year earlier American businessmen were unsympathetic with the plight of Britain and France. Now the majority supported assisting both counties in defeating Hitler, even though most hoped they themselves wouldn't have to fight. Roosevelt used a metaphor to describe the situation: If your neighbor's house is on fire, Roosevelt said, and he wants to borrow your garden hose, you don't ask to be paid, you just want your hose back. "There is far less chance of the United States getting into war if we do all what we can now to support the nations defending themselves against the attack by the Axis than if we acquiesce in their defeat," Roosevelt told the nation over the radio in a fireside chat.

In mid-May of '41, with many players poised to quit the Army team because they were so run down from the nonstop blocking and tackling drills, Blaik finally had his team start practicing basic plays. One of Blaik's staple plays was "41 Pitch," a simple pitch sweep to a back. Blaik told his team that this would be one of the primary offensive plays that they'd run throughout the season. This meant that his players had to master it to perfection before they could start learning other plays. "Precision, precision, precision," Blaik repeatedly told his team as they worked on perfecting the one play they were taught.

Robin Olds quickly grew to detest "41 Pitch." Even though he would only be a sophomore (second class) next season, Olds had quickly worked his way into the starting lineup. By May he was a first-string offensive and defensive tackle on the varsity. When he was on offense, his assignment on "41 pitch" was to block a defensive tackle named James McKinney. Before he'd arrived at West Point, McKinney had worked as an attendant at a sanitarium. One of his duties was to keep the patients in line. If, for example, a patient became physical with another patient or a staff member, it was McKinney's job to subdue that patient. This meant that McKinney, who stood 6' 0" and weighed 220 pounds, had a lot of experience in grappling with people one-on-one. McKinney also had a wild streak—he was known to deliver more than a few late hits—and occasionally acted as if he should be living *in* an asylum rather than working at one. "I've been thinking about hitting you all day long," McKinney would sometimes tell Olds before they lined up. "I got a lot of anger I need to take out on you."

In spite of his heated talk, nine times out of ten Olds prevented McKinney from making the tackle—or even disrupting the flow of the play. But the leather helmet that Olds wore didn't protect his ears, and McKinney frequently smacked Olds' ears when he'd club Olds with his forearms in an attempt to knock him off balance. After a week, Olds' right ear was so cauliflowered that he had to go to the campus infirmary to have it pierced and drained. A few days later, he started to lose hearing out of that ear.

"Coach, could we at least mix the plays up so the defense doesn't know what we're running all the time?" Olds asked Blaik after practice one afternoon. "They're beating us up out there because they know exactly how we're going to block them. Could we at least run it in the other direction?"

"We can't do that," replied Blaik. "We're making this as hard as possible on you, Robin, because once we run this play in a game against a team that doesn't know it's coming, you shouldn't have any problems making the right blocks."

When he spoke during practice, Blaik rarely raised his voice. Always wearing his Army baseball cap, sweatshirt, football pants that were cut off below the knee, wool socks, and black cleats, Blaik stood alone as he watched his players perform one drill after the next. If he saw something that bothered him on the practice field, he sometimes blurted out, "Jesus Katy!" but usually he would stand stoically off to the side, a liquid glimmer of intensity flickering in his eyes as he scanned the field, absorbing the action. If he did need to correct a player, Blaik would calmly call him over and quietly explain what he did wrong, leaning over close to his ear. Blaik was a literalist, not a storyteller who had a gift with words, and he always cut straight to the chase, no matter what the setting.

Along with Blaik's outwardly detached demeanor—Henry Romanek once remarked to a teammate that Blaik was as "warm as a cold bottle of piss"—he also had a bullish aura. The players never challenged him, though several came close to saying something to him about his method for conditioning the team. Blaik always saved his toughest drill for the end of practice. He wanted the players' legs to be already burning when he instructed his boys to line up on the goal line and try to make a series of goal-line stands. These were often the most intensive few minutes of practice. Standing on the goal line with a whistle in his mouth, Blaik would ask his players to dig deep, to find that last kernel of energy and give all that they had for just a few more plays. He would tell his players to imagine that it was the fourth quarter against Navy and all that stood between a victory and a loss was a mere three yards. *Do you have what it takes to stop them?* Blaik asked. *Are you strong enough? Are you man enough?* "Give me your all right now!" he'd yell to his squad.

To the players, it sometimes felt like Blaik and his assistants were the Hounds of Hell, always snapping at their ankles, chasing them around the practice field, barking one directive after the next. But the staff's intensive approach worked. Because by the time October rolled around and Army was preparing to play its first game against the Citadel, the Cadet players had been transformed. The spring practice that began in the chill of January, continued through the sleets of March, and concluded in the heat of August had succeeded in changing the attitude, the conditioning, and the skill level of the players. This was a team that had been remade in Blaik's image: They were fundamentally sound, mentally tough, and emotionally starving for success. "I like this team," Blaik told Murphy one afternoon before the season opener. "I like it because no one knows how good we're going to be. This means we've got something that our opponents don't: the element of surprise."

Down at Navy, on August 18, Swede Larson held the initial team meeting of the Midshipmen's 1941 season. Wearing a dark sweatshirt, gray sweatpants and football knickers, Larson spoke to his team in the wrestling loft. Larson was normally an upbeat person—he constantly had a piano-key smile on his face—but he was also famous for his Midwestern reserve, so he rarely let his emotions bubble up to the surface. Yet now as he prepared to speak to the hundred players who were trying out for the team, he couldn't stop himself from getting excited. There was promise in the air. Larson knew that, unlike many of their upcoming opponents, graduation hadn't hit the Middies hard. They had lost only eight lettermen from the top two strings. So as Larson looked out at his players, he knew he was staring at a team that could seriously challenge for the national championship, and he told his players as much.

"We have a chance to be one of the best Navy teams in the history of Navy football," said Larson. "But at this point, it's just a chance. We have to work hard and stay focused from now until the season is over."

Before the 1941 season began, the era of single platoon football came to an end when the NCAA passed a rule allowing free player substitutions except during the last two minutes of the first half. Up until then, player substitutions could only be made between quarters. Larson liked the idea of single platoon football, and in 1940 he had successfully employed what he called "The Two Ocean Navy." Because Larson felt he had an abundance of talented players, he typically played his first string in the first and fourth quarters and his second string in the second and third. Even though all the players played both offense and defense, they didn't get fatigued because they only played half the game. The majority of college coaches were opposed to the new substitution rule of '41, believing that football players should be all-around talents and be good on both sides of the ball. Most coaches also felt that the rule rewarded specialization. In spite of the new rule, Larson told his team that they'd again be operating "The Two Ocean Navy."

Larson also announced to his players that they'd be wearing a new type of helmet for the '41 season. Instead of donning leather caps, the Middies would be wearing a plastic helmet with a blue stripe down the middle. Larson noted to his players that in 1940 a few college teams had

worn these helmets—which didn't include face guards—and they had dramatically reduced the number of head injuries that the players had suffered. All of this made sense to Busik, Kauffman, and the others in the
room, even if the helmets did, in their estimation, look a little like something Buck Rogers would wear.

The other cosmetic change that Larson told his players about was
the numbering system. Instead of allowing players to wear whatever
number they desired, the NCAA had recently issued guidelines for a
player's number based on the position that he played. Wingbacks were to
be numbered 10 to 19, blocking backs 20 to 29, fullbacks 30 to 39, tailbacks 40 to 49, centers 50 to 59, guards 60 to 69, tackles 70 to 79, and
ends 80 to 89. These new requirements didn't sit well with a number of
the returning players, especially those who felt that their old numbers
had brought them good luck. Larson, not wanting anyone to feel jinxed,
allowed his returning lettermen to keep their number if they desired, but
all the new players had to abide by the NCAA guidelines. Busik was relieved. As tailback, he wore number 63. It didn't make sense to him to don
a jersey that had a number in the forties. "It looks funny when I don't
wear 63," Busik told a teammate. "That's my number, simple as that."

When the Navy team finally hit the practice field during the last days of
August, Larson wasn't disappointed. As he walked from one group of
players performing a drill to the next, he was pleased with the effort and
talent level that he saw. Unlike Army's Blaik, Larson left much of the actual coaching to his stable of assistants. Larson's top lieutenant was Rip
Miller. A hearty, amiable man, Miller coached Navy's offensive and defensive lines. Many of the players considered him a surrogate father, mostly
because he was the reason that nearly all of them were there. Miller, who
also served as Navy's recruiting coordinator, was a noted ball-player
bloodhound who could sniff talent from thousands of miles away. By
1941, his Bird-Dog recruiting system—having dozens of scouts across the
country on the prowl for talent—was starting to be copied by schools all
across the country. But no one in the recruiting game was as plugged in as
Miller, whose connections extended all the way to the White House.

Throughout the late '30s and early '40s, Miller made several trips to
visit President Roosevelt, who was a rabid Navy football fan. Roosevelt
kept a miniature wheel of a ship on his desk in the oval office and he was
always snooping around for inside information on the Midshipmen football team. On numerous occasions during his trips to Washington, Miller

would bring a silent reel of film from the most recent Army-Navy contest and, usually in the president's private quarters, the two would sit and watch the game. Miller would narrate the action to the President, but he was always careful with his words. Because the President could issue ten appointments to each academy, Miller stressed to Roosevelt that it would greatly help the Navy program if the President doled out his appointments to potential football players. One time, on the tape, Navy was outfitted in white uniforms and Army was dressed in black—on the video, black always made the players look bigger than they actually were—and Miller tried to pull the wool over the President's eyes, noting to Roosevelt, "Look, Mr. President. Just look at how much bigger those Army boys are than us. We have a hell of time beating them."

"Well, Rip, what do you plan to do about it?" the President asked.

"That's where we were hoping you'd come in, sir," Miller replied. "We could really use your ten appointments. I've got boys all around the country lined up, but it's tough to get all of them congressional appointments."

Rip's plan worked. "Well, Rip," replied the President, after considering the situation, "I'll tell you what I'll do. I'll do my best to give you all ten. We gotta do whatever it takes to beat Army."

On the practice field, Miller often lined up against his players. Miller believed that the best way to teach proper blocking and tackling technique was through example, and he relished putting on the pads and mixing it up with lineman who were twenty years his junior. Miller was so passionate about line play that he wrote a two thousand word article on the subject in the November 1926 edition of *The Athletic Journal*. "The main objective of the offensive lineman," wrote Miller, "is to obtain quick contact and above all things to keep that contact. Whether a lineman uses a shoulder charge to drive a man out of the way of a play, or whether he reverts to a body block to prevent a drifting defensive opponent from slicing into a play, or whether he runs interference in the open field, the thing uppermost in his mind at all times is—to keep contact. Too many offensive lineman give up easily."

As Miller coached the offensive line, telling his players over and over at practice, "Damn it, you gotta be tough," Keith Molesworth was busy teaching both the offensive and defensive backs. Molesworth had been a star quarterback with the Chicago Bears from 1931 to '37 and his success in the NFL gave him instant credibility among the Navy players. When he talked to them, it was as if his words came thundering down from

Mt. Olympus, so attentive were the players to his every suggestion and command. Larson felt comfortable letting Miller and Molesworth oversee the Xs and Os of the game; Larson was more at ease acting as the leader who made the big-picture decisions. So at practices Larson floated from one group to the next, a serious look etched on his face, imploring his kids to work harder, but rarely did he delve into the nuances of the game with them.

As Navy's first game against William & Mary approached on September 27, the players badly wanted to win for their coaches—especially their head coach. Because even though Larson hadn't told them yet, the players figured that this was going to be his last season as Navy's coach. The clouds of war were gathering, and they knew Larson would soon have to fight in the approaching storm.

That storm was intensifying by the day. In late June of '41, as the Navy boys continued practicing in Annapolis, Germany attacked Russia, its former ally. Speaking on a radio broadcast on the morning after the invasion, Hitler boasted that Germany's army movements were "the greatest the world has ever seen."

Days later Japan conscripted a million men into its army and recalled all of its merchant ships from the Atlantic. The Japanese government was preparing for a possible war against Britain and the United States over Indochina, which Japan had invaded in September 1940 and by June of '41 had established control over the entire country. On the afternoon of the announcement of troops being called up, the war minister, Hideki Tojo, made a rare appearance at an imperial conference. He emphatically told the Japanese cabinet that the time for action had come. Based on Germany's success in Europe, the war minister insisted that the Japanese empire needed to expand immediately—or risk missing a rare opportunity in history.

The British and U.S. governments responded by signing the Atlantic Charter. Meeting in secrecy on board the American cruiser *Augusta* and British battleship *Prince of Wales* at Placentia Bay in Newfoundland, President Roosevelt and Prime Minister Winston Churchill signed a joint declaration of common principles. The two countries were bound together like family, and both Roosevelt and Churchill insisted that, no matter what the outcome of the approaching storm, neither country would seek territorial gains from the war.

. . .

Like most high school, college, and pro football teams in 1941, Army and Navy both ran the single wing offense. In the Cadets' and the Midshipmen's versions of the single wings, the center could snap the ball to the tailback, fullback, quarterback, or wingback in motion. The center had to be one of the most skilled players on the offense, because he was required to accurately hike the ball in different directions based on the play call. The center usually looked through his legs when he made the snap, which left him vulnerable to a hard-charging defensive lineman. But even more important than the center in the single wing was the tailback, because he received the majority of the snaps and then either ran, passed, or punted. Indeed, most of the great triple threats in football history were single-wing tailbacks, players such as Red Grange, George Gipp, Sammy Baugh, Tom Harmon, and Doak Walker.

Sometimes after receiving the ball the tailback would hand the ball to the fullback, who would take a step forward and then spin 180 degrees. With his back to the line, the fullback had several options: He could hand off to another back, fake a handoff and run, or turn back toward the line of scrimmage and run straight into the middle of the line. The quarterback, for his part, rarely touched the ball. His most important role was to be the lead blocker, which made him more of a glorified guard than anything else.

What made the offense so hard to defend was that all the backs in the single wing were constantly spinning, reversing, faking handoffs, making handoffs, running the ball, passing the ball, blocking, and receiving. Confusing the defense was what Pop Warner had in mind when he devised the offense in 1906 while he was the coach at Carlisle (Pennsylvania) Indian School. In 1912, Warner wrote a book on the formation and its popularity spread quickly. Blaik and Larson had by now tweaked the offense, but the single wing was the dominant formation that each squad practiced prior to the '41 season kickoff.

"The offense is hard to defend because of its deception," Larson told reporters one day during preseason practice. "I know some teams are starting to get away from the single wing, but we'll still use it. After all, we've got a tailback named Bill Busik, and I'd be crazy not to run the single wing with him."

7

THE 1941 SEASON

ON THE PORTABLE RADIOS that many of the Cadets and Midshipmen kept in their rooms, the sports news crackled out, story after story in the summer of '41. Joe DiMaggio, the Yankee Clipper, hit safely in fifty-six straight games. The Red Sox's Ted Williams, the sweet swingin' lefty, was hitting .400 heading into the final day of baseball's regular season. Instead of protecting that magical number by sitting on the bench that last day, Williams played in both games of a double-header against Cleveland. He went six for nine, leaving his season-ending average at .406.

There was more. On June 18, Billy Conn, known as the "Pittsburgh Kid," met Joe Louis in a boxing ring at the Polo Grounds in New York. Conn was the definition of an underdog. He weighed 168 pounds. Louis, the champ, already an American folk hero, checked in at 202 pounds. But through the first ten rounds of the bout, Conn was clubbing Louis, winning on all three of the judges' cards. At the end of the twelfth, Conn landed a devastating right that nailed Louis flush in the face. After the round Conn boldly told his corner that he was going to be the first man to knock the great Joe Louis out. Conn's corner begged their fighter to stay away, telling him that he had the fight won on points but Conn, sensing a historic KO, didn't listen.

Conn came out in the thirteenth firing one punch after the next, tiring with each shot. Louis waited and waited, taking the punishment, absorbing all that the challenger could give, then . . . *BAM!* Louis unleashed a right-hand cross that hit Conn square in the jaw. For the first time all night, the challenger, having just spent so much energy trying to flatten the champ, staggered. Louis followed with seven straight punches—all of them connected. The eighth punch, another right to the jaw, was enough. It sent Conn sprawling onto the canvas. He was counted out. After he came to his senses, Conn, who was as Irish as a shamrock, was asked why he didn't try to win the bout on points. Without missing a beat, he replied, "What's the sense of being Irish if you can't be dumb?"

Then there was Whirlaway, the handsome little red colt that captivated the imagination of racing fans across the nation. Nicknamed Mr. Longtail because of his uncommonly long, flowing black tail that shot up at a 90-degree angle when he ran, Whirlaway had a hard-charging, come-from-behind style not seen since the great Seabiscuit from the late '30s. In the '41 Kentucky Derby, Whirlaway, ridden by jockey Eddie Arcaro, was foundering at the back of the pack with a quarter mile left—but then blazed to victory, winning by eight lengths. In the Preakness, he again started slowly, closed in the last quarter and won by five and a half lengths. And in the Belmont, he broke out of the gate quickly, opened up a seven-length lead and won by two and a half lengths to capture the Triple Crown. The horse was a little nuts—he often veered wildly all over the track until trainer Ben Jones fashioned a special hood with a one-eyed blinker that kept the colt from bearing to the outside—but by the end of the summer Whirlaway was as beloved as any thoroughbred of his time. "There may be better horses," Ben Jones said after winning the Triple Crown, "but there can be only one Whirlaway."

None of these riveting stories was lost on Robin Olds or Henry Romanek. It seemed that in sport anything was possible in the summer of '41, so why not a rebirth of Army football? From listening to the radio and reading the newspapers, Olds and Romanek knew that DiMaggio had done the unexpected, as had Williams, as had Whirlaway, as had the Pittsburgh Kid. To Romanek and Olds, it was now Army's turn. Certainly, the Cadets had worked harder than any college or pro team since the start of the year. They also had Earl "Red" Blaik, who, like a Baptist preacher, had won a squad full of converts. Indeed, in the summer of '41, for the first time since Olds and Romanek got their first stains on their Army football uniforms, hope was rolling high at the Point.

Half a world away during this stellar summer of sport, Japanese Admiral Isokyro Yamamoto sat in his cabin aboard the 42,000-ton battleship *Nagato*. The date was August 10, 1941. Though he was the commander in chief of Japan's Combined Fleet, Yamamoto was not an imposing figure. At 5' 3" Yamamoto, even by Japanese standards, was considered short. He had a straight, large nose and pointed eyebrows, which usually gave Yamamoto the appearance of having a inquisitive look. On this morning the commander's dress uniform overflowed with medals and honors.

Aboard the *Nagato*, which was anchored in Saeki Bay, Yamamoto summoned one of his old friends, Admiral Zengo Yoshida, to his cabin. In their younger days Yamamoto and Yoshida had been classmates, and they trusted each other without question. Once Yoshida walked into the cabin, the commander told his old classmate about a secret plan that he'd been crafting for months. "Japan must deal the U.S. Navy a fatal blow at the outset of the war," Yamamoto told Yoshida in Japanese. "It is the only way she can fight with any reasonable prospect of success. An attack is necessary to give Japan a free hand in the southern operation."

"How will it be possible to send a task force so far from Japan with the present radius of action of the fleet?" asked Yoshida.

"The task force will refuel at sea," replied Yamamoto. "Prospects are favorable for its success."

Army opened the 1941 season by pounding the Citadel, 19–6. The next week the Cadets squeaked past VMI, 27–20. By the time Army faced an undefeated Notre Dame team at Yankee Stadium on November 1, the Cadets were 4–0 and the surprise team of the nation. In just over a month, Army, a team that began the season unranked, had risen to Number 14 in the AP poll. "There's no reason we can't beat Notre Dame," Olds told reporters a few days before Army traveled to New York. "Sure, they're a great team, but we've been through so much together already that we feel like we can conquer any challenge."

"This team has come along fast," added Blaik. "Actually, it's come along even faster than I expected. Right now, I think we can give anyone in the country a great battle."

Army's quick start had all of West Point abuzz. After their 20–7 win at Yale on October 18 in New Haven, hundreds of cadets met the team at the train depot on the Hudson. The cadets ushered the players into horse-drawn carts. But instead of having horses pull the players, the plebes grabbed the carts and dragged the team up the steep hill and into the central area of the campus for a celebratory pep rally. The plebes in particular were ecstatic over Army's four wins to begin the season. When the Cadets were victorious, the plebes were afforded the luxury of falling out for the next week, meaning they weren't hazed for six whole days after the game. The prospect of falling out always prompted the plebes to cheer like they were in a shouting contest whenever they sat in the stands at games, many screaming so loudly they became hoarse for days afterward.

With the team undefeated, cadets began gathering at the old parade grounds to watch practice. Standing in groups of ten and twenty along the marked-off sideline, the cadets constantly encouraged the players to hit harder, to play well for the entire army. The Corp also started cheering the team each night at mess hall, the yells of support loudly reverberating off the hall's concrete walls. The student-body excitement reached a crescendo on October 31, the eve of the Notre Dame game at Yankee Stadium in New York City. Before the squad left for the Knollwood Country Club in White Plains, New York, the eighteen hundred cadets held a boisterous mess-hall rally. Then they marched outside and had a torch-lit parade, capped by a bonfire on the practice field. As the tongues of flames licked the autumn sky on this Halloween night, the entire school seemed reinvigorated by its football team. The student body chanted that they wanted to squash Notre Dame, that they wanted to flatten the Fighting Irish. This kind of school spirit was exactly what Eichelberger had hoped Blaik would generate when he hired him away from Dartmouth, but not even Eichelberger thought Blaik could fashion a winning team at Army so quickly. His wildest dreams never reached that far.

The next day newspaper men from around the country traveled to Yankee Stadium for the Army-Notre Dame contest, which was billed by many as the best game to date of the 1941 college football season. "While over two-hundred games will splash across the gridirons of this broad land today, none compares in public interest and enthusiasm with the meeting of the Cadets and Irish," stated the *New York Daily News*. Dating back to 1923, when Army and Notre Dame first played each other at Ebbets Field in Brooklyn, this game had been the showpiece of New York football. Big Apple businessmen had long used it as an opportunity to invite out-of-town customers to Gotham. And even fans who only had a moderate interest in football—including scores of women—marked it on their calendars months in advance. This was as much a social event as it was a football game, and New York blue bloods, dressed in their mink coats and tailored suits, wouldn't dream of being no-shows.

On the morning of the game, which had a 12:30 P.M. kickoff, the skies over the South Bronx turned dark. The rain started at 11:00 A.M. and wouldn't stop for some ten hours. Nonetheless, a capacity crowd of seventy-six thousand filled Yankee Stadium. The stands and boxes were an ocean of umbrellas, oilskins, cellophane coverings, and plastic ponchos. Most fans carried a thermos of hot cocoa—some spiked it with mint schnapps—and the drinks helped the fans stay warm on this miserable afternoon.

When the Notre Dame players ran out from their locker room and into the gloom, they made football history: The Irish became the first college team to wear nylon football pants. Notre Dame coach Frank Leahy, in his first year on the job, made the decision to have his players wear these newfangled pants once he learned that the weather forecast called for thunderstorms. The gold nylon pants, which weighed only four and a half ounces—or half the weight of the standard cotton football pants—shed water rather than absorbed it. Notre Dame had always been considered the sartorial leader of the gridiron, but to Leahy, this was about football strategy, not about making a fashion statement.

Even though a tarp covered the field until just minutes before kickoff, the field quickly became a large pit of mud. The poor playing conditions favored Army. The slow, slick field helped mitigate Notre Dame's size advantage: The Irish outweighed the Cadets by an average of fifteen pounds per man on both the offensive and defensive lines. Ranked sixth in the nation in the AP poll, Notre Dame entered the game as a three-to-one favorite over the fourteenth ranked Cadets, yet Army threatened to score first. Late in the first period the Irish's Dippy Evans, lining up to punt at his own 21-yard line, had the ball slide off the side of his foot as he went to kick; the ball fluttered out of bounds 13 yards beyond the line of scrimmage at Notre Dame's 34. Army suddenly had an opportunity to gain the early advantage.

After a few runs by the Cadets' Hank Mazur, Army faced a fourth and one at the Irish 10-yard line. All throughout the first quarter Mazur had been brilliant, running through the slop like a gifted mudder at Churchill Downs. A native of Lowell, Massachusetts, Mazur had attended Boston College for two years before enrolling at West Point. He was considered one of the best backs in the nation by most newspapermen and, if the season went well, a darkhorse candidate for the Heisman Trophy. Now on fourth and one, Mazur took the handoff, ran off tackle and gained two yards. First down. But then Mazur noticed a yellow flag laying on the sloppy field: Army was offside. On fourth and six, Blaik chose to go for it again, to gamble and try to get an early touchdown. He called for another off-tackle run—Army had had success with this play—but the Irish held Army to only a 2-yard gain. After the Cadets gave up possession, Blaik looked like a man in search of a wall to punch as he paced back and forth on the sideline. He knew a precious opportunity had slipped away. Worse, it had slipped away because of a mental error.

But Notre Dame, led by star runner and passer Angelo Bertelli, couldn't seize the momentum. Not only was the muddy field slowing down the Irish, but Notre Dame's offensive line couldn't consistently block Robin Olds, who was having the best game of his life. Playing the full 60 minutes on both the offensive and defensive lines, Olds made about a dozen tackles. That Olds could have such an impact on the game was a testament to his toughness. A few weeks before fall practice began, Olds and a few friends spent a lazy afternoon at Delafield Pond, a popular swimming hole just north of West Point. Delafield had three diving platforms and Olds decided to attempt a simple swan dive off the highest platform. But he hit the water at an awkward angle—it was one of the first times in his life that he looked woefully unathletic—and both of his arms were pushed back behind his head. Pain immediately pulsed through his body. Underwater, Olds couldn't move either of his arms. He kicked his legs, pushing himself above the surface. He took a big gulp of air, relieved that he didn't drown, then kicked his way to the beach.

Later that night, his arms were still numb, almost lifeless. In the mess hall the next day he couldn't even lift a pitcher of water off the table with his right hand. Olds never told Blaik about the injury, fearing that he'd lose his starting position, but often in practice and in games his right arm would go dead if he took a direct shot to the arm. Midway through the second quarter against Notre Dame this happened—the hit sent a shot of pain that flowed to every part of his body—and for the rest of the game Olds essentially played with only one good arm.

Olds' teammates knew that he was injured. They saw him in the hot tub after every practice, nursing his sore right shoulder. And they saw him struggle simply to lift his right arm when he was putting on his shirt. Seeing this, his teammates came to view Olds with renewed respect. Even though he was in his first year on the varsity squad, whenever Olds rose to speak in the locker room, his teammates would quiet down and listen as intently as if Coach Blaik was talking. The respect Olds commanded was deep, and he never held his tongue when he had something on his mind. His teammates were reminded of this in the third quarter against the Irish, the score still 0–0, when Olds nearly blew a gasket in the huddle.

Army faced a first and ten from its own two yard line. Olds, like all of his linemates, was now completely slathered in mud; the fans were unable even to see his uniform number of 75. All you could see was the whites of his eyes. "I feel like a goddamn pig," Olds told one of his teammates in the huddle. "But this is fun."

With the ball on their own two-yard line in the third quarter, Blaik sent in a backup tailback, whose uniform was spotless because he hadn't played all day. The tailback was charged with making the play call and he decided to open the series with a reverse, a risky play given Army's field position and the poor playing conditions. "Like hell we're going to run that play," Olds yelled in the huddle. "We've busted our asses all afternoon, and we're not going to throw away this game with that stupid play call of yours."

"Shut up, Olds, or I'll throw your ass off the field," replied the tailback.

"You and who else," countered Olds.

But that's as far as the argument went. In spite of Olds' objections, the Cadets went ahead and ran the reverse. If not for a last-second lunge by end James Kelleher, the Irish would have tackled Kelleher in the end zone for a safety. But as it stood, Army faced a second and 11 from its own 2-inch line. Instead of risking a safety by running another play, Blaik opted to punt on second down. That near safety, it turned out, was the closest that either team would come to scoring all afternoon. The game ended in a 0–0 tie. Army had more first downs than the Irish (5 to 4) and more total yards of offense (120 to 96), but neither team even attempted a field goal. Though Blaik wouldn't admit it, the tie amounted to a moral victory for the underdog Cadets. It proved that they could play with any team in the nation, and it proved that Blaik had his team moving in the right direction.

"Army doesn't like ties," Blaik said tersely to the press after the game outside the locker room. Blaik then walked away from the newspapermen, anxious to return to West Point and study the game film of their next opponent, Harvard. Blaik feared his team would suffer an emotional letdown against the Crimson; he knew that his Cadets were beat-up and exhausted. But for the first time since he took over the Army program, Blaik privately experienced an emotion for his players that he hadn't experienced since his days at Dartmouth: He was proud. Damn proud, in fact. Even Blaik, a natural-born pessimist, started to believe in his boys, believe that they could do something special in '41.

Before the 1941 season kicked off, the Cadet and Midshipmen football players were given some sobering news: Because of the increasingly volatile situations in Europe and the Far East, academic programs at both academies would be accelerated. The demand for more army and navy officers was rapidly growing, and the quickest way to fill that need was to expedite the pace of study at the academies. This meant that Olds and Romanek, for example, would graduate after only three years at the school in June 1943 instead of June 1944. Busik and Kauffman, meanwhile, would finish their studies in June 1942 instead of June 1943. This eliminated one year of football eligibility from every player at the academies, so they all knew that they had to make this season count, that they had to pack two years worth of dreams into one season. This redlined everyone's intensity.

Before Navy's third game of the 1941 season against Lafayette, which was played on a warm early October day in Annapolis, that sense of intensity was written all over the face of Swede Larson. Navy had blown out its first two opponents of the season, William & Mary (34–0) and West Virginia (40–0), but that didn't offer much comfort to Larson in the moments before the Lafayette game. As Larson put on his sports jacket and gray felt fedora in the coach's locker room, he smoked one Lucky Strike after the next. Larson made it a point not to smoke during games and practices, but he felt that having a cigarette before the game—or, hell, half a pack on occasion—helped calm his nerves. Once dressed, Larson then met with his team in the wrestling loft an hour before kickoff. "Go out there and fight like your life depends on it," Larson emphatically told his boys. "Go out and do the things that we practiced and be disciplined and this game is ours. Now let's do it!"

Larson led his boys on their long walk across campus to the football stadium. Many midshipmen and local fans walked with the players to the field, slapping the players on their shoulder pads and shouting encouragement. Once they reached the stadium, the 21,660 fans—which included Vice President Henry A. Wallace—gave the Middies a standing ovation. From his seat in a box, Wallace appeared to be in especially high spirits.

A smile stretched across his face like a rubber band as he watched Navy exert its dominance right away. Busik led the Midshipmen on three pile-driving touchdown marches to give Navy a 21–0 lead midway through the second quarter. The Midshipmen were a heavy favorite, and several marines who were in attendance had bet that Navy would shut out the undermanned Lafayette squad. For most of the first half, those bets looked as safe as a bar of gold in Fort Knox. But then Busik fielded a punt on his own one yard line. Instead of pushing forward for an easy five yards, Busik stepped back two yards while he cut to his left, thinking that he had a wall of blockers set up for him. But just as he was making the turn upfield, he was tackled by Lafayette's Bob Leopard for a safety. After the game, which Navy won 41–2, the marines accosted Busik as he walked back across campus to the locker room, telling him that his mistake had cost them a thick wad of bills.

"I'm just trying to do my best, fellas," Busik told the angry marines. "Sorry about your bet, but even if I had known about it, I wouldn't have changed a thing. If you got a problem with it, tough luck."

Busik then stopped in his tracks and coldly eyed the group of marines. He said nothing for a full minute, daring one of the marines to offer a challenge. When none was proffered, Busik turned and slowly walked away, his head held high.

On the Monday evening after the Lafayette victory—like every Monday evening after a game—the Navy team gathered in the team's projection room to watch the eight-millimeter, black-and-white film of Saturday's contest. Holding narrow wooden sticks that served as their pointers, Larson and his lieutenants went over every play in excruciating detail. After Larson gave his initial remarks on the play, the position coaches would point out what each of the Middies did well and what they did poorly on the play. A few Navy staffers were assigned to take still photographs during the game, and these were analyzed on Monday nights with the same intensity as the film. By the end of the 90-minute session following the Lafayette game, it was clear to the coaches and the rest of the team that Busik was playing better than any back in the country. "Busik is the most well-rounded tailback I've ever coached," Larson told reporters shortly after the Lafayette game. "There's really not anything he can't do. He can run inside, outside, and boy, he can really wing the ball when we have to pass."

The next week Navy beat Cornell, 14–0. Seven days later the Middies traveled to Cambridge, Massachusetts, to face Harvard. Many columnists in the East had Navy sitting atop their national poll. Jesse A. Linthicum of the *Baltimore Sun*, for example, ranked Navy number one, Minnesota two, and Michigan three. Because of Navy's growing reputation, the Middies were a four-to-one favorite over Harvard, but all week prior to the game Larson was as worried as an expectant father on his baby's due date. He repeatedly told his team to be wary of the Crimson, mainly because they were coached by Dick Harlow, who was one of the most cunning coaches of his time. Harlow often developed off-beat, wild gameplans that employed strategies and formations that no other coach in the nation used, such as the slanting line defense. As the *New York Sun* put it a day before the game, "Harlow . . . is noted for his ability to harness the power of a stronger opponent and occasionally upset a rival by means of ambuscade, surprise, and everything but fifth-column activity."

On the eve of the game, Larson took his players to a movie theater in Boston and showed them a motion picture of the 1937 Harvard-Navy game. The players munched on popcorn and drank soda in the dark as they watched the game end in a scoreless tie. "We need to execute, execute, and execute some more to make sure that what happened to Navy in 1937 doesn't happen in 1941," Larson told his players after watching the film. "Every man will win his own individual battle on every play, and then we'll have no problem winning the team battle."

But the next afternoon, just as Larson had anticipated, Harvard coach Dick Harlow did have a surprise for the Middies. Moments before the Navy offense hiked the ball, the Crimson defense shifted multiple players, trying to confuse the Midshipmen. What's more, on almost every defensive play both of Harvard's ends looped to the outside of their blockers in an effort to force all the plays to the inside. In their scouting and film study, Navy had never seen Harvard play this kind of defense. It rattled the Midshipmen—especially Busik. He fumbled three times and had one punt sail off the side of his foot, a shank that only traveled 10 yards. This was by far the worst, and most embarrassing, game of Busik's career. The final score, just like in '37, was 0–0.

In the locker room Larson consoled his players by telling them that the 1926 Navy team had won the national title even though they had tied a game. This team could repeat that feat, Larson said over and over as he shook the hand of each player in the locker room. Then, as was his custom, Larson walked over to the Harvard locker room and congratulated the Crimson. He rarely left the opponents' locker room until he had shaken the hand of every player, from the star tailback who played all 60 minutes to the lowest reserve who didn't even make it onto the field.

Three days after the Harvard game, Larson traveled to New York to attend a luncheon for New York football writers. As he nibbled on a steak, he received a telegram stating that Rose Bowl officials had offered the naval academy a bid to play in their New Year's Day game. Larson was stunned—and not just because his team hadn't played in a bowl game in seventeen years. Larson was surprised by the bid because Navy was only halfway through its schedule—the three giants of Pennsylvania, Notre Dame, and Army still remained—but already his boys were attracting nationwide attention.

"We are still seeking to instill confidence in the boys for any and every situation which must face them," Larson said at the luncheon after he had time to put some perspective on the Rose Bowl invite. "I certainly hope we go through the season unbeaten, because I'd like to see the boys get a chance to play in such a game as the Rose Bowl. We have four games left to play and even if we win them, we have another difficulty to overcome. We're on an accelerated academic program because there's a war coming. And our boys are going to fight."

During the luncheon, Larson also was peppered with questions about a rumor that suggested he was going to become the next commissioner of the NFL. Washington Redskins' owner George Marshall had been touting Larson's credentials for weeks. But Larson, wearing a coat and tie, told the writers that his future was tied to the armed forces. "I don't have time to think about a job in the NFL," Larson said, "I've got a football team and a war to worry about."

On November 1, the same rainstorm that fell on New York City as Army played Notre Dame also drenched Philadelphia, where the Midshipmen were facing Penn. The constant rain swirled in the cross-wind at Franklin Field, forcing many of the 73,391 fans to watch the game from the covered runways in the doubled-decked, horseshoe stadium. But nearly everyone stayed in the stadium because this was the first time since the series between Navy and Penn originated in 1922 that both teams entered the game ranked in the Eastern rankings' Top 10 (Penn was second, Navy was third) and in the Top 20 in the AP national rankings (Penn was eighth; Navy was eleventh).

Navy struck first. The Middies marched 51 yards on their first drive to score a touchdown on a 12-yard pass from Busik to Sammy Booth. For the rest of the first half and seven minutes into the third quarter, neither team could push the ball into the end zone. Navy had only given up two points all season—and that was on Busik's safety against Lafayette—so the defense was virtually impenetrable. Then midway through the third the Middies got some breathing room; back Archie Clarke took a pitch from Busik and crossed over the goal line. The point after sailed wide right, but Navy had a 13–0 lead.

When the Middies got the ball back after a Penn punt, they again began to move the ball. Facing a third and three early in the fourth quarter, Busik took the center snap, spun, and ran to his right. After getting the first down, he was tackled by a Penn lineman. With Busik lying prone on the ground in front of the Navy bench, another out-of-control Quaker player jumped on Busik, hitting him with a flying elbow to the head, knocking Busik out cold. None of the referees saw the cheap shot, but Navy assistant Rip Miller did.

"Laboon!" Miller yelled down the bench. He wanted Jake Laboon, a strapping, 6' 4", 220-pound sophomore tackle. Laboon grabbed his helmet and sprinted toward Miller.

"Laboon, did you see what just happened to Busik?" Miller shouted.

"Yes sir!" replied Laboon.

"Well, you get in there and I don't want that end to be in this game much longer. Do you understand me, Laboon?" Miller asked.

"Yes sir!" again replied Laboon, who then jogged onto the soggy field.

Busik still lay on the ground, motionless. The elbow blow had hit him in the forehead, which was left exposed by his plastic helmet. Finally, after a few minutes, he groggily got up and was helped to the bench. In the huddle all the Navy players knew Laboon's mission. They didn't say anything outright; they just looked at Laboon and nodded their heads. When Navy broke the huddle and approached the line of scrimmage, Laboon sized up the end he was told to take out, his nostrils flaring. A few of Laboon's teammates later swore they'd never seen a scarier face.

The ball was snapped. Laboon grabbed a fistful of mud and slung it in the end's face. As the play drifted to the opposite side of the field, leaving Laboon and the end standing face-to-face some twenty yards from the action, Laboon drew a fist. The end was trying to get the mud off of his face, his hands rubbing his eyes. Laboon then threw a haymaker, hitting the player in the nose with all his might. The Penn player fell to the ground, sprawled out in a whirling daze. His nose was broken and his face, which was already covered in mud, quickly reddened as a reservoir of blood pooled. He tried to get up, but he swayed like a tall wheat stalk in the wind, and fell back to the ground. The officials—and most of the fans—had seen this retaliatory act, and Laboon was tossed out of the game. He walked to the sideline, took off his helmet, and spoke to Miller. Now in the cool and wet air smoke rose off Laboon's head as if from a smoldering camp fire.

"Laboon, I didn't tell you to take him out in front of everybody," Miller told Laboon as the assistant coach escorted his player to the locker room. "I meant for you to be a little more subtle about it."

"Sorry coach," replied Laboon.

"It's okay, Jake," said Miller. "You did good. You protected our star."

Late in the third quarter Penn scored, but Navy won the game, 13–6. The Fighting Irish, who earlier on this day had tied Army, were up next.

At precisely the same time that the Navy players were slugging it out with the boys from Penn, a ship named the *Taiyo Maru* eased into Honolulu Harbor. The *Taiyo Maru* was a passenger vessel from Japan, and the U.S. government allowed her to enter the waters of Hawaii in the hope of deflating the growing tensions between the United States and Japan. (On this very day, Joseph C. Grew, the U.S. ambassador to Japan, sent a telegram to President Roosevelt from Tokyo. In it Grew warned Roosevelt that the Japanese may be planning a "surprise attack.")

On the bridge of the *Taiyo Maru*, with binoculars held to their eyes, were what appeared to be two Japanese tourists. Suguru Suzuki and Toshihide Maejima each looked at the Navy port on Oahu carefully, as if they were studying a piece of art from afar. They were particularly interested in the ship and personnel movements at Pearl Harbor. It was 8:30 A.M. local time and on this crystal-clear Saturday Suzuki and Maejima were afforded an almost perfect perspective on what the early morning conditions around Pearl Harbor looked like on the weekend. Most of the base appeared to be resting, the two Japanese men said to each other.

The U.S. government didn't know it, but Suzuki was a lieutenant in the Japanese Air Force, Maejima a submarine expert in the Japanese Navy. They were spies.

In the Navy locker room after defeating Penn, at about the same time that Suzuki and Maejima were peering though their binoculars at Pearl, the Midshipmen coaches and players slapped Laboon on the back and congratulated him on obeying the instructions of his coach. Yet Laboon was deeply disturbed by his action. One of the most popular Midshipmen at the naval academy, Laboon had a clear idea of the line between right and wrong, and he felt he had crossed it. A native of Pittsburgh, Pennsylvania, Laboon came from a deeply religious Catholic family. The first day he arrived at the academy, Laboon joined the Newman Club (a Catholic club) and every Sunday morning he led all the Catholic midshipmen in the mile-long march to St. Mary's, an old brick church where they would attend mass. Laboon had a notion that he might one day pursue the priesthood, but like most young men, he wasn't sure what the future held for him. "I really like helping others," Laboon told his roommate William Leahy one day during their plebe year. "I just need to figure out what's the best way to do that."

Even though Laboon sucker-punched the Penn player—and even though he often liked to blow off steam by banging his fists into walls—there was a sweetness in his character that endeared him to admirals, midshipmen, and janitors alike. He talked to everybody about everything; no subjects were off limits. *Is Jackson Pollack the greatest living painter? Is Spam, that new kind of canned meat, as tasty as everyone says? Is Rita Hayworth, the movies' Love Goddess, the sexiest woman alive?* Always with an ear-to-ear grin on his face, Laboon flapped his gums on all these topics, and his teammates quickly came to regard him as the biggest talker on the team.

The very large Laboon, who was also an All-American lacrosse player, decided in his first year at the academy that he would enter the Naval branch of submarines after he graduated from Annapolis. Laboon figured since he was already ducking every time he walked inside a naval academy building, life in a sub wouldn't be that drastic of a change. "Subs fascinate me," Laboon told his friend Leahy. "And mark my words: They're going to be critical in the war."

The decision to join the subs would ultimately be the most important of his life. Because in a few years, while out at sea, Jake Laboon would do something that sailors would end up talking about for decades, an act that would seal Laboon's fate.

The Navy players considered Notre Dame their second-biggest game of the season, right behind their blood feud with Army. In the days before taking on the Fighting Irish, Larson told reporters that he was most concerned about stopping Notre Dame's Angelo Bertelli, one of the best passers in college football. When the Irish played Army the previous week at muddy Yankee Stadium, the poor playing conditions had limited what Bertelli could do. Larson now fretted that Bertelli was due, but he still believed the Navy defense could shut him down.

"If our plans centering around Mr. Bertelli work out, I think there's a good chance we'll win this game," Larson said. "Anyway, we expect to do some scoring. Maybe people think we play defensive football, but we spend far more time on our offense, and I hope our attack will really get going on Saturday."

Though Navy hadn't defeated the Irish since 1936, the Midshipmen exuded an air of confidence as they practiced and prepared for Notre Dame. Hundreds of midshipmen attended each practice, sometimes sitting in the rain to watch and support their football team. There was plenty to see, because Larson put his team through three scrimmages in the five days before the game. About a dozen reporters attended the scrimmages, and though none of them noted it in their columns, Hal Kauffman once again proved his value as a sixth-string back. Working on the scout team, Kauffman impersonated Notre Dame's Dippy Evans, a small, fast back who was a threat to go the distance whenever he touched the ball.

Every time Kauffman's number was called, the Midshipmen's first-string defense pounded him. But Kauffman always popped up after being tackled and congratulated his teammates on their powerful defense. Kauffman knew he wouldn't play a single down against the Irish, so he treated these scrimmages as his game, his moment to shine. Showing as much courage as anyone on the team, Kauffman was still as introspective off the field as he was when he was in high school. But once he stepped between the lines, he ran the ball as furiously as Busik—even though he wasn't as big or as fast as his buddy from Pasadena.

Kauffman was a coach's dream. He wasn't listed on the official team roster, but Kauffman was one of a handful of Midshipmen who was allowed to practice with the team because he showed as much heart on the field as Larson had ever seen. As a reward for his hard work, Larson promised Kauffman something that, to Kauffman, was more delicious than chocolate: An opportunity to suit up and stand on the sideline for the Army game.

"You've got to be the best scout-back in America," Busik told Kauffman once. "Nobody works harder in practice than you."

"I just like playing," Kauffman replied. "I feel free out there on the field."

Two and half years since arriving at Annapolis, Busik and Kauffman remained close. Though there was little time for socializing, they still double-dated every so often, taking their ladies to formal hop dances at the academy on Saturday nights after football games. The two friends also talked frequently about the future, and where they'd end up. "It's time for the Germans to be stopped," Kauffman told Busik one afternoon after practice. "And I think the Japanese are going to have to be dealt with at some point as well. I don't know about you, but I'm ready to fight."

"So am I," said Busik. "But I'd sure like to win a national championship before we go overseas. That would be the perfect way to end our football careers."

A cold front blew into Baltimore on the morning of kickoff of the Notre Dame game, dropping the temperature into the high thirties. But the sun shone brightly and more than seventy-six thousand filled Baltimore's Municipal Stadium, including a third of the president's cabinet who had arrived via train from Washington. Notre Dame brought with them their one-hundred-piece band, and they entertained the crowd before the game by playing an assortment of tunes, including repeated renditions of the Irish fight song, "Notre Dame Victory March." Football fans from across the country tuned into NBC radio to hear the broadcast. Out in California a dozen Rose Bowl representatives adjusted their radio dials to listen to the game, anxious to see if Navy could keep its unbeaten record.

Notre Dame, a slight underdog, won the toss and elected to kick. The Middies' Johnny Harrell returned the ball to the 25. On first down Navy ran for 3 yards; on second down they were flagged for offsides. After the penalty, the Middies faced a second and 12 from their 23. Busik called for a quick-kick, and it worked to near perfection: The ball covered 56 yards, rolling out of bounds at Notre Dame's 21-yard line. After two ineffectual plays, the Irish also quick-kicked. Busik, playing deep, returned the ball to his own 48-yard line. It was early, but Navy was winning the battle for field position.

But in the second quarter, Bertelli got on a roll. After receiving the snap, Bertelli would often drop 10 to 15 yards behind the line of scrimmage before he'd look downfield for a prospective receiver. Only a few teams in the country relied so much on down-the-field passes. Even though Navy had spent the entire week preparing for it, now that they were facing this novel kind of offensive attack, they couldn't stop it. Bertelli's skinny right arm propelled the Irish on two touchdown drives in the second quarter as Notre Dame stormed to a 13–7 halftime lead. Navy kept the game close in the second half, but lost 20–13. Bertelli completed 12 of his 18 passes for 232 yards—by far the most passing yards Navy had given up in more than three years.

After the game, Swede Larson's wife jumped out of her seat and ran onto the field. Upset over Navy's loss, she was especially irate with Navy tackle Gene Flathman for playing a poor game, in her opinion. Dressed in a fur coat and wearing high heels, Mrs. Larson, a petite brunette, nearly stumbled as she approached Flathman. Away from the football field, Mrs. Larson was as warm as hot cocoa on Christmas morning. On Sundays she invited the entire team to her house for cake, cookies, and milk. Swede occasionally talked football to his players as they munched on Mrs. Larson's treats, but that wasn't the real purpose of these gatherings. Rather, Mrs. Larson wanted the players to feel as if she was a second mother to them, and she tried to make her home as welcoming as possible. Many of the players even took to calling her "Mama Larson," and they never left her home without giving her a big hug.

But once Mama Larson walked into the stadium and started watching a game, she yelled louder than any midshipman and she took the losses just as hard as her husband. When she finally found Flathman on the field after the Notre Dame game, Mama Larson grabbed him by the jersey, pulling his face close to hers. "Why didn't you play better?" she screamed at the 6' 4", 220-pound Flathman. "We could have won the game if you had played better." The diatribe continued for a few minutes, and it left Flathman near tears.

In the locker room, Larson was much more composed than his wife. He spoke calmly and with a reassuring tone, like a father telling his kids that everything will be okay. "It just wasn't our day today, boys," Larson said. "But our season is not over. We have Princeton and Army left. You know and I know that all that really matters is beating Army. We'll get them in a few weeks. But now let's just prepare real hard to play Princeton next week and we'll worry about Army later. Forget what the scoreboard says. I'm proud of you boys."

While Larson was speaking to his players, Red Blaik was giving a similar speech to the Army players at Cambridge. Blaik's worst fears had come true: his players, still recovering physically from the game in the mud against Notre Dame, seemed a step slower against Harvard. In front of a crowd of fifty-three thousand at Harvard Stadium—the largest attendance total since 1937—the Crimson thoroughly dominated the battered

Cadets, winning 20–6. Army couldn't consistently stop Harvard's modified T-formation on offense. And it didn't help that both Olds and Romanek were still sore from the previous week's game. Both had trouble making blocks on offense and shedding blockers on defense.

"We will get over this loss," Blaik said sternly in the locker room. "We will go back and we will practice and we will improve. We've still got some football to play this season. And, remember, we've still got Navy. Never forget that."

In Washington, relations with Japan continued to cool. Five days after Army's loss to Harvard, President Roosevelt rejected a peace proposal from Japanese Premier Hideki Tojo. United States Secretary of State Cordell Hull said that U.S. acceptance would be tantamount to "aiding and abetting Japan in her efforts to create a Japanese hegemony in and over the western Pacific."

Few around the world were surprised by the Secretary's dismissive attitude. After all, Japan's proposed peace agreement with the United States called for the United States to lift its oil embargo on Japan, supply Japan with one million tons of aviation fuel each month, and help the country acquire whatever oil it needed from the Dutch East Indies. Japan was desperate for oil. The United States and Britain imposed an embargo after Japan invaded Indochina. Japan imported 88 percent of her oil—and its supply was dwindling. Her need was growing by the hour.

The Midshipmen did not overlook their next opponent, Princeton. Before a crowd of forty-two thousand at Tiger Stadium—which included Secretary of the Navy Frank Knox—Navy played its best game of the season, defeating the Tigers 23–0 on November 22. Busik ripped off runs of 46, 35, and 20 yards in leading the Midshipmen to their fourth shutout victory of 1941.

After the game, the white-capped Midshipmen stormed out of the stands and onto the field to congratulate their players. They were met by hundreds of Tiger fans who also poured onto the field. A few brawls started and just when it appeared to the fans remaining in the stands—including Secretary Knox—that a full-scale melee would break out, the Navy band, hoping to diffuse the situation, struck into "The Star Spangled Banner." The Midshipmen and the Tiger fans quickly came to attention, and the fighting ceased. When the song was over, no one had the spirit to raise their fists. Everyone left the field in peace.

"We knew we couldn't look ahead to the Army game," Busik told reporters after the game. "We had to focus all of our attention on Princeton because we thought they would be tough. But now, finally, we can think about Army and Army alone. It's going to be my last game for Navy, and I plan on making it memorable. I'll be heading overseas soon, and I want to be able to tell everyone I serve with about how we beat Army in my last game."

After losing to Harvard, Blaik took it easy on his Army players during practice. He had no other choice. With five starters nursing injuries and several second-team players also hurt, Blaik didn't hold a single scrimmage in the days before the Cadets hosted Pennsylvania.

On the eve of the game Blaik reminded his team that the Quakers had embarrassed Army last season, defeating the Cadets 48–0. "Remember what happened last year," Blaik said, his voice rising. "Let's make up for that tomorrow. We may be a little banged up right now, but remember how hard we've worked. Remember when we were out there in the cold and practicing in January. No team has worked harder than us this year. Let's make all of that work pay off for us tomorrow."

In spite of Blaik's passionate words, the next day the injury-riddled Cadets couldn't consistently move the ball on offense and lost 14–7—a 41-point improvement in the outcome from the previous year. The next week Army again struggled, but hung on to down West Virginia, 7–6. Navy had destroyed the Mountaineers 40–0 earlier in the season—a fact that many of the Cadet players talked about in the locker room after the game.

"I don't care how many points Navy beat West Virginia by, I think we have a real good chance at beating the guys from Navy next week," Olds told reporters. "We're starting to get healthy again and when we're healthy, we feel like we can beat anybody in the nation. Even Navy."

"I know two things," Romanek told anyone with a press badge and a notebook. "One, we'll show up to play next Saturday. And two, we'll give it our all. Navy has a way of bringing out the best in us."

The 1941 Army-Navy game was seven days away.

8

THE BUILDUP

FIVE DAYS BEFORE the Army-Navy game kicked off, clerks at Philadelphia's Municipal Stadium were besieged with mail. More than two thousand requests for tickets from all corners of the country piled up in the stadium box office. Municipal could hold a standing room crowd of more than 102,000 fans, but the game had been sold out for months. Thus, the clerks spent much of the week sending out preprinted forms regretting that the ticket supply had run dry long ago. This overwhelming demand for tickets underscored the fact that, even though neither team was undefeated, the nationwide interest in the game was as high as it'd ever been since the two teams first played each other in 1890. A few days before kickoff, the *Philadelphia Sun* captured the magnitude of this Army-Navy matchup when the paper reported, "There probably never was a time when interest in the game was greater than it is today, the international situation being as it is, the eyes of this nation being on its young men in the military and naval academies."

Trying to capitalize on the demand to see the game, a local television station in Philadelphia decided to broadcast the game on closed-circuit television—one of the first times in college football history that this bold new innovation was used. At two different locations in Philly, fans could pay $2 to watch the game on a TV screen. "The entire country and our armed forces around the world will be following this game," Larson told his players early in the week. "Remember that you're not playing for yourself or for this team. You're playing for the entire navy."

At both academies, the week of the game was unlike any other. Pep rallies were held every day on both campuses. In Annapolis, the Middies hung posters and bed sheets with painted words on them all around Bancroft Hall urging their team to defeat Army. A large sign at the main entrance to Bancroft read: BEAT ARMY! Every evening at dusk those words above Bancroft's entrance became illuminated by electrical lights, serving as a late-night reminder of what was truly important at the naval academy this week. The Middies also posted a sign in the gymnasium, which was changed daily, that counted down the days to kickoff, FIVE DAYS ARMY, FOUR DAYS ARMY, THREE DAYS ARMY.

At West Point, the cadets were just as juiced. Though Blaik had closed practices both to the media and to the corps for fear of spy scouts, the players were greeted by hundreds of cadets each time they walked off the practice field. The energy on campus hung in the air like a mist, and the cadets were so excited that they hardly needed sleep to get through this week. The scream of "Beat Navy" could be heard echoing off the stone buildings and pines several times a day, and whenever Romanek and Olds walked to class several of their fellow cadets would always pat them on the back, telling them that it was Army's turn to win the big game. Everyone on campus knew the recent history: The Cadets had not beaten Navy in three years— their longest winless streak against the Midshipmen since 1921. This fostered such a sense of urgency at the Point that even those few cadets who didn't know a first down from a touchdown could detect the immensity of this particular Army-Navy game.

"Army has one of its best teams in years," Larson told reporters four days before kickoff. "Army is offensively minded and has a diversified attack. There are sixteen letter winners from last year, they're all six-footers with the exception of two, and they're going to give us all the trouble anybody can handle for one afternoon."

Larson had an intimate understanding of Army's team. Navy had sent at least one scout to every game that the Cadets had played. The scouts took notes on Army's coaching tendencies and its players' strengths and weaknesses. Based on all the information that he'd accumulated over the course of the season, Larson felt that Navy would have success running the ball straight at the Army defense. The Midshipmen had a decided size advantage on the line, and Busik had flourished all season when he put his head down and bulldozed between the tackles.

Out on the Navy practice field this week was a special block of wood. It was the remains of one of the goalposts that had been torn down after the '40 game, and a few players made sure to touch it for good luck at the end of every practice. One late afternoon, as several players made their way toward the wood after the final whistle of practice had sounded, Rip Miller noticed a man on the sideline whom he'd never seen before. The Navy practices were open to reporters, but Miller didn't think this man dressed in a trenchcoat was a reporter. "Look at him, he's a spy from West Point," Miller told a player as he subtly pointed toward the man. The next day the mysterious man appeared again. But this time as Miller walked off the field he purposely dropped Navy's playbook within eyeshot of the stranger. Miller had spent part of the morning drawing up a bogus playbook, complete with formations, terminology, and plays that Navy never used. Later that night Miller returned to the practice field to see if the phony playbook still lay in the grass. Much to his delight, it was gone.

On Wednesday morning, a bulletin was issued to all of America's armed forces. REPEAT. PACIFIC, NOVEMBER 26, 1941: JAPANESE CARRIER FORCE LEAVES BASE, MOVING EAST . . .

At 6:00 A.M. Japan time on November 26—which was 11:00 A.M. November 25 at Pearl Harbor—the task force pulled out of Hitokappu Bay, the task force's assembly point off the coast of Japan. Amid snow that blew over the cold and choppy water, thirty vessels set sail in the half light, their destination thirty-five hundred miles across the Pacific. The armada boasted six carriers, led by the flagship, the *Akagi;* four hundred warplanes; two battleships; three cruisers; nine destroyers; and ten other surface ships. They would travel at an average of thirteen knots. Its orders stated that "in the event an agreement is reached in the negotiations with the United States, the task force will immediately return to Japan," but none of the officers on board these thirty ships expected to be turning around.

On Thursday afternoon the Midshipmen boarded a train for Philadelphia. They were sent off like princes, as the entire regiment gathered for a rally in the Yard. Larson said a few words, thanking everyone for their support, then the team hopped on the Toonerville Trolley. On the ride to Philly the players were uncharacteristically quiet, everyone deep in thought. The game was still 48 hours away, but already the players had begun their pregame routine. Most simply looked out the window and watched the countryside fly by as the train jiggled northward.

Army also left for Philly on Thursday afternoon. Like the Navy squad, they were given a hero's sendoff as they stepped onto the train at the Hudson River depot. It had already been a remarkable season for the Cadets, and even though they had lost two of their last three games, the players now reflected the quiet confidence of their coach. With Blaik, it seemed that anything was possible, that Army could beat any team on any day, and this was the attitude the players took with them as the train pulled out of the depot and began to snake its way southward along the river. They had nothing to lose, the players figured, because they'd already accomplished more in the 1941 season than anyone could have possibly predicted. This relaxed the players, and now 48 hours before kickoff, many of them took naps as they sat in their rail cars.

Navy stayed at a country club located on the northern outskirts of Philadelphia. After checking into their rooms, Larson met the players on an open grass field behind the hotel that was surrounded by trees turned golden by autumn. The team held a quick, padless workout. What really caught the attention of the players was how quiet it was as the team practiced. Aside from the squawks of a few blackbirds, the only sounds were the voices of the coaches and the grunts of the players as they went over a few basic plays. It was oddly peaceful. At the end of session, just as the late-November sun bled across the western sky, Larson asked his players to gather around. "Let's use this time out here to focus on what we need to do on Saturday," he said. "You'll remember this game for the rest of your lives, I promise you."

Army was quartered at a hotel on the southern outskirts of Philadelphia. Their special train was delayed arriving into Philly, which meant that the players didn't check into their rooms until 7:00 P.M. Instead of holding a workout, the cadets ate dinner and were in bed by 10:00 P.M. The next morning the team rode on two buses to Municipal Stadium for a light practice. As Olds and Romanek walked into the empty stadium, it appeared bigger to them than it had last year when they attended the game as plebes and sat in the stands. Then it was full of screaming fans. Now the wind howled and whipped around the vacant horseshoe structure. Olds imagined what the place would be like tomorrow, and the mere thought of it gave him a rush of adrenaline. Like every other Army player, Olds didn't think gameday could come fast enough.

Early that evening the two teams went to different local theaters. Before either movie came on, though, both teams were shown newsreels that depicted the deteriorating situations in the Far East and Europe. As they munched on buttery popcorn, the players sat wide-eyed as they watched the news unfold, fantasizing not about what would transpire the next day on the football field, but what would happen once they entered the field of combat. For the 10 minutes that the black-and-white images flickered on the big screens, not one player on either team uttered a word. They were all transfixed by the images that unspooled before them, which included pictures of innocent civilians already dead in the growing conflict. The players understood that tomorrow's game meant nothing compared to the war overseas, and seeing these newsreels reminded every Cadet and every Midshipmen that they were bound together by a cause bigger than the game.

"Boy, I can't wait to start fighting," Olds told a teammate. "I say we kill every one of those goddamn Nazis."

About forty-eight hours before kickoff, the War Department sent Pearl Harbor and other American outposts around the world a "war warning." "Negotiations with Japan appear to be terminated to all practical purposes," said the message from George Marshall, the army chief of staff. "Japanese future action is unpredictable but hostile action possible at any moment. . . . You are directed to undertake such reconnaissance and other measures as you deem necessary, but these measures should be carried out so as not, repeat, not to alarm civil population or disclose intent."

The commanding officers at Pearl Harbor responded to the warning by taking steps to avoid sabotage, like locking up all ammunition supplies. When these antisabotage measures were reported to the War Department, Marshall felt satisfied that the commanding officers at Pearl had adequately fulfilled his request.

On the eve of the game the players on both teams had their lights out by 8:45. Tomorrow would be a long day—one that would go down in American history as one of the last carefree afternoons before America entered World War II. But before the players retired for the evening, both Blaik and Larson read to their players a statement that the president had made to the American public that afternoon.

> *"Thinking about people in other countries that have been overrun and about those who have been doing the attacking, I think we can offer up a little silent prayer that those people, we hope, next year will be able to hold a Thanksgiving more like an American Thanksgiving,"* Roosevelt said. *"That is something to dream about perhaps. In days like these it is always possible that our boys who are now at the naval and military academies may be actually fighting for the defense of these American institutions of ours. . . . Great games run in the spirit of peoples and the right kind of national spirit of peace is necessary for that Army-Navy game. How many other countries have things like that going on now?*

The next morning at the country club, after a steak-and-potatoes breakfast, Larson told his Navy players to walk around the golf course and clear their heads. Busik and Kauffman strolled along a fairway and each privately marveled at how far they'd come since that May day in 1939 when they boarded the train in Pasadena. Busik was now a national sports figure—nearly everywhere he went, little boys would ask for his autograph—but in many ways he was still the same California kid who rode the train across the nation. He still was as friendly as a favorite uncle, and he still never got too upset or too overjoyed at anything. The biggest change in Busik was that he was now hardened. Like many in his class, the sense of optimism about the future that he brought to the academy had eroded. He once thought he could change the world; now he felt he'd be lucky if he survived the next five years.

Hal Kauffman had also changed. Though he still daydreamed of being a professional singer—a dream that he never shared with his classmates—Kauffman was no longer the overly sensitive boy who had stepped onto the train with Busik. Since arriving at the naval academy, Kauffman had emerged from his shell, becoming more talkative and animated. He now was as confident as any of his classmates in his ability to accomplish whatever task was before him. This newfound certainty in him stemmed from the fact that Kauffman had steadily climbed the class rank ladder, and now he was one of the top academic students at the academy. One day he hoped to be the captain of a destroyer, and based on his performance at the academy, his instructors thought it was just a matter of time before that happened.

Indeed, Busik and Kauffman had grown up. Their last game as Midshipmen was hours away, and then they didn't know where they'd be off to. Perhaps the Atlantic. Maybe the Pacific. All they really knew was that their futures were clouded and suffused with peril. But on this morning, as they strolled on the golf course through the cool and fresh November air, life was peaceful. They were Navy football players, and in a few hours the ears of a nation and the eyes of one hundred thousand fans would be riveted on the game. As Busik and Kauffman and a few other players tossed a football around in the quiet of the golf course, it felt to them as if they were standing on the summit of life.

9

THE ARRIVAL

FROM ALL ACROSS the Eastern Seaboard, they came by plane, train, and automobile to the great concrete horseshoe that stood on the marshy flats of the Delaware River. Located on the south side of Philadelphia, at the corner of Broad and Pattison, Municipal Stadium was a sprawling, single-deck ballyard that could seat 98,620 people—with standing room only, the crowd could swell to 102,000. On this cool, still, foggy morning, fans started arriving at the stadium at 7:30 A.M. for the 1:30 kickoff. Like an electrical storm, anticipation charged the air.

For two days, long lines of reserved trains carrying football fans from New York and Washington, all of whom were packed tight in the compartments, creaked along the rusty rails that led into the heart of Philly. On this Saturday after Thanksgiving—the Army-Navy game's traditional date—the trains dropped off passengers right at the gates of the stadium.

For the 1936 Army-Navy contest, the Pennsylvania Railroad had scheduled thirty-eight special trains. By '41 the Pennsy, as it was called, ran forty-two special locomotives—making this one of the most complex single-day operations in passenger railroad history. Railroad executives held planning sessions for this one event throughout the year to nail down the logistics. In the days leading up to kickoff all the railcars were repaired and cleaned; the trains' exteriors were waxed and polished. On game day wreck crews were deployed up and down the Eastern Seaboard, just in case, and extra crew members were added to all the locomotives.

For those passengers who arrived the night before the game, they found downtown Philadelphia teeming with Army and Navy fans. All the hotels were booked. Restaurants turned away customers and the pubs overflowed with revelers. Indeed, the city was transformed into a rollicking festival that surged with patriotism; Army's colors of black, gold, and gray and Navy's blue and gold bathed the entire area. In the crowd at the Benjamin Franklin Hotel, where the Army backers made their headquarters, were ranking officers from both Washington and from forts and camps all over the country—officers, who, somehow, had arranged to get leave for the game. At the Bellevue Stratford, where the Midshipmen supporters were staying, were navy officers from ships and ports all over the world. And from Iceland to the Straits of Singapore, from Alaska to the West Indies and beyond, soldiers, sailors, and marines huddled around short-wave radios to catch broadcasts of the game.

Perhaps no one in the world, though, looked forward to this game more than Alan Shapley, who was stationed aboard the U.S.S. *Arizona* off the coast of Oahu Island. When Shapley was at the naval academy from 1923 to '26, he earned twelve varsity letters in the three major sports of football, basketball, and track—a mark that has never been equaled. Of all the sports he played, though, his favorite was football. A four-year starting quarterback, Shapley helped the '23 team capture a 14–14 tie against the University of Washington in the Rose Bowl. Three years later, in his final season at the academy, he led Navy straight into the history books, guiding the Midshipmen to their first and only national championship.

Navy bolted to a 9–0 start in 1926 behind Shapley's passing and running. All that remained was a game against Army at recently finished Soldier Field in Chicago. The game, the first-ever gridiron contest held at Soldier Field, also marked the first time that Army and Navy had ever played each other in the Midwest. The lure of the game was so strong in the heartland that more than half a million people requested tickets. Notre Dame coach Knute Rockne even abandoned his team on game day—the Irish played Carnegie Tech on the same afternoon—to sit in the stands and watch the Army-Navy matchup. (Without their coach, Notre Dame wound up getting upset by Carnegie Tech 19–0).

More than 110,000 fans filled Soldier Field. Army's first-year coach Biff Jones tried to surprise Navy by starting his second-team unit. The plan backfired: The Middies stormed to a 14–0 lead. But Army came back, and late in the fourth quarter, with about four minutes to play, it led the Midshipmen 21–14. The Cadets now had the ball and were trying to kill the clock, but Navy intercepted a pass with less than two minutes left and got the ball back on its own 35-yard line. Pointing to the end zone 65 yards away, Shapley told his teammates in the huddle, "We're going to cross the line."

As Navy moved the ball down the field, it started to get dark. The field was rimmed with snow and the players were covered in mud, making it difficult for fans to discern what players belonged to which team. Finally, Navy faced a fourth and goal from the eight-yard line. The Middies called a double reverse. Halfback Howard Ransford faked a run to the right and slipped the ball to Shapley, who broke a tackle and pushed the ball over the goal line with just seconds to play. A hush fell over the crowd as Shapley dropkicked the ball through the goal posts to tie the game at 21–21, which would be the final score. The Navy boys were ecstatic over the tie; because they were the only unbeaten team in the country, it meant they'd won the national championship. That evening Shapley was the toast of the town in Chicago, as he and his teammates met up with their dates who had traveled to the Windy City from different towns in the Midwest. Together, they danced to tunes such as "Bye, Bye Blackbird," by Ray Henderson and Mort Dixon, and, "When the Red, Red Robin Comes, Bob, Bob, Bobbin' Along" by Harry Woods. It was one of those special nights that they'd all talk about for the rest of their lives.

Fifteen years later, Shapley could still vividly recall that 1926 Army game in his mind. He could tell anyone who was interested all about that chilly late-afternoon in the Windy City. Now he was aboard the U.S.S. *Arizona*, and Shapley still followed the team as if he were living in Bancroft Hall. On this late November day in 1941, the *Arizona* was running drills and playing war. In a few days she would dock at Pearl Harbor. But now, out in the blue ocean, Shapley arranged for the broadcast of the Army-Navy game to be piped through the ship's public address system. He had to hear it, and he was the kind of person who made things happen.

Shapley was the commanding officer of the marine detachment aboard the *Arizona*. He was also a close friend to Navy assistant coach Rip Miller. Whenever Shapley got the chance, he'd phone or telegram Miller and ask for information on the current state of the Navy football team. He was always looking for scouting reports and inside information—just like he did when he was a player. Back when he was the golden boy of Annapolis, Shapley, a sandy-haired, handsome midshipmen, was known for his strong right arm and quick thinking on the field. Those same characteristics still held true fifteen years later. On the *Arizona* he often threw a football around with his marines, and he was the coach of the marines' whaleboat race-team. When his marine whaleboat team beat all the other teams on the *Arizona*, Shapley approached the *Arizona*'s Captain, Van Valkenburgh, and asked that his marines represent the ship in future competitions with other ships rather than assembling an all-star team, which was what had been done in the past. Valkenburgh reluctantly agreed, and each morning while nearly everyone else on the ship was still sleeping, Shapley and his marines were up and practicing rowing their whaleboat in the gray, early-morning light. The work ethic he learned playing football at Navy was still with him.

Though Shapley didn't know it, the battleship *Arizona* was featured in a picture in the 212-page 1941 Army-Navy game program, which cost 50 cents. On page 180 the *Arizona* was shown plowing into a huge swell. The caption read: "It is significant that, despite the claims of air enthusiasts, no battleship has yet been sunk by bombs."

In its heyday, Municipal Stadium held concerts and sporting events that attracted more than one hundred thousand people. On September 23, 1926, 120,757 packed into the massive venue to watch Gene Tunney's heavyweight title victory over Jack Dempsey. Only Chicago's Soldier Field and the Memorial Coliseum in Los Angeles could hold a larger crowd than Municipal. And for two reasons the stadium's sixty-acre site was the logical choice to host the Army-Navy game: It was big enough to accommodate the intense interest in the game and it was located between Annapolis, Maryland, and West Point, New York.

Situated at 2601 South Broad Street, Municipal was fifteen years old in 1941 and still living on an allowance from the taxpayers. The stadium was built in connection with Philadelphia's Sesquicentennial celebration and in its first years was under the control of the Sesquicentennial Association. Planned to give the city the "biggest stadium in the world," one that was suitable for the staging of Olympic Games and other marquee events, construction of the stadium was authorized by the City Council on March 3, 1925. It was completed on May 15, 1926, at a cost nearly twice the original estimate of $2 million. Financing was done with miscellaneous city funds plus a fifty-year bond issue of more than $2 million.

In 1941, small cracks in the stadium's concrete facade pinstriped the outer walls. Many fans pointed to these cracks as they entered the stadium, wondering aloud if the venue was safe to hold a standing-room-only crowd of more than one hundred thousand. A few fans went so far as to ask ushers if they thought the whole place was going to buckle. Still, even with cracks spiderwebbing toward the sky in some places at Municipal, fans arrived in droves on November 29. At 10:45 A.M., a squad of thirty men began removing the eight tarpaulins that covered the entire playing field. The stadium slowly began to fill up. Among the first in the stadium were two navy enlisted men who were assigned a most peculiar task: They were to warm the seat cushions of a few high-ranking navy officers who weren't scheduled to arrive at the field for another two hours. So, following orders, the two enlisted men wiggled their backsides on the officers's seat cushions, moving side to side in their wool pants, keeping the cushions cozy for the navy brass hats, as the enlisted men called them.

At 11:00, the early-morning fog lifted and soft beams of sunlight burst though the torn sky. Suddenly, it was a perfect afternoon for football. A mild breeze fluttered the flags on the rim of the stadium and it strummed the bunting that was draped on the stands surrounding the field. The temperature was a comfortable 61 degrees. If this late November afternoon had been a painting, the brushstrokes on the canvas couldn't have been more beautiful.

The security on this day was unprecedented for a sporting event. Outside the stadium, more than one hundred patrolmen were on duty. Inside, one hundred and fifty police officers had been assigned to various posts. There were also seven hundred Pinkerton men, several hundred schoolboy ushers, and dozens of detectives stationed inside the stadium. Sixty Internal Revenue agents, most from Washington, D.C., were on hand to make sure that the scalpers didn't sell any tickets for more than the $4.40 face value and to spot counterfeit tickets. In the first aid room, located in the bowels of the stadium, four hospital cots stood ready for any game-day casualties. Chief Police Surgeon Mike Keegan and eleven other police surgeons manned the first aid room. During the previous year's game some fifty cases were treated; most were fans who'd had a little too much beer with their cheer.

Outside the stadium, merchandise and concessions sales were stellar.

The thick glossy programs, which weighed almost two pounds, were being nabbed up quickly. At 8:30 A.M., Irving Fried, the senior partner of Fried and Gerber Concessionaires, hauled truckloads of hot dogs, soft drinks, and sandwiches into the stadium. About three hundred members of Fried's staff were local high school boys employed for the day, who were, according to Fried, "jumping out of their socks for a chance to see the game."

At the Navy Stock Yard, which stood adjacent to the stadium, a vendor sold his supply of five hundred blue-and-gold Navy buttons to workers entering the main gate by 7:00 A.M., clearing his inventory in less than an hour. The men who bought the buttons proudly pinned them to their work overalls, trying to do their part to support their team, and they didn't take the buttons off as they worked on the ships in the Yard. The Navy Yard's twenty-five thousand employees only worked a 6-hour shift on the day of the game, in order to avert congestion of northbound traffic on Broad Street. Everybody went to work 15 minutes early, with orders to quit 2 hours early. This meant they would be able to listen to the game on the radio and cheer for their beloved Midshipmen.

As Army officers left the Benjamin Franklin hotel, they were given box lunches, which were stacked high in the lobby, that included a ham sandwich and an apple. Weaving their way to the stadium, many officers bought chrysanthemums at local flower shops, which sold for $1.25 a piece. Two hours before kickoff, more than thirty people stood in line to buy the flowers from a street vendor on Broad. The officers either affixed the chrysanthemums to their overcoats or gave them to their girls. In just a few hours, flower merchants all around the stadium made a week's worth of profit.

Finally, at precisely 12:15 in the afternoon, the castle-like gates at the northeast end of the stadium swung open and the boys from the academies who weren't football players made a Caesar-entering-Rome kind of entrance. Since Army was the host team, the Midshipmen marched into the stadium first. Many of the Midshipmen had been standing on the rise just outside the gate, and now the seventy-five-piece Navy band led them inside, playing "Anchors Aweigh." The song's booming notes split the air, bouncing off every corner of the colossal, echoing bowl as the entire navy academy complement—3,110 midshipmen—confidently marched in.

At first, the fans in the crowd were hushed as the Middies appeared before their eyes. Then applause erupted, as the men, women, and children in the stands rose to their feet and shouted their support—not just for Navy, but for America. The twenty midshipmen companies marched around the track and past the Army stands. Company by company filed onto the field and then, arriving at their designated position on the field, stood as still as statues beneath the north goal posts while the band played.

At 12:40 the army cadets entered the stadium. Dressed in service grays, eighteen hundred cadets and a ninety-two-piece enlisted men's band marched in. The band first played "Anchors Aweigh" as a mark of courtesy to the navy, but then it broke into, "Fight On, Old Army Team," as the cadets marched past the Navy stands. By 12:50, the cadets and midshipmen were all in their seats. Now it was time for the real pageantry to begin.

Upon arriving at the railroad station south of the stadium, Eleanor Roosevelt, accompanied by Vice President Henry Wallace, rode in a car to the stadium. The First Lady, who was guarded by two secret service agents, was helped out of the vehicle at the stadium entrance and then walked in, strolling onto the field. First she looked to the Navy side and bowed and waved to Rear Admiral Russell Wilson, the superintendent of the naval academy. Wearing a black wool suit with a blue skirt, a fur coat, and a black felt hat with a shallow crown, she slowly walked around the south end of the field, accompanied by Major General Robert L. Eichelberger, superintendent of the military academy, and other army officers, to view the first half of the game. The First Lady planned to watch the first two quarters on the Army side of the field with British Ambassador Lord Halifax. Not wanting to appear partial, she would then move to the Navy side for the game's second half.

Forty years earlier, in 1901, President Theodore Roosevelt also tried to act like he didn't care who won the Army-Navy game at Franklin Field in Philadelphia. In the first half, Roosevelt sat on the Midshipmen's side; at halftime, he switched over to the Army bleachers. But when Navy tied the score 5–5 in the fourth quarter, Roosevelt, who had been assistant secretary of the navy under President McKinley, couldn't contain his enthusiasm. He rose from his box seat, ran past his Secret Service guards, leaped over a railing and jogged to the Navy bench to congratulate the players. The president whooped and hollered the entire time, as he shed all appearances of impartiality. But as happy as the president was when the Midshipmen tied the score, he was equally dejected when Army scored a late touchdown and won the game, 11–5.

. . .

A few hours before kickoff of the 1941 game, Franklin Roosevelt was on the tail end of a nineteen-hour train and car trip from Washington to Warm Springs, Georgia, where the president would enjoy a brief vacation. The president had wanted to come to Warm Springs for more than a week, but felt that he couldn't leave the White House with America's immediate future in such a fragile state. But on the evening of November 28, the president and his staff decided he should take a break and head to Warm Springs for a few days. Special arrangements were made so that the president could respond quickly to a sudden crisis. When the president's train stopped in Atlanta for 10 minutes, a secret telephone was connected to his vehicle in the motorcade that was being transported on the train so that he could be kept abreast of breaking international developments once he got off the train. Contrary to custom, the journey was interrupted at Newman, Georgia, where the presidential party left the train and drove by car the remaining forty-three miles to Warm Springs. Under a cloudless sky on the morning of November 29, the motorcade sped past scrubby pinewoods and fields of cotton, traveling deep into the Georgia countryside. When the President finally reached his cottage on a hilltop in Warm Springs, he wanted to do just one thing: get in his car, turn on the radio, and listen to the game.

To relax while he listened, the president spent the afternoon being driven in his own car through Warm Springs. He tuned the radio to the game, straining to hear every drip of information that was coming out of the speakers. He listened as the car tooled though the pleasant land of white houses and ploughed fields, all the while imagining what the action on the field looked like. Hours later the president related to reporters what raced through his mind as he took in the action from Philadelphia. "The game was run in the spirit of peace, and the spirit of peace is necessary for this game," he said. "I think we ought to be thankful that since 1918 we have been able to hold our gains—in health and education and in a great many volunteer lines. We're one of the largest nations of the world and nearly all other large nations are at war or defending themselves or conquered."

A few hours after making this statement, presidential advisers announced to reporters that the president's vacation would be cut short. That evening the president received a phone call from Secretary of State Cordell Hull. Hull had received some extracts of a speech that Premier Tojo of Japan was scheduled to deliver the following day. Tojo was going to say that his country was taking steps to wipe out the "exploitation" in the Far East being perpetrated by the United States and Britain. Hull informed Roosevelt of the inflammatory speech and stressed "the imminent danger of a Japanese attack." Hull asked the president to cut his trip short and return to Washington to consult with his advisers. The president agreed to return on December 1. World civilization, slowly but surely, was falling apart.

Robin Olds, West Point Class of June '43
(U.S. Military Academy Library, Special Collections and Archives Division, National Archives Record Group 404, White Studio Collection)

Henry Romanek, West Point Class of June '43 *(U.S. Military Academy Library, Special Collections and Archives Division, National Archives Record Group 404, White Studio Collection)*

Hal Kauffman, Naval Academy Class of '43 *(Naval Academy Special Collections and Archives)*

William S. Busik, Naval Academy Class of '43 *(Naval Academy Special Collections and Archives)*

Navy player Bill Chewning. He wouldn't survive the war. *(Courtesy Chewning family)*

John Frances Laboon, Naval Academy Class of '44 *(Naval Academy Special Collections and Archives)*

William Francis Leahy, Naval Academy Class of '44 *(Naval Academy Special Collections and Archives)*

Alan Shapley, Naval Academy Class of '27 *(Naval Academy Special Collections and Archives)*

**Army coach Red Blaik
diagrams plays for his team.**

**Coach Blaik (*far left*) on the
sideline during a game**

*(U.S. Military Academy Library,
Special Collections and Archives
Division, National Archives Record
Group 404, White Studio Collection)*

**Navy coach Swede Larson
(*far left*) with assistants
Keith Moelsworth (*center*)
and Rip Miller (*right*) in
1940** *(Courtesy Swede Larson, Jr.)*

A 1940 intrasquad
scrimmage at the
Naval Academy
(*L. McNally, Baltimore
News Post*)

Bill Busik *(with ball)*
struggles for yards in
a 1940 intrasquad
scrimmage. (*L. McNally,
Baltimore News Post*)

Bill Busik *(bottom left)* with
several of his Navy teammates
after a practice in 1940 (*Courtesy
Bill Busik*)

Navy's Bill Busik in the fall of 1941 *(Naval Academy Special Collections and Archives)*

A Notre Dame back carries the ball against Navy in 1941. The Fighting Irish beat the Midshipmen 20-13. *(Courtesy Bill Busik)*

Navy players run sprints during 1941 preseason practice. *(Naval Academy Special Collections and Archives)*

Both Academies march on the field prior to the 1941 Army-Navy game. (*Naval Academy Special Collections and Archives*)

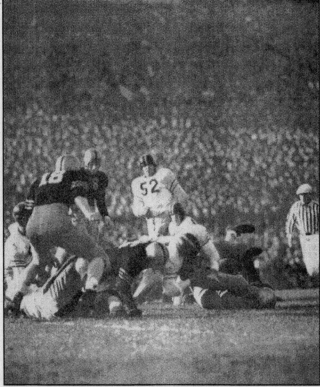

Bill Busik carries the ball against Army during the 1941 game. (*Naval Academy Special Collections and Archives*)

**Program from the 1941
Army-Navy football
game** *(Naval Academy Special
Collections and Archives)*

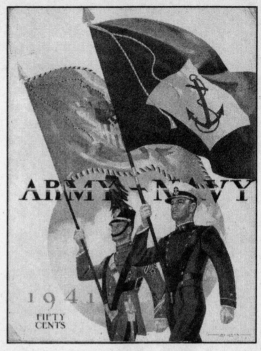

A day after the big game, Swede Larson is surrounded by Annapolis locals and midshipmen as he rings the Gokokuji Bell to celebrate Navy's 14-6 victory over Army. *(Courtesy Swede Larson, Jr.)*

Swede Larson, in his Marine Corps uniform, removes his name tag from his locker
for the final time as he heads off to war. He would lose his life in November, 1945.
(Courtesy Swede Larson, Jr.)

IO

THE GAME

WITH SIRENS WAILING, two police cars escorted the two yellow school buses full of Navy players and coaches down Broad Street. As the cavalcade motored through heavy traffic, fans on the sidewalks shouted encouragement and pounded their hands on the sides of the buses. A few players stuck their heads out the windows and shook hands with the fans as if they were running for governor. Kickoff was still three hours away, but already the Navy players could sense the building emotion of the gathering crowd. Even fans wearing Army black and gold cheered the Navy buses as they slowly rolled through the bright sunshine toward the stadium.

To the Navy players, this was an overwhelming sight, seeing Army fans stopping in their tracks and zealously cheering as the buses of Midshipmen approached. The whole town seemed to be performing a human drum roll as the buses inched their way to the stadium for the big showdown. Men, women, and small children waved American flags at the buses. A few old men held their canes—which had red, white, and blue streamers flowing from them—up high as the boys from Annapolis went by. Many fans blew on horns, whistles, and trumpets; others shook rattles and large brass hand bells.

Army was the first team to arrive at the stadium. Before having his team dress and don their pads and uniforms, Blaik led them through the locker room and out onto the field. Kickoff was two and a half hours away, but already a smattering of hard-core fans had taken their seats. Blaik wanted his team to get familiar with the field, and he instructed his players to walk around and acquire a feel for the grass and the footing. He also told his players to imagine what they'd be doing once the whistle blew and the game started. The crowd will be deafening, he warned them, but don't let that blur your focus. Some players, as they strolled down the sidelines, looked up into the mostly empty stands, which stretched up and up and up, like the floor of heaven rested just above the top rim of the stadium. None of the players said it, but all of them knew it: Their moment was at hand.

Around the time the Army players retreated to the locker room to put on their uniforms, the Navy buses pulled into the stadium parking lot. The players went straight to the locker room, where Larson gave his team 45 minutes to suit up and take care of whatever pregame business they needed to attend to—doing some extra stretching, studying their plays, or just concentrating on what they needed to do to be successful. Larson didn't script his players' pregame activities as thoroughly as Blaik, who planned every minute of his players' actions for the two hours before kickoff, because Larson insisted on putting a lot of faith in his players' ability to get ready on their own. "I figure I've got some of the most responsible young men in the country," Larson once told a friend, "so I trust them to do what's right until they prove me wrong. And you know what? They never do."

By the time the Midshipmen were ready to jog out onto the field and warm up, the stadium was almost half full. Navy hadn't stepped foot on the Municipal Stadium field since 1940—they had practiced at Temple the day before—so when the boys ran out of the locker room and into the late-fall afternoon they were overwhelmed by what greeted them. It was as if a powder keg of excitement had burst. Even Busik, who had played in the game the year before, didn't expect the hyped atmosphere that he and his teammates now stood in the middle of. The crowd was producing thunder, and the noise rattled around the concrete horseshoe. Unlike many of the stadiums in which Navy had played, the fans at Municipal seemed right on top of the field. Municipal was built with watching football in mind; there was an unusually high tilt to the bleachers. The fans also appeared more animated than the previous year. Very few sat and many fans brought large signs that they placed all around the stadium. Already, some thirty minutes before kickoff, the place seemed to be rumbling.

"This is the most amazing thing I've ever seen," Busik told a teammate on the field. "This is something I'll never forget."

A few minutes later, the Cadets came out for their warm-ups and were given a similar greeting. As the players stretched, Blaik and Larson met at midfield. The two coaches shook hands and congratulated each other on their seasons. Though neither coach was a small-talker, the topic of the crowd made for an easy, free-flowing conversation. There was a hum in the stadium even as the teams sat on the ground and stretched. In all their years on the sidelines, neither coach had ever been swaddled in a more robust football atmosphere than what they were standing in the midst of just then. A few minutes later, the two shook hands again and parted.

After warm-ups, both teams retreated to their respective locker rooms one final time before kickoff. Coach Blaik, looking into the eyes of his players, felt that they were too anxious, wound a little too tight. To settle his team down, Blaik told everyone to lie down on the floor. He wanted his players to take deep breaths and visualize what they were going to do on the field. This yoga-style exercise was before its time, and many of the players thought it was odd, including Olds. As he lay on the cold concrete floor of the locker room, Olds suspected that Navy was going to try to run right at him. As a result of the diving accident months earlier, he still had trouble raising his right arm, and he figured that the Midshipmen had noticed that in their film studies. Nonetheless, Olds couldn't wait to get on the field. It was something he'd been thinking about almost every day since he sat in the stands and watched Navy beat Army last year 14–0.

A similar thought floated through Romanek's head. With his eyes closed, Romanek visualized making strong, solid blocks on offense and sure-handed tackles on defense. He knew that if unranked Army was going to have a chance to upset the eleventh-ranked Midshipmen—Navy was a four-to-one favorite—then the Cadets needed to control the line of scrimmage on both sides of the ball. It was as simple as that. As Romanek and Olds lay there, the stadium seemed to shake above them, the crowd sizzling with an emotional fever.

Across the field, in the Navy locker room, Larson made a stunning announcement to his players: This was going to be his last game as Navy's coach. "There's a war coming boys, and like all of you, I'm going to go fight in it," Larson said. "All of us in this room have a more important duty than playing football." As Larson spoke, he appeared as serious as he'd ever been. Many of the Navy boys felt the urge to run up and hug their coach, but instead they all stayed sitting on the benches in front of the lockers, unsure of how to react. The players had suspected that this might be Larson's last game, but none of them thought he'd make the announcement right before kickoff. In the long history of pregame speeches, no five words—not even, "Win one for the Gipper," which Notre Dame's Knute Rockne uttered in 1928 before the Irish's game against Army—had a more meaningful impact than Larson's, "I'm going to go fight." As soon as those words floated from his lips, the boys in the locker room were prepared to do whatever it took to win this last game for their beloved coach, to send him out with a victory.

Larson went on to tell his players that he'd never lost to Army. As a Midshipman player back in the '20s, Larson went 3–0 against the Cadets. In his first two seasons as a coach, he'd defeated Army both seasons. Now just 60 minutes of football stood between him and a perfect record against his rivals from West Point.

After speaking for a few minutes about how much this final game meant to him, Larson then took his team on a trip back through the mists of time, giving them a crash-course history lesson on the Army-Navy game—a history that dated back fifty-one years to the day, when on November 29, 1890, the schools first met on a cool autumn afternoon at the Point . . .

On that chilly November afternoon in 1890, Dennis Michie paced back and forth up on the cliffs at West Point, looking out across the Hudson River. Michie, a cadet, had been waiting for this day for more than a year. Then, in the distance, Michie saw them: On a wooden ferryboat, the naval academy football team was chugging across the river. Minutes earlier the Midshipmen had arrived on a train at the rail station directly across from West Point on the East side of the Hudson. Then the Navy players, who were all carrying a canvas bag that contained a football uniform, boarded the ferryboat for West Point. The first football game between the schools was minutes away.

Michie was the driving force behind this historical matchup; he had spent much of that fall trying to organize a game. Now a crowd of more than 1,000 people—which included cadets, the army band, a few dozen

West Point officers (many of whom had fought in the Civil War), their wives, visitors from outside the post, and a group of navy officers—had already gathered around a makeshift football field that had been laid out on the southeast corner of the parade grounds.

Months earlier, in the summer of 1890, Michie was one of only three cadets at the military academy who had ever played in an organized football game. In the 1880s the sport had been revolutionized by Walter Camp, an advisory coach at Yale who created rules such as the play from scrimmage and the eleven player on-field limit for each team. By laying out a standardized set of rules, Camp ended much of the chaos in the game. (But it was still a brutal sport; after the 1905 season President Theodore Roosevelt suggested that colleges ban it after eighteen players died as a result of collisions in a game.)

Because of Camp's alterations, football had become popular at eastern colleges such as Yale, Harvard, and Princeton by 1890, but it was slow to catch on at West Point. Navy, conversely, had a comparatively rich tradition. The Middies had played their first game in 1879, and by the beginning of 1890 had a cumulative record of 14–12–2. Bill Maxwell, who was a Midshipman in 1879 and served as the team's captain that season, had been credited by Camp with developing the first football uniform. Maxwell fashioned some athletic wear for his team only after he learned that the squad from the Baltimore Athletic Club, the only opponent of the Naval Academy in 1879, outweighed the Midshipmen by an average of ten pounds per player. Determined to make his players heavier for that game, Maxwell visited the academy's tailor, who proceeded to make heavy sleeveless jackets for the players. They consisted of double-lined canvas and were laced down the front and drawn tightly to fit snugly around a player's body. The Midshipmen, wearing these strange, heavy, newfangled getups, wound up tying the team from the Baltimore Athletic Club, 0–0.

At West Point Michie was one of the few cadets who even knew the rules of football. Nonetheless, he wanted to found a football team at West Point, and he figured there was only one way to do it: Get the boys at Navy to challenge Army to a football game. This way the power brokers at Army, with their pride on the line, would be forced to accept the matchup. Weeks later, after Michie had written a few clandestine letters to midshipmen that he knew, a letter arrived for him from Annapolis. The missive was a formal challenge to a football game. Michie took the letter to his father, Lieutenant Colonel Peter Michie, a philosophy instructor at West Point who had served in the Civil War. With his father backing him, Michie didn't have to ask twice to get permission from Superintendent Colonel John Wilson to accept the challenge.

Not everyone was pleased that this game was going to take place. Two months before the showdown, the *New York Times* ran a story on faculty upheaval at West Point. Many instructors argued that it made no sense for young cadets and midshipmen to hit and bloody each other on a football field, given that someday they may have to rely on each other in the field of combat. Yet in spite of these objections, Michie and his father kept lobbying the superintendent and others that the game would ultimately benefit both the academies and bring them closer together. The superintendent agreed with the Michies, and he refused to stop the game.

Now all young Michie had to do was assemble a twenty-one-man team, tutor the players in the essentials of the game, and whip them into playing shape. A classmate of Michie's, John A. Palmer, later recalled what those first weeks of Army football were like in *The Assembly*, a U.S. Army magazine.

> *"Dennis now had his hands full. He was captain, coach, trainer, and business manager of a nonexistent team that must play a championship game at the end of eight weeks. Dennis had scant time to teach the simplest fundamentals to his raw recruits. They had no practices except for a few riotous scrimmages against an even more inexperienced second team. There was no time for coaching except in the brief intervals between military duties.*
>
> *"Only on Saturday afternoons when the weather was too bad for drill and dress parade could Dennis count on any time for continuous practice. Dennis was able to rouse his teammates at 5:30 A.M., half an hour before reveille, for a run around the Plain, down and back Flirtation Walk, over past Thayer Hall, around the Supe's headquarters, and then back to the barracks in time for reveille."*

When the naval academy squad finally arrived on the West Bank of the Hudson on their ferryboat, the Middies were in high spirits. Many town residents of West Point stood in their front yards and chatted with the young Navy players as they made their way up to the Plain.

Once the Navy players finally made it to the football field, they were surprised to see several New York newspaper men, all clutching a notebook and a pencil, waiting to ask them questions. Beyond them were hundreds of people, all circled around the field, curious to see what this relatively new game of football was all about. In the front were scores of women, all wearing their finest Sunday dresses and sitting on folding chairs that had been swiped from classrooms. Everyone else stood around the field, in some cases three deep. When the two teams jogged out for the opening kickoff, virtually the entire crowd leaned inward, all anxious to see if the young men from West Point could give Navy a run for their money.

Then the referees, who all had on big black hats, signaled that it was time to start the game. Army kicked the ball. Navy's Charles Emerich, behind a V-formation, caught the ball and headed straight upfield. What followed was a massive collision, as the two teams—all the Navy players wore wool caps, the Army players were bareheaded—ran into each other at full speed. To the fans, it sounded like concrete slabs ramming into each other. Immediately, a few players from each team dropped to the earth, as if they'd suddenly been rendered unconscious. Many in the crowd gasped and yelled for Army to make the tackle, but Emerich broke free from the pileup and scampered 20 more yards before he was tackled by a group of Army players led by Michie. The opening kickoff turned out to be a preview of coming attractions: Navy was better in all phases of the game and won 24–0.

It wasn't until the matchup was over that everyone involved realized the savagery of the game. One Army player lost three teeth. Another Cadet had a piece of his ear bitten off while yet another Army player had his nose broken. The next day the *New York Times* placed their story of the game on the front page, hailing the contest as "the greatest victory the Navy has achieved since Decatur and John Paul Jones . . . The result was watched with national interest . . . It was generally regarded as the beginning of new era in the athletic training of two institutions."

This new era, however, almost ended before it could gather steam. By 1893 the game had grown progressively more violent. Not only were fights common on the field, but also skirmishes along the sidelines frequently broke out between cadets and midshipmen. A few hours after the game in 1893 the rivalry between the two institutions was so white-hot that a general and an admiral challenged each other to a duel at the Army-Navy Club in Washington, D.C. The duel was averted, but clearly something needed to be done about the mounting animosity between the two schools.

"The excitement attending [the game] exceeds all reasonable limits," said Major Oswald Ernst, who had replaced Wilson as the military academy's superintendent.

At the urging of Ernst and others, President Grover Cleveland con-vened a special Cabinet meeting to discuss Army-Navy football in Febru-ary 1894. Shortly after the Cabinet meeting was over, both the secretaries of the army and the navy issued edicts that, in effect, canceled the game. Not until 1899 was it resumed on an annual basis. But by then, Michie, who had been the key figure in organizing the first Army-Navy game, was dead. He'd been killed in the Spanish-American War in 1898. The only Naval officer killed in that conflict was Worth Bagley—a four-year let-terman for Navy's football team. Michie and Bagley were two of the first football players from Army or Navy to die in combat on foreign soil.

After Larson delivered his history lesson, he told his boys to get out on the field and make the entire Navy proud. Let's play like this is the last game of our lives, Larson told his team. The players then bolted out of the locker room, primed for the challenge.

Navy was the first team on the Municipal Stadium field. The Mid-dies were clad in white jerseys with blue numbers, their pants gold. Less than a minute later the Army players, adorned in black jerseys with gold numbers and also outfitted with gold pants, jogged to their sideline. Each team's offense practiced a few plays in their single-wing formations while the captains were beckoned to the center of the field. There, Army's Ray Murphy and Navy's Bob Froude shook hands and made a friendly wager: The losing captain would have to give the winner his football helmet. The regiments had been making bets against each other all week long. Bathrobes, sweaters, cuff links, even full uniforms were put on the line between cadets and midshipmen. These items carried little monetary value, but their symbolic and personal worth would be priceless to the winners, as precious as family heirlooms packed in a cedar chest.

Army won the toss and elected to kick off—as most teams did in 1941 in the hope of acquiring superior field position. As the players lined up in kickoff formation, a burr of expectation filled the stadium, which was now stuffed to capacity, making this game the most heavily attended football, baseball, or basketball contest of 1941. Over one hundred writers in the press box grabbed their pencils and prepared to take notes. Broadcasters from three separate radio networks—National, Columbia, and Mutual—all cleared their throats as they readied to speak to national audiences, and in some cases global. Calling the game on NBC radio were Fort Pearson, who gave the color description, and Bill Stern, who handled the play-by-play duties. Both Pearson and Stern were considered two of the top football announcers of their time, and this game was the plummiest assignment anyone in sports radio could land. In the pregame portion of their broadcast Pearson and Stern interviewed former Notre Dame coach Elmer Layden, Columbia coach Lou Little, Minnesota coach Bernie Bierman, Colgate coach Andy Kerr, and sportswriter Grantland Rice. All the guests agreed that Army would have to play a near-perfect game to beat Navy, a team that simply was bigger and had more experience than the Cadets.

With the fans standing on their feet in the grandstands, which were a sea of black, brown, and gray fedoras, Army's John Roberts, using a straight-on approach, kicked off. The ball sailed low and rolled out of bounds at Navy's 35-yard line. In the Navy huddle Busik called for a run up the middle on the Middies' first play. Larson had told Busik all week long that he wanted to wear down the Cadet lineman, and to accomplish that Larson instructed Busik to hammer the ball between the tackles. But three straight runs into the line produced only five yards. On fourth and 5, Busik punted the ball to the Army 35-yard line, where it rolled out of bounds. Now Army's offense got its first shot.

On first down, Hank Mazur, the left back, received the direct snap and plowed straight over the left tackle for 2 yards. On second down Mazur, lined up 7 yards behind the left tackle, again received the direct snap. Instead of running, though, he quick-kicked the ball. The surprise worked, as the ball rolled to a stop at the Navy 16-yard line. The 47-yard kick prompted a clapping of the hands from Coach Blaik on the sideline. It was blue-moon rare for coaches to call plays in 1941—they usually left it up to their star back—but during the previous week in practice Blaik repeatedly told Mazur that he should be conservative with his play-calling on offense. This meant, Blaik said, that in many cases the best play call on a second and long would be a quick kick.

Navy's offense began its second series. On first down Busik took the direct snap and ran to his right. Not seeing any daylight, he put his head down and bulled forward. Just as he was falling to the ground, Romanek slid over from his defensive end position and put a wicked helmet-to-helmet shot on Busik. For a split second, Busik, who had lost a yard on the play, didn't know where he was. But he quickly regained his wits and was able to get up without any help.

In the huddle, Busik was frustrated. He felt like he'd just run into a stone wall and he wasn't getting any help from his blockers. Tired of being pummeled, he called for another quick kick with the ball on the 15-yard line. The Army defensive backs had anticipated the play, but Busik un-corked the best kick of his life. After receiving the direct snap 8 yards behind the line of scrimmage, Busik took one step back with his left foot, then one forward with his left foot, then dropped the ball. His right foot swung up like a massive pendulum in motion and connected with the sweet spot of the ball. The Army backs, in full sprint, were at midfield when they looked up into the cobalt-blue sky and saw the foot-ball some 20 yards directly above them. The ball landed on the Army 20 and then it rolled. It came to a dead stop at the Cadet one-foot line. Busik had out-kicked not only his coverage, but also Army's returners. The ball sat perfectly stone-still for a couple of seconds before anyone on the field could reach it. The punt had traveled 85 yards, by far the longest in Navy history.

Busik was taught how to punt by Snede Schmidt, a Navy assistant coach who had graduated from the academy in 1936. After practice, Schmidt, Busik, and the team's center would often stay until darkness fell to work on their quick-kicks. Holding a stopwatch, Schmidt would chart the amount of time it took Busik to get each punt off. When Busik was a plebe, Schmidt thought that Busik, who was using a two-step approach, was taking too much time. So Schmidt taught his young pupil the rocker step. Busik would line up 8 yards behind the line of scrimmage with his legs together. Once he was hiked the ball, he'd take one step back with his left foot, then a step forward with his left foot, and then kick the ball with his right foot. Busik could tell when he unleashed a good kick by the fact that he wouldn't feel or hear the punt. Schmidt instructed Busik to drive the ball and not to worry about hang time, because all he needed to do was get the ball beyond the defense's deep safety and let it roll. But against Army, Busik had driven the ball and booted it high enough so that it trav-eled the arc of a big, beautiful rainbow. "The perfect punt," was how Lar-son would later describe it.

At first, the crowd reacted quietly to this "perfect" punt. As soon as the ball left Busik's foot, it was so hushed in the stadium that Busik could hear his cleats crunch against the thick green grass as he ran upfield. The crowd seemed to be in momentary disbelief, as if they'd never seen a ball travel so high into the sky before. But when the ball began its descent, the crowd came alive. This was the first big play of the game, and the fans had been waiting for nearly a quarter to roar. Now, they let it all out. By the time the ball rolled to a stop, the noise in Municipal Stadium could practically be heard on the other side of town. Busik, like most of his teammates, jumped wildly up and down as he ran to take his position on defense. The Midshipmen on the sideline were also ecstatic. Hal Kauffman had often stayed after practice and shagged balls for Busik as he worked on his punting. Now Kauffman yelled to his friend to keep the pressure on Army. Kauffman knew it would take an act of divine intervention for him to play in the game, but he felt like he played a small part in Busik's magical punt. It wasn't much, but it was something he was proud of.

On first down, backed up to their one-foot line, Army's Mazur didn't want to risk a safety or a turnover deep in Army territory, so he quick-kicked the ball back to Navy. Under the circumstances, it was a splendid kick. Busik caught the ball at Army's 48-yard line and, making a few deft cuts, returned it to the 31, where he slipped and fell. On first down, Busik received the snap, gyrated, faked a pass, then ran around the right end for 8 yards. It was early, but Navy already appeared to be taking control of the line of scrimmage. In the huddle Busik called for a sweep to the left side. But as the snap was centered to him, Busik looked up before the ball was in his hands. There was a gaping hole he could have run through—perhaps he even could have scored—but he never gained control of the ball. It fell to the ground and bounced away from him. Army's George Seip, who had been blocked and was out of position to make the tackle, was in perfect position to recover the fumble, which he did on the 28-yard line. The play prompted almost every Midshipmen in the stands to either stomp his foot or put his hands on his head in utter exasperation.

The rest of the first quarter was a defensive struggle. After four punts were exchanged, Navy faced a third and one from Army's 48. Busik had yet to attempt a pass, and he thought that switching to an aerial game would surprise the Cadets. He dropped back into the pocket and saw one of his ends cutting across the middle of the field. Busik lofted the ball, but Army's Robert Evans, who was the team's middle guard, had dropped off the line and back into coverage. Evans leaped high into the air, tipped the ball, and made a spectacular interception. For an interior lineman, it was an unexpectedly athletic play—exactly the type of effort that Coach Blaik knew he'd need to win this game. The Cadets in the stands yelled as Evans returned the ball to Navy's 44-yard line. At the end of the play, the whistle blew, signaling the end of the first quarter.

Earlier in the day, the Japanese consulate in San Francisco received an important message from their Foreign Ministry back in Tokyo. The consulate was to make full reports of the name, nationality, port of departure, port of destination, and departure date "of all foreign commercial and war ships now in the Pacific, Indian Ocean, and South China Sea." Four days had passed since the task force of thirty ships sailed away from Hitokappu Bay, and officials in Tokyo wanted to know if any foreign vessels leaving the port of San Francisco might sail within sight of Japan's war ships.

As the boys from Army and Navy fought it out on the football field, the Japanese ships had sailed about a third of the distance to Pearl Harbor, creeping closer toward their date with history.

As the teams switched ends of the field after the first quarter, Larson called all of his players over to him. He was going to insert his entire second team for the second quarter—earlier in the week he had contemplated playing only his first string in the game, but eventually decided he didn't want to stray from the substitution pattern he'd employed all season. But before the second team went onto the field, he wanted to give them a pep talk. "Everybody do your job and trust your teammates," Larson told his players. "We will wear this team out because we have better depth and we're bigger. Just stay patient."

Over on the Army sideline, Coach Blaik wasn't talking. In fact, he didn't say a word to his players because he was reasonably pleased with how his team had performed in the first quarter. Before the game he was concerned that Navy might jump all over his boys early because they had more experience in big games. But now that fear had been allayed, and Coach Blaik felt like the game was anybody's to win.

Facing Navy's second team at the start of the second quarter, Army still couldn't move the ball. Three runs into the line netted just 5 yards, forcing Mazur to punt again; this time the ball bounced into the end zone. Fearful of making a mistake, Navy punted the ball back on second down, giving Army the ball back on its own 47. Two plays later, Mazur made the first big offensive play of the game. Receiving the snap, Mazur faked a run into the line, then dropped 15 yards behind the line of scrimmage to pass. He fired a long bomb to James Kelleher, who made a graceful leaping catch at the Navy 15. It was Mazur's first pass of the afternoon, and not a single Midshipman lineman got within five yards of Mazur when he dropped back in the pocket. Olds, Romanek, and the rest of the line neutralized the Navy rush, giving Mazur all the time he needed to find the open receiver.

Navy's defense quickly stiffened. Three plays after the long pass, Army faced a fourth and 10 from the 15. Instead of attempting a fairly easy field goal, Coach Blaik opted to go for it. He steadfastly believed that field position was almost as important as points, so even if his team didn't convert the fourth down, his thinking went, Navy would still be pinned deep in their own territory. On fourth down Mazur again had a few seconds to pass, but this time he overthrew his intended receiver. Navy got the ball back on downs.

The next 5 minutes of the second quarter was a festival of punts. Navy kicked the ball three times, Army twice. But before Navy's third kick, late in the second quarter, Coach Blaik instructed his returners to run a trick play that they'd practiced all week. In film study Coach Blaik noticed that one of the things that the Midshipmen did very well on punt coverage was to pursue the ball carrier. The Navy players went after the returner like bulls to a red-waving flag, and Blaik thought that a well-conceived reverse on a punt return could be successful because the Midshipmen, at least initially, would be zeroed in on the wrong player. After a week of practices, the Army return team had perfected this trick return.

With a little less than 5 minutes remaining in the first half, Mazur received the punt on his own 20 near the Army sideline. He immediately sprinted to the other side of the field, drawing to him all the Navy defenders, who were hurtling in his direction. Running down the Navy sideline in the direction of Mazur was Cadet wingback Ralph Hill, one of the fastest players on the Army team. Just before Mazur got tackled, he flipped the ball to Hill. The reverse fooled the Midshipmen. As soon as Hill got the ball, he appeared to be startled by how much open field lay in front of him. He nearly tripped, but regained his balance as he eyed the end zone. The crowd rose to its feet as he sprinted up the Army sideline.

Hill was at midfield. Still no Navy defender around. He was at the 40. The 30. He was running as hard as he could, his legs pumping like pistons. Finally, at the 22-yard line, a Midshipman who had gained ground on Hill only because he had the angle, pushed him out of bounds. Now the momentum was with the Cadets. Feeling confident, Coach Blaik ordered his team to operate out of the T-formation—something he'd never done before at Army. The Cadets had only practiced it for a few days, but that was also why Blaik thought it could be effective: Blaik knew that Navy hadn't had a chance to prepare for it in their pregame practices. And, sure enough, the switch in formations confused the Midshipmen. On first down, Kelleher gained 5 yards on an end around. On second down Mazur ran for 11. Three plays later, fullback Jim Watkins plowed through the center of the line for a 1-yard touchdown plunge. The

Cadets in the stands went delirious, producing a noise that echoed throughout the concrete horseshoe. Suddenly, an upset seemed possible.

Yet the Navy players were a reflection of Larson—their emotional equilibrium never got too out of whack, no matter what the circumstances—and as the teams lined up for the extra point, Navy lineman Arthur Knox nudged Dick Fedon, also an interior lineman for the Midshipmen. The two made eye contact and flashed each other a knowing nod. Ever since Knox was in prep school, he excelled at what he called "pulling the center," which years later would be deemed holding. An accomplished wrestler, Knox lined up over the center on extra points. As soon as the ball was centered, he'd perform the move: First he'd leap and grab the center by his shoulder pads. Then, holding onto the center's pads, Knox would twist and throw his feet up off the ground so that the center would be holding all of Knox's weight. Using his leverage, Knox would then pull the center to his left. Once the center was out of the way, a teammate—in this case Fedon—would loop behind Knox and have a straight shot at the kicker.

Against Army the move worked to perfection. Knox fired off the line of scrimmage, grabbed the center, twisted, then threw him out of the way. Fedon slid into the gaping hole and smothered the kick. He arrived at the ball at almost the same time as the kicker. As soon as the kick was blocked, the Navy sideline, where most of the players and coaches had been sitting on folding chairs, erupted. "I knew we could get 'em on that one," Knox shouted to Fedon as they jogged to the sideline. "It's the oldest trick in the book." Other than Busik's long punt, this was the first game-altering play Navy had made all afternoon, and it injected the team with a shot of confidence. The scoreboard read: Army 6, Navy 0.

Navy's second-string offensive unit had time for one more drive before halftime. On a second-down play from their own 11-yard line, Alex Zechella caught a pass over the middle from Sherwood Werner. Just as Zechella was being tackled at the Navy 20-yard line, he lateraled the ball to teammate Bob Woods, who then ran up the Navy sideline to the Cadets' 45. Less than one minute remained in the half. Back Howie Clark, who was the second team player in charge of play-calling, opted to try another pass. As he dropped back deep into the pocket, though, Romanek beat his man off the right edge. Coming from Clark's blind side, Romanek had a clear shot at making the sack. But instead of going strictly for Clark, Romanek went for the ball, stripping it cleanly, swiping the pigskin directly out of Clark's arms. The Army players on the sideline leapt from their chairs, screaming for Romanek to run.

Romanek saw no one between him and the end zone, 40 yards away. The Cadets in the stands yelled deliriously. If Army could score here, it would be a devastating blow to Navy. But just as Romanek secured the ball and started to run—just as the vision of him scoring a touchdown began to gloriously unfold in his mind—Clark lunged at Romanek and poked the ball just hard enough to jar it loose from Romanek's grasp. Army ultimately recovered the fumble, but failed to advance the ball any farther upfield. Only seconds remained in the half.

The Cadets ran one play and then let the clock expire. As Romanek headed off the field for the locker room, he couldn't believe he hadn't return the fumble for a touchdown. He figured that play would haunt him for the rest of his life. "I should have scored," he muttered to himself over and over as he neared the locker room. "Goddamn it, I should have scored."

In the Navy locker room, the overwhelming sentiment was anger. The players felt like they'd played their worst half of football of the season. They let Army dictate the tempo and flow of the game on both sides of the ball and, worse, they seemed to be playing as if they were afraid to lose rather than wanting to win. Larson nervously paced back and forth from one end of the locker room to the other, trying to figure out what he should say to his team. He was searching for magical words, for a few sentences that would make his boys play to the top of their potential in the last 30 minutes of the game—the last 30 minutes of his coaching career. Then it came to him.

"Boys, today is our last war together," said Coach Larson. "We have a chance to win this war together on this battlefield. Now listen, you boys are fine football players, and you will make even better officers. The nation will need you. You will need each other. In these last 30 minutes, let's show the nation what kind of football players you are and what kind of officers you will be." Larson's voice grew louder. "Let's play these last 30 minutes of football like they're the last 30 minutes of our lives, because what you do right now you will remember for the rest of your lives. Now let's go get 'em."

As soon as Larson stopped speaking, every player in the locker room jumped from his seat on the bench and yelled. Never before had they seen their coach so passionate and intense. They were so ready for action that they would have run through barbed wire to get out of the locker room, if that's what it took to get back on that field and get another crack at Army.

As fire and brimstone flew from Larson's lips in the Navy quarters, Coach Blaik was coolly assessing the situation with his assistants in the opposite locker room. The consensus was that their boys had played their best half of football of the season. Blaik hadn't expected to move the ball much on offense, and that was holding true. Blaik believed that the only way the Cadets would maintain their lead was if they could continue to win the minigame of field position and make one more game-changing play on special teams. Blaik knew that the more talented players resided on the other side of the field, which meant he needed to outfox Larson in the second half. "We're doing great," Coach Blaik calmly told his team. "Let's just keep being precise in everything we do—with our blocking, tackling, and running—and we'll win this game."

During halftime, Mrs. Roosevelt and her entourage slowly walked across the field to take their seats on the Navy side of the stadium. Because of her husband's long-standing interest in the Army-Navy clash, the First Lady had a good grasp of the rules of the game and was well versed in its nuances. As she strolled across the field she waved to the Navy fans, all of whom gave her an enthusiastic welcome. Some in the stands even figured she'd bring the Midshipmen good luck. After all, they figured, the underdog Cadets did score a touchdown when she sat on *their* side.

Navy had the option to kick or receive to begin the second half, and Larson chose to go on offense first. His best player was Busik, and he wanted the ball in Busik's hands for as much of the second half as possible. When Busik received the kickoff at his goal line, he sprinted upfield, broke two tackles, and was finally dragged down on Navy's 32-yard line. Before calling the first play of the drive, Busik looked around in the huddle, locking eyes with his teammates. "This is why we play football, fellas," Busik said above the crowd noise, "for moments like this. Let's do what we have to and win this game for coach."

Busik then called his own number—as he did for eight of the next nine plays. None of these runs or passes was particularly spectacular, but each time Busik made positive gains. He'd get 3 yards running up the middle. Then 5 to the outside. Then 3 more up the middle in a cloud of dust. Then 6 on a pass to the Army sideline. Eventually, Busik led the

Midshipmen to the Army 16-yard line, where Navy faced a fourth and 6. The key moment of the game—up to this point—had arrived.

On the sideline, Larson knew exactly what Busik should call: a run around the right end. But the play call was Busik's. Larson, though, was so sure that he knew the right play to call that, suddenly, he yelled at the top of his lungs, "Gebert!" Tackle Wes Gebert quickly got up off his metal folding chair, grabbed his helmet, and sprinted up to his coach. Larson told Gebert what play he wanted Busik to run and then he pushed Gebert out onto the field, subbing him in for another tackle. Even though a rule was implemented at the beginning of the 1941 season that allowed coaches to shuttle players and play calls in from the sideline, Larson had never done it before. He trusted his players on the field to make the play calls. Larson figured they had a better feel for what would work because they were more intimately involved in the action. But this was such an important moment in the game that Larson made the snap decision to send in his first midquarter substitution of the season and call the first play of his coaching career. He felt, right now, that he had a golden touch, a sure thing, and he obeyed his instincts.

When Gebert got to the huddle and relayed the information, Busik was shocked. He looked to coach Larson on the sideline, who nodded his head and motioned that Busik should get to the line of scrimmage. The Army players were equally surprised to see Gebert run onto the field. A few players thought that a trick play was coming; others thought that Gebert would attempt a field goal. The confusion on the Cadet side seemed to linger once Busik was hiked the ball. He sprinted around the right end—it was almost as if he were flying—and he gained 15 yards to the Army 1-foot line. On the next play, backup Phil Hurt bulled through the middle to score Navy's first touchdown of the afternoon. The extra point was good and 8 minutes into the third quarter Navy held a 7–6 lead. The fans on the Navy side of the field were in a frenzy, shouting at the top of their lungs.

On the Army sideline, Coach Blaik weighed his options for what to do next. According to the rules in 1941, once a team surrendered a touchdown it had the choice of either receiving the ball or kicking off for a second straight time. It was virtually unheard of for a coach to use this rule and kick off after his team was just scored upon, but the idea intrigued Blaik. He figured Navy's offense was just as tired as his defense, and if they could hold the Midshipmen inside their 30, then the Cadets would be able to acquire good field position. With his team gathered around him on the sideline, Coach Blaik quickly made up his mind: He called for the kickoff squad to get back on the field. Many of his players looked at Blaik like he'd gone made, but again Blaik barked his instructions.

The Navy players were as surprised by Blaik's decision as the Army players. The Midshipmen kickoff team was already on the field when the referee signaled that the Cadets would be kicking off. Many fans didn't understand the move either, as a quizzical groan emanated from Army supporters in the stands. Nonetheless, Blaik saw this as a chance to eventually put his offense in a favorable position to score, which to Blaik was the key to the game. He didn't think his offense could drive the ball any distance and push the ball into the end zone.

Again Busik returned the ball and again he advanced it to Navy's 32-yard line. On the sideline before the kick, Larson had told Busik to pound the ball, really pound it, between the tackles. Larson added that 37 Buck, which was a fullback plunge up the middle, would be a good play to run. Larson thought the play would further wear down the undersized Cadets, and Larson was right. Mixing 37 Buck with an assortment of short passes, the Midshipmen moved the ball methodically down the field. They faced only one third down—a third and two at Army's 37—and converted it with a 12-yard run by Busik.

One of the players that Navy was successfully blocking was Olds. When healthy, Olds had all-American potential. He thought the adrenaline rush brought on by the game would propel him for four quarters, would make his pain go away, but by now his right shoulder had been hit so many times that his entire right arm was virtually limp. If he had two good arms, Olds may have been able to stop the Midshipmen on the drive that they were now embarking on—Olds was that talented, no question—but not by playing at only 50 percent. Navy knew that Olds was injured, and the Midshipmen didn't hesitate running the ball in his direction, a tactic they never would have pursued had Olds not been hurt.

The twelve-play drive concluded with another 1-yard touchdown run, this one by back Howie Clark. The extra point kicked by Bob Leonard split the uprights and, with less than a minute remaining in the third quarter, Navy had a 14–6 lead. The Midshipmen in the stands, sensing that their team was closing in on victory, celebrated exuberantly. If the Navy fans had been worn out by the nearly three quarters of tense football, it didn't show, because they continued to yell like their pants were on fire.

This time Blaik didn't elect to kick off. Mazur, who felt like he hadn't had the ball in his hands for hours, received the kick at the goal line and returned it 36 yards. Playing with a sense of urgency, Mazur on first down threw deep over the middle. The pass was incomplete, but Navy was flagged for interference, giving the Cadets a 22-yard gain to Navy's 42. After the referees marched off the penalty yards, the quarter came to an end. Fifteen minutes of football remained.

Coach Larson asked the entire Navy squad to gather around him on the sideline. "This is it, one more quarter," Larson yelled. "Give it your all right now, and we'll win this game."

After the teams changed sides, Mazur threw another beautiful long pass. He hit Ralph Hill in stride as Hill streaked down the Navy sideline. Hill was pushed out of bounds at the Middies' 17-yard line. Suddenly, the Cadets in the stands were bouncing up and down again. The game, which had seemed like a lost cause just moments ago, suddenly was exciting again. Trying to capitalize on his hot hand, Mazur called for another pass play in the huddle. He dropped back 10 yards behind the line of scrimmage, sprinted to his left, then saw what he believed to be an open man cutting across the field at Navy's 5-yard line. Mazur threw the ball as hard as could, trying to squeeze it between two defenders, but Busik, playing defensive back, reacted quickly and intercepted the ball at the 5. He returned it 6 yards to the 11, where he was pushed out of bounds. Some 13 minutes remained in the game, but to Larson and to everyone else who was on the Navy sideline this appeared to be the play of the game.

When Busik came to the bench—the second team was now in on offense—the first player to greet him was Hal Kauffman. All game long Kauffman had intensely watched the game from the bench. He had agonized over every play, every block, and now his buddy from California had at least momentarily saved the game. They embraced on the sideline—a long, tight, heart-felt embrace. Right now Kauffman almost felt like he was a brother to Busik, so proud was he of his friend.

Navy again ran the ball between the tackles, trying to bleed as much time off the clock as possible. They gained two first downs before Army finally forced a punt. But when the Cadets got the ball back at their own 25 with 6 minutes to play, they were a demoralized—and a dog tired—squad. Mazur ran for one first down, but the Navy defense stiffened and forced another punt. When the Middies gained possession of the ball only 3 minutes remained. Now the Navy supporters in the stands were in full-scale party-mode, as they smiled and hugged and laughed in the bleachers.

On the other side of the stadium it was perfectly quiet. Some fans cried while others consoled. Yet not a single fan filed out of the stadium.

Navy slammed the ball between the tackles on three straight plays and gained a first down. Then the final gun sounded. The game was over. The undermanned Cadet players had fought as hard as Vikings, but the Midshipmen prevailed 14–6.

As Army and Navy players began to walk across the field, the Midshipmen band struck into its alma mater song, causing players from both teams to stand at attention. Cadets, holding their helmets under their arms, wept as the Midshipmen players all proudly sang along. Minutes later, the Cadet band broke into its alma mater song, and the Navy players stood at attention out of respect for Army. Up in the stands, men, women, and children all teared up as they watched the young men on the field, standing shoulder-to-shoulder in the growing afternoon shadows.

It took Larson about ten minutes to reach Navy's locker room. After the playing of the alma mater songs, fans spilled onto the field, impeding Larson's route. The Midshipmen fans climbed on top of both goalposts and, as both bands now played the "Star Spangled Banner," the posts tipped down until their roots were unearthed. After the national anthem was over—the entire stadium had sung together—Larson shook hands with Coach Blaik and several of the Army players and then waded through the crush of fans that had congregated on the field. A full 20 minutes after the game was over, the stadium was still packed. No one wanted to leave. Everyone understood that this was one memory worth stretching out as long as possible.

A group of reporters was waiting for Larson when he walked into the locker room. Now a big smile lighted Larson's long, slender face. "Those Army lads were as hot as firecrackers!" Larson shouted. "But we showed them a few plays they hadn't seen before."

Just then, tackle Bill Chewning, his uniform smeared with dirt, blood, and grass stains, approached Larson with the game ball. "Here you are, coach," said Chewning as he handed Larson the ball.

"Thanks, Billy," replied Larson. "You played a marvelous game."

On the other side of the stadium, in the corridor just outside the Army locker room, Blaik stood straight and tall. Though his heart was sick, he still looked all the reporters in the eye. "If we had a few boys to stick in that backfield, we could have done better," he said. "You saw how it was. Navy not only had two lines but two backfields. I'm definitely not satisfied. I'm a bad loser. I thought we might upset them. We had them on the run for awhile, but a few little things in there hurt us and helped Navy."

That night players from both teams celebrated the end of their seasons. Most the Midshipmen attended a party at the Bellevue Hotel and gorged on the nectar of glory. They danced with their dates until the sun peeked over the horizon, moving their feet to songs like "Waltzing Matilda," by Banjo Patterson. The scene was similar at the Franklin Hotel. Even though the Cadets had lost a heartbreaking game, most of the players were still in a festive mood. "You can't cry all day," Romanek told a few of his teammates who were crestfallen and holding pity parties in their rooms at the hotel. "You gotta move on. After all, who knows where we'll be in the next month, the next year, or the next two years."

In the morning each team made its way back to its respective campus. At West Point, their fellow classmates and a few hundred locals greeted the Cadet players at the train depot. Everyone cheered as the team stepped off the train. This one last show of support by their fans somehow made the loss bearable.

At the naval academy, it seemed that the entire city of Annapolis turned out to meet the Middies. The Toonerville Trolley carried the team straight into the Yard. From there, players and fans walked over to Tecumseh Court and rang the Gokokuji Bell. The bell, which Commodore Matthew Perry brought to the United States in 1854 from Japan, tolled only after a Navy victory over Army. And now each player and coach rang the bell fourteen times—for the fourteen points they scored against the Cadets—as the throng of midshipmen and fans cheered. The bell clanged and clattered deep into the night, the sounds echoing through the trees and all across campus.

"I'm glad I decided to play football," Busik told a teammate as they waited their turn. "It's probably one of the best decisions I ever made. I'll never forget this win."

The date was November 30, 1941. For the next few days, Busik and his teammates would swap tales—some a little taller than others—about their exploits from that dream day. For seven days the glory of the game seemed to lighten everyone's spirit at the naval academy. Fellow midshipmen and Annapolis locals alike all sought out Busik, greeting him like a conquering hero and asking him for an autograph. Even the academy instructors went out of their way to congratulate the players, even guys like Hal Kauffman who didn't get into the game.

Indeed, these were golden moments for Busik and Kauffman. Graduation was just months away, and then they'd be sent off into the real world as officers in the United States Navy. But for now, for the next few days, they reveled in the warm glow of victory.

II

PEARL HARBOR

AFTER THE NAVY VICTORY Alan Shapley took every opportunity to chat about the game. Whenever he so much as bumped into one of the eighty-seven marines he was in charge of aboard the U.S.S. *Arizona* who hadn't paid close attention to the radio broadcast of the Army-Navy contest, Shapley would put a hand on his shoulder and tell him all about it, sparring no detail. Normally stingy with his words, Shapley would talk a blue streak when it came to discussing Navy football—particularly when it involved beating Army. The Midshipmen's victory over the Cadets on November 29 had tickled his heart, filling Shapley with so much pride that it was as if his own blood brothers had won the game.

Now, on the morning of December 7, 1941, as Shapley walked into the *Arizona*'s wardroom for breakfast, he was still beaming. The widest of smiles illuminated his angular face. With his sandy-hair, big blue eyes, and athletic, slender build, Shapley still could be taken for the Big Man On Campus, even though it had been fifteen years since he led the Midshipmen to the 1926 national title. Now Shapley took a seat. The *Arizona* was moored in the still waters of Pearl Harbor. Along with the *Arizona*, there were seven other battleships, eight cruisers, thirty destroyers, and four submarines resting at the Navy base.

Outside it was a peaceful, quiet morning. The air was moist and mild. Blue waves glistened in the winter sunshine. A soft breeze fluffed the palm trees on the island. Sunday was generally regarded as a day of leisure at Pearl, so there was little activity at the base. Inside the *Arizona*, Shapley had more than just Navy's victory over Army to be happy about. The previous afternoon he had been promoted to major. His new orders were to report to the First Marine Amphibious Corps at Camp Elliot, located outside of San Diego, as soon as possible. Though he had been relieved of his duties aboard the *Arizona*, which had recently returned to Pearl Harbor after performing exercises in the Pacific, the next transportation ship back to California wasn't scheduled to leave until the morning of December 8, a Monday. The delay suited Shapley just fine. He was both the coach and first baseman of the *Arizona*'s baseball team, and on this Sunday morning the U.S.S. *Arizona* had a game scheduled against the U.S.S. *Enterprise*. But Shapley had time to enjoy his breakfast because the *Enterprise* was still due in from Wake Island, an atoll in the North Pacific Ocean where she had delivered planes to reinforce the Marine garrison. So Shapley was in no hurry as he drank coffee and ate eggs and hot cakes with two dozen other officers in the wardroom.

At about 7:50, Shapley rose from his seat and stretched his legs. He walked outside the wardroom and started chatting with a few other officers. He explained to them that he had mixed feelings about leaving. On one hand, he was thrilled that he'd see his wife and two young children once he made it stateside. They lived in Detroit, some five thousand miles away from Pearl Harbor. Shapley, like many officers stationed at Pearl, chose to leave his family in the States out of concern for a possible war erupting in the Pacific. But as happy as Shapley was that he'd get to see his loved ones, he was heartbroken that he'd have to leave his men. "They're like family to me," Shapley said on numerous occasions of his marines. "It just doesn't seem right leaving them."

The marine detachment of eighty-seven men on the *Arizona*, which had a total crew of 1,731, was charged with several duties. They acted as orderlies and messengers for the senior officers on board. They stood watch at the brig in four-hour shifts. They served as gun crews and they performed ceremonial duties, such as keeping track of the time of day by ringing the ship's bell. And the marines were the only ones aboard the ship who carried loaded guns—an old tradition based on the theory that the marines were present to protect the senior officers in the event of a mutiny. When the marines weren't on duty, they spent a good deal of their free time shining shoes, pressing their uniforms, and polishing their belt buckles. This wasn't a particularly glamorous way of life, but Shapley—ever the quarterback, the leader of his team—tried to make his men feel important. One of the first things that Shapley did when he assumed command of the detachment was to memorize as well as he could the biographies of all his men. He then took a genuine interest in all of them and talked to each of them about his family, his hopes, his dreams, his fears. This fostered a closeness between Shapley and his men that was rare in the world of marine detachments.

At approximately 7:56, Shapley left the officers standing outside the wardroom and began walking to his stateroom, his living quarters. There he planned to put on his baseball uniform and, if he had time, pack his bags for his transfer to the States. But just as he turned to start walking he felt a jolt, which rocked the ship and forced him to put his hands on the wall to keep his balance. A loud thud followed. He figured that perhaps one of the forty-foot boats had been accidentally dropped off the crane onto the stern of the ship.

Alarmed but hardly panicked, Shapley climbed the ladder to the deck just to make sure that everything was okay. There he saw a group of sailors standing on the rail and peering across the harbor at the big Number 1 dry dock. In the dry dock were the flagship U.S.S. *Pennsylvania* and two destroyers, the U.S.S. *Cassin* and the U.S.S. *Downs*. The sailors were watching dozens of airplanes zoom over the Pearl Harbor shipyard. "This is the best damn drill that the Army Air Force has ever put on," remarked one sailor to Shapley as Shapley kept his gaze fastened on the harbor. A few seconds later, to everyone's horror, one of the destroyers burst into flames. A mushroom cloud of black, brackish smoke swelled into the sky. The boom of the explosion shot across the water; it was so strong that Shapley and the others could feel a sharp thump in their chests. A voice shouted over the *Arizona's* loudspeaker for all disengaged personnel to get below the third deck, where they would have the protection of armor plating. Moments later, the flagship *Pennsylvania*, which was now engulfed in flames, countermanded, which overruled the last order, and ran up the signal for general quarters, signaling for everyone to get to their battle stations. They were under attack.

Shapley immediately recognized the planes as Japanese, since the red ball on the underside of the wings was a telltale marking. Shapley's battlestation for general quarters, along with thirteen enlisted Marines and one of his lieutenants, was to man the gunnery director station up in the Arizona's mainmast and, if necessary, the two .50 caliber machine guns that were fastened at the very top of the mast in a post known as the "bird bath," which sat more than one hundred feet above the waterline. The *Arizona*'s mainmast—the ship's tallest mast—had three positions that could be manned. The first was the searchlight platform, which was forty feet in the air. The next was the gunnery director station, which was ninety feet up. The third was the "bird bath," fifteen feet above the gunnery station. Shapley headed for the gunnery station, on the double.

On the deck, men were running in all directions, trying to get either to their battle stations or into the belly of the ship for protection. Some of the younger men—some weren't even shaving yet—looked panicked, unsure of what to do, as they frantically scrambled around the deck. As Shapley ran toward the ladder that led up to the bird bath, he saw Second Lieutenant Carleton Simensen, a graduate of North Dakota University and one of the junior officers in the detachment. Simensen had already rounded up a group of marines and they were all running to the tripod mainmast. Shapley calmly told everyone to remember their training. This, he reminded everyone in a loud voice, was the real thing.

Simensen was the first marine to reach the metal ladder. Hand over hand, he began climbing. Shapley was next. As they moved upward, more planes appeared, dotting the sky like a swarm of killer bees. The planes bore down on the ships, releasing bombs that whistled as they fell and detonated with a thunder when they blew gaping holes into the ships. As Shapley climbed, he could see that the planes were also strafing the men who were topside on the ships with machine guns; men would fall in an eyeblink once they were struck. Torpedoes also rained from the sky. Once they hit the water, they moved like sharks after meat toward their intended targets. Shapley felt each explosion reverberate against him as he continued the push to his battlestation.

Just as Simensen, the lead climber, reached for the last rung before the searchlight platform—forty feet in the air—he lost his grasp. He fell backward onto Shapley, lifeless as a rag doll. With one hand gripping a rung, Shapley caught hold of Simensen with his free arm. Shapley pushed him across his shoulders and, exerting all the strength he had, managed to carry Simensen up three feet and lay him on the searchlight platform. Out of breath, Shapley quickly inspected Simensen. His shirtfront was soaked with blood, and he wasn't breathing. Simensen had been hit by machine gun fire, killed instantly. Shapley looked down the ladder and saw that four other marines had also been struck and fallen off the ladder. They were all dead.

In a firm voice, Shapley instructed his men who were still alive that they had to keep climbing; they had to reach their battlestation. They continued to climb, up, up, up. Shapley and his eight marines could see some of the faces of the Japanese pilots as they whizzed by. Many of the planes had their canopies open, and Shapley was so close to one pilot that their eyes met. For a moment that seemed to occur in slow motion, Shapley and the pilot looked hard at each other. It was almost like they were communicating . . . then, in a flash, the pilot and the plane were out of sight, gone to drop more death on Pearl.

When Shapley and eight of his men finally finished the climb to the director platform, they went to man the five-inch guns—but it was a futile task. The guns weren't designed to blast enemy aircraft; they were made to shoot at other ships. Shapley and his men desperately tried to elevate the guns so they could target the planes that circled Pearl like buzzards, but they wouldn't budge. All Shapley and his men could do was watch the destruction. From their perch they saw a torpedo ram into the U.S.S. *Oklahoma*, which was moored just ahead of the *Arizona* in Battleship Row. The blast caused the *Oklahoma* to roll over on her back and pitch hundreds of her crew into the water. Shapley and his men watched dozens of injured men drown within a few feet of land.

The whole scene had a dreamlike unreal feel to it. In the distance Shapley and his men could see Hickem Field, which was an Army Air Force base, and closer by was Ford Island, where a naval air station was located. Japanese aircraft were attacking both. As they witnessed the destruction with their panoramic view of Pearl, chips of metal and paint struck Shapley and his men, the result of enemy gunfire hitting the ship. Realizing there was nothing they could do at their battlestation, Shapley looked for a clear path down. He examined each of the tripod legs, but each one led directly into a towering ball of flames. For the moment, there was no way out. The ship was burning from bow to stern and, after spending about 10 minutes up in the director platform, the heat was becoming unbearable.

"We're cooking up here," a sergeant told Shapley.

"I'll get you out of this," Shapley replied, his hair standing on edge from the nonstop concussions of shock waves that were being produced by the explosions. "I promise I'll get you out of this. We're not going to die."

Just then, Shapley noticed that one of the tripod legs of the main-mast had become clear of flames. This was their opportunity to get to the main deck and abandon ship, and he ordered his men to start the descent. The metal ladder was now so hot that it burned their hands when they touched it, but Shapley encouraged his men by telling them that burned hands and burned feet will heal. Shapley was the last to leave the platform and he climbed down as fast as he could. When he reached the searchlight platform he again checked the status of Simensen, confirming he was dead. As Shapley got back on the ladder and started his final descent, he looked up and saw a bomb fall from the sky, heading straight for the *Arizona*. Shapley—and the rest of his men who saw this bomb coming—took a deep breath and braced for the explosion, clenching their teeth and wrapping their hands tight around the hot metal ladder.

The 1,760-pound armor-piercing shell struck the *Arizona* near the Number 2 turret, igniting a fire. The flames spread quickly through a hatch that the men inside the *Arizona* didn't have time to shut. Within seconds the fire reached the ship's munitions rooms where one hundred tons of gunpowder rested. First there was a silent white flash, then a blast erupted like a volcano from inside of the ship. In an instant, more than two-thirds of the crew were dead.

A putrid rush of air came at Shapley, who was still on the ladder, forty feet above the water line. Then the explosion lifted him off the ladder, throwing him high into the air. He landed in the water some thirty feet from the ship, unconscious. All around him debris fell from the sky and plopped into the water—parts of the ship, human body parts, and charred sailors. As Shapley started to sink, he came to and—miraculously—he was physically unharmed except that he felt sick to his stomach. All of his clothes either burned or blew off and he was momentarily deafened by the blast—but he was still alive.

When Shapley emerged from beneath the water, he took a gasping breath of air. Looking around him, it was as if he was glimpsing a boiling, screaming hell. Men were splashing in their own blood, crying for help. Others were swallowed in flames. Much of the surface of the water was on fire; the *Arizona* had some ninety-three thousand barrels of oil aboard, and when she was hit the fuel spewed out and ignited.

In the distance Shapley saw five of his marines in the water, most struggling to stay afloat. Shapley always was a strong swimmer and he kicked and paddled to his men, gliding by several body parts and charred bodies that were floating in the water. When he reached his marines—like Shapley, they were all covered in oil—Shapley explained to them how they should swim through burning water. He told them to swim underwater and then, when they had to come up for air, they were to perform a quick twirl to keep from catching on fire. Then, Shapley told them, they should get back under water as quickly as they could. Shapley also said that they should swim directly into the breeze when possible, because that made them less likely to catch fire when they bobbed up for air. Shapley then lead five men toward a water-supply pipeline that was about halfway between them and Ford Island, which was about 150 yards away.

As the group swam though the oily water, Shapley shouted encouragement. "We can do this," he told them. "All of us can. We've trained and we can do this. All of us will make it." When Shapley noticed that Russ McCurdy, one of his marines, was struggling, Shapley swam over to him and told McCurdy not to give up. "You're a great whaleboat man so I know you can do this," Shapley told his marine, who he also coached on the whaleboat team. "Be strong. Just be strong."

Bombs continued to fall from the sky like hail, one after the other, as Shapley and his men swam. From their perspective, when they looked up it seemed as if each bomb was headed straight for them, as if they had bull's-eyes tattooed on their foreheads. Whenever a bomb detonated in the water, the reverberation was so great that it jiggled the men's flesh. About halfway to the pipeline, Shapley saw that corporal Earl Nightengale, who was swimming nearby, was losing strength. Shapley maneuvered close to Nightengale and told him, "Come on, son, you can do it. We'll get out of this together. Keep fighting."

But Nightengale's strength was completely sapped. He told Shapley to go on without him. "Grab my shoulders," Shapley said. Though he was a dozen years older than most of his men, Shapley was still more athletic than any of them. His natural endurance helped him now as he attempted to tow Nightengale to the pipeline, which was still some twenty yards away.

For the first few yards, Shapley felt as if he and Nightengale would make it. But then, as quick as a room light being turned off, a wave of fatigue overwhelmed him. It felt as if lead weights were draped around his legs. He started bobbing in the water. Nightengale let go. He told Shapley to save himself, that he was ready to die. Shapley looked up at the pipeline and it was still ten yards away, but to him it seemed on the other side of the ocean. Shapley told his men that he was letting go as well. Nightengale, just before he disappeared beneath the water, brought his trembling fingers to his forehead, his final salute to a commanding officer.

Shapley then descended into the water, dropping like a bag of rocks, all hope lost. But suddenly, eight feet down, his feet touched the bottom. Shapley was shocked. He had figured the water was much deeper. He tapped his feet on the muddy surface, just to make sure he was actually feeling the bottom. Revitalized and refueled with hope, he bolted back up above the water, pushing with his legs, and resumed the struggle.

When the men saw Shapley fighting to stay alive, it lifted their spirits. After coming up for a breath of air, Shapley dove back down, grabbed Nightengale by the shirt, and yanked him back up. Gritting his teeth, Shapley dragged Nightengale the rest of the way to the pipeline. Soon the other men joined. They were now about halfway to Ford Island, where they could find safety in a bomb shelter. Behind them the *Arizona* was sunk, though a thick stream of black smoke still poured out of part of the ship's superstructure that was above the surface. "Let's make this a quick rest and then we'll move on," Shapley told his men as they all clung to the pipeline. "We're going to do this."

After a few minutes, the group began the final leg of their swim. The bombs kept falling and planes peppered the water with bullets. One bomb whose target was apparently the U.S.S. *Nevada* strayed far off course. It landed about fifty feet from the men, and the vibration in the water was so great that the men felt as if the flesh and muscle was being pulled off their bodies. Shapley, though, never lost his focus. As the group got closer and closer to Ford Island, he continued to shout encouragement to his men. Finally, after about 30 minutes of swimming, the entire group reached Ford Island. As Shapley got out of the water, he was in a daze, not really sure what had just happened to him. For a few moments he wandered around the island with a confused look on his face, but he was eventually recognized by a chief petty officer. The officer gave Shapley an official boat cloak and a bottle of whiskey, which he had taken out of the officers' club. Shapley took a big swig, and then, along with the other men he was in the water with, was escorted to the bomb shelter. Shapley stayed there for about 90 minutes, dazed but sure of one thing: The Japanese would one day pay dearly for this attack.

Some six thousand miles away, an hour after the first bomb had exploded at Pearl Harbor, hordes of fans were pushing their way through the turnstiles at Washington D.C.'s Griffith Stadium. The final pro football game of the 1941 season for the Washington Redskins and Philadelphia Eagles was scheduled to kick off at 2:00 P.M. local time—9:00 A.M. in Hawaii. More than twenty-seven thousand fans filled Washington's old ballpark at Seventh Street and V Street NW. Many of the men wore suits and ties under their overcoats while most of the women were decked out in long dresses and furs. It was a chilly December morning—in the cold air, everyone's breath burst out of their mouths in white puffs—but the weather didn't bother members of the Navy B squad (the backup players) who had made the trip from Annapolis to see the game. They were just thrilled to witness an NFL contest, which for most of the players was a first.

William Leahy, a second-year reserve player at Navy who in less than four years would play a pivotal role in D-day, was especially enthralled. A native of Philadelphia, Leahy liked the Eagles even more than cake when he was growing up in the City of Brotherly Love. The Eagles were the heroes of his youth, players like quarterback Davey O'Brien (an Eagle in 1939–40), end Don Looney (1940), and running back Swede Hanson (1933–37). On this afternoon Leahy was interested in seeing if the Philadelphia defense could slow down the Washington offense, which was led by Slingin' Sammy Baugh. As the Redskins' tobacco-juice-spitting quarterback, Baugh threw a pretty ball, and he could chuck it better than any other player of his day. Though neither the Redskins nor the Eagles were going to advance to the playoffs, Leahy considered this game to be as important as the NFL Championship. After all, this was the first time that Leahy had gotten a chance to see his beloved Eagles play all season.

After traveling to the stadium on a school bus, the Navy B squad players took their seats behind the visitor's bench at about the 30-yard line. Just before kickoff, high above them in the press box, a reporter for the Associated Press named Pat O'Brien received a message from his editor ordering him to keep his story short. When O'Brien complained, he received a second message: "The Japanese have kicked off. War Now!" O'Brien was shocked. He ran up and down the press box announcing that the Japanese had attacked the United States. O'Brien relayed the information to Redskins President George Marshall and General Manager Jack Espey. By this time the game had already started and, midway through the first quarter, Philadelphia held a 7-0 lead. After considering what they should do for a few minutes, Marshall and Espey decided not to inform the crowd of the events at Pear Harbor, fearing that panicked fans could injure each other as they stampeded for the exits. "We don't want to contribute to any hysteria," said Espey. A few moments later, in a box on the 50-yard line, Jesse Jones, the secretary of commerce, was handed a message and quickly departed from the game.

Even without the official announcement, it soon became clear to the fans that something monumental had happened. Every few minutes a voice would come over the public address system and announce that a certain admiral or major was being summoned to his office. "Admiral W. H. P. Blandy is asked to report to his office at once!" said the PA announcer midway through the first quarter. "The Resident Commissioner of the Philippines, Mr. Joaquin Elizalde, is urged to report to his office immediately!" came another announcement. By the end of the first half, after more than a dozen people had been urgently paged, a rumor had spread through the crowd that most of the United States' Pacific Fleet had been destroyed at Pearl Harbor.

In the press box, only a few reporters remained. Editors from the *Washington Post* and the *Washington Times Herald*—D.C.'s two morning newspapers—had been frantically calling the press box ever since the opening kickoff. They needed all of their reporters back in the office so they could help put out a special afternoon edition. One wife of a reporter took matters into her own hands. She instructed Western Union to deliver a telegram to Section P, Top Row, Seat 27, opposite 25-yard line, on the east side that read: "War with Japan. Get to office." Down on the field, only one photographer remained. The rest had been told to go to the Japanese Embassy or to the White House or to Capitol Hill.

Midway through the third quarter the most pressing announcement of the day was made: All military personnel, whether on leave or just away from their stations, were to report to their stations immediately. Upon hearing this, Leahy and all the other Midshipmen quickly rose from their seats and headed for the exit. But as soon as Leahy got to the aisle, one female fan after the next rushed up to him and gave him a hug and a kiss on the cheek. Leahy looked around and saw that the same thing was happening to his teammates. "That was the most attention I've ever gotten," Leahy told one of his teammates when they finally reached the bus. "I've never been kissed that much in my whole life!"

The B squad didn't get a chance to see the finish of the game. Late in the fourth quarter, Baugh threw his third touchdown pass of the day to rookie end Joe Aguirre to cement the Redskins' 20–14 victory. After the game, exuberant Washington fans rushed the field and tore down the goal posts. It marked the last football celebration of an era. Just outside the stadium, newsboys held swag sacks that were full of special-edition papers. These boys were screaming the most important news in the western hemisphere since November 11, 1918, when the armistice ended World War I. "United States attacked!" the boys shouted. "United States attacked!"

Forty-five miles northeast of Washington, the party at the superintendent's quarters in Annapolis was just getting into full swing when the Redskins and Eagles kicked off. The superintendent at Navy had promised the Navy varsity players that if they beat Army he'd invite them over to celebrate. When the players arrived attired in their dress uniforms with their drags (dates) on their arms, they saw a mouth-watering spread of food. Various meats, fruits, vegetables, cheeses, and desserts were laid out on several tables. The food perfumed the air, and the players couldn't wait to dig in.

At the party, Busik shared some surprising news with his teammates: Two days earlier he had received a telegram from Earl (Curly) Lambeau, the head coach of the Green Bay Packers. Lambeau had listened to the Army-Navy game and he had been mighty impressed with Busik's all-around play. Even though he'd never seen any tape of Busik, Lambeau still wanted to offer Busik a tryout with the Packers. In the telegram, Lambeau said that the Packers were interested in Busik both as a back and as a punter. "Can you believe that the Packers actually want me to try out?" Busik laughed as he discussed the matter with a few teammates, including Hal Kauffman, at the superintendent's party. "Don't they realize that I'm committed to the navy? But maybe someday I'll give it a try, who knows?"

Thirty minutes into the party, at about 2:30 local time, a waiter informed the superintendent that he had an important telephone call. The urgency and quaver in the waiter's voice caught everyone's attention. Conversations stopped and every set of eyes followed the superintendent as he went to the top of a winding stairway to speak in private. The teammates moved toward the base of the stairs with a premonition that something was terribly wrong. When the superintendent hung up the phone and came back down the stairs, his face was ashen, his eyes wide with alarm. He informed the team that Pearl Harbor had been attacked and that thousands of Americans were dead. Several recent academy graduates, more than likely, were also dead. "We are now at war, gentlemen," the superintendent told the players. "Return to quarters and await further orders."

At first Busik and Kauffman, like most of the players, were too numb to move. By the time that the boys reached Bancroft Hall, armed guards were already standing outside the entrance of the dorm. Busik and Kauffman were both shaken. Suddenly, combat was no longer something that existed only in the abstract, on the pages of books. Now it was something they'd wake up to every day, and soon be face to face with. In an instant, the world had changed.

At West Point, Henry Romanek sat crosslegged on a folding chair in the gymnasium theater. He and several other cadets were spending their Sunday afternoon watching a movie. When Romanek walked out of the theater, he saw several cadets running wildly around the campus, screaming something he couldn't understand. When he finally cornered one of them, he was told about Pearl Harbor. "Isn't this great?!" the cadet gleefully shouted at Romanek. "Now we get to graduate early. We'll be off to war before you know it!"

Romanek didn't think it was great. Neither did John Buckner, one of Romanek's teammates. He was down near the Hudson River on a flat path known as Flirtation Walk. This was a popular place to bring dates, which was what Buckner did on this December afternoon. He and his honey were sitting on a rock. They looked across the Hudson, watching the dappled sunlight bounce off the water, and they were listening to a hand-held radio when the announcement came over the airwaves. Both Buckner and his date turned to look at each other, overwhelmed by the news. She started crying uncontrollably, saying how much she didn't want him to leave. Buckner tried to console her, softly and sweetly telling her that everything would be okay. What he didn't tell her was that he also couldn't wait to get overseas. He'd been in flight training for more than two years and now he felt it was time for the United States to flex its military muscle. "Everything will be just fine," Buckner told his date. "Don't worry, nobody's going to kill *me*."

At mess hall the next evening, the administrators at West Point piped into the PA system the president's war message to Congress. As soon as the President uttered his first sentence, no one at West Point spoke or ate. Every cadet was transfixed by the president's words, which were delivered in a clear, confident voice, a voice that was perfect for radio.

Mr. Vice President, Mr. Speaker, members of the Senate and of the
House of Representatives. Yesterday, December 7, 1941, a date which

will live in infamy, the United States of America was suddenly and de-
liberately attacked by naval and air forces of the Empire of Japan. The
United States was at peace with that nation and at the solicitation of
Japan, was still in conversation with its government and its emperor
looking toward the maintenance of peace in the Pacific . . .

The attack yesterday on the Hawaiian Islands has caused severe
damage to American naval and military forces. I regret to tell you that
many American lives have been lost. In addition, American ships have
been reported torpedoed on the high seas between San Francisco and
Honolulu . . .

No matter how long it may take us to overcome this premeditated
invasion, the American people in their righteous might will win a thor-
ough to absolute victory. I believe I interpret the will of the Congress
and of the people when I assert that we will not only defend ourselves to
the uttermost but will make it very certain that this form of treachery
shall never again endanger us.

Hostilities exist. There is no blinking at the fact that our people,
our territory, and our interests are in grave danger. With confidence in
our armed forces, with the unbounding determination of our people, we
will gain the inevitable triumph — so help us God.

I ask that the Congress declare that since the unprovoked and das-
tardly attack by Japan on Sunday, December 7, a state of war has ex-
isted between the United States and the Japanese empire.

As soon as the president finished speaking, the mess hall at West
Point erupted. The winds of war were blowing, and every cadet in the
hall—even the quietest of them all—stood on his feet and clapped, some
applauding so hard that they bruised their palms. The emotion and energy in the room bounced off the walls, the intensity of this moment unlike anything any of these young men had ever experienced before. A
similar outburst occurred at the naval academy, where many of the midshipmen also listened to the speech in their mess hall.

For Busik, Kauffman, Olds, and Romanek, the direction of their
lives had just taken an unexpected turn. The battle was joined.

PART TWO

12

THE *MEREDITH*

AS HAL KAUFFMAN SLOWLY walked along the topside of the destroyer U.S.S. *Meredith* on the morning of October 15, 1942, he enjoyed a beautiful sunrise. The first blush of pink light danced over the rippling waters of the South Pacific Ocean and, for a brief moment, Kauffman allowed himself to forget where he was. Nearly eleven months had passed since the attack on Pearl Harbor, but to Kauffman it seemed like decades since he was carrying his books around the leafy Annapolis campus and taking out his frustrations at football practice. Now aboard the *Meredith*, a destroyer that was commissioned on March 4, 1941, Kauffman and his shipmates were pushing straight into the heart of one of the most volatile regions on the planet. The *Meredith* was escorting ships between Espiritu Santo—an Island in the Coral Sea controlled by Allied Forces—and Guadalcanal. Known as "Bloody Guad" because of the fierce fighting taking place on the island, Guadalcanal lay east of the southern tip of New Guinea. On this clear, bright morning, the *Meredith* was escorting a convoy of troop carriers and a tug with two barges filled with aviation gasoline.

As Kauffman continued to stroll on the deck of the *Meredith*, he marveled at how much his life had changed in the four months since he and 610 other midshipmen graduated from the Academy and became officers in the navy. On June 19, 1942, Admiral Ernest J. King, the commander in chief of the United States fleet, welcomed the largest class in the ninety-seven-year history of the naval academy to the brotherhood of naval officers. Speaking to the class at Dahlgren Hall, which overflowed with classmates, friends, and family, Admiral King began his remarks by saying it was an appropriate time to recall Prime Minister Winston Churchill's notable phrase, "I have nothing to offer you but blood, toil, sweat, and tears." Admiral King then added that victory would come only at the cost of "unremitting labor and a multitude of heartaches and sacrifices such as this country has never known before."

Sitting close to Bill Busik and several other of his football teammates, Kauffman was surprised by the brutal frankness of the Admiral's words—as were many of the family members in attendance. A few of the mothers in the crowd began to weep as the Admiral continued to talk, crying out of joy and fear for their sons. "Victory will bring us not only the preservation of your own freedom and the restoration of the lost liberties of uncounted millions," the Admiral said, "but also the firm confidence that when we have won this war, we Americans—under the leadership of the president—will take steps to see to it that the ability of any person or of any people to enslave others physically or mentally or spiritually, shall forever be destroyed."

The ceremony concluded with the traditional singing by the graduates of the "Navy Blue and Gold" alma mater song, followed by a cheer of the regiment "for those about to leave," a cheer for "those we leave behind," and the tossing of the graduates' white midshipmen caps into the air. Each cap immediately became the center of a scrum, as every Middie wanted to save one as a momento. From Dahlgren Hall, the graduates marched to Bancroft Hall to take the officers' oath. Many of the graduates had their new bars and officers' shoulder boards pinned on by their mothers and sweethearts. After their oath, they were told that they had ten days to report to active duty. Every newly minted officer in attendance planned to pack as much fun in the next ten days as possible, as they all knew that these could be the last ten unfettered days for a long time.

Busik's and Kauffman's last months at the Academy were frantic. Because their course of study had been truncated from four to three years, the instructors overloaded the midshipmen with work. There was so much to study. The soon-to-be-officers learned all they could about new weapons systems (such as gun directors) that were being added to many of the ships. They also were tutored on the rapidly developing technology known as radar, which the instructors said would one day play a critical role in the war. Busik and Kauffman absorbed as much as they could, often studying until four in the morning.

In these months Busik and Kauffman also began to view themselves differently. Soon they would be officers. They would be in charge of many young men and making decisions that would impact hundreds of lives. People had always looked up to Busik because of his superior athletic ability, but in war men would look to him for answers because of the bars on his shoulders. Busik and Kauffman frequently talked about this awesome responsibility in late-night bull sessions with friends, and Busik became more earnest in everything he did. If you're going to be a leader, Busik told his friends one night, you need to act like one all the time. His words may have sounded hokey in different, more peaceful times, but not one of his friends disagreed with what he said.

Kauffman felt the same way. Though he was the senior class president of his high school, Kauffman was never as sought-after as Busik. His natural tendency was to shy away from people rather than seek them out, but he was much more outgoing now than when he arrived at the academy in July of 1939. Like Busik, Kauffman grew more serious-minded as his time in Annapolis dwindled.

Part of the reason why Busik and Kauffman had changed was because of the mail they received during their final spring at the academy. Almost every day a frightening letter from a former classmate would arrive that detailed the cold reality of combat. In these missives Busik and Kauffman read about what it was like to have a man die in your arms, and what it was like to take the life of a stranger. These were troubling letters, yes, but they also emboldened the young, would-be sailors. By the time they graduated, Busik and Kauffman were anxious to join their friends and fellow Americans on the battlefield. This was their destiny, and they wanted to fight, consequences be damned.

A few hours after graduation, with his friends and family watching from the pews in the Naval Academy Chapel, the kiss sparked a small fire in Hal Kauffman. Kauffman had fantasized about this kiss ever since he first laid eyes on Lois Bradburg, that pretty girl in his tenth grade English class at Glendale High in California. They had started dating shortly after he first saw her, and Kauffman often took her to the beach, to weekend dances, and on daytrips to Hollywood. Now, the day after his graduation from the naval academy, Kauffman stood at the altar of the academy chapel wearing his white officers' uniform. As Bradburg glided down the aisle in a traditional satin white wedding dress, Busik sat near the front of the chapel, nodding in approval at the groom.

Kauffman and Bradburg were one of 180 couples to tie the knot at the academy chapel in the days following graduation. A few months earlier the Navy Department rescinded a rule that forbade newly commissioned officers from marrying in their first two years of service. As soon as Kauffman learned that the rule was no longer in effect, he wrote Bradburg a letter asking for her hand. A week later, Kauffman received a note with her one-word answer: Yes.

Now aboard the U.S.S. *Meredith* as she headed toward Guadalcanal, the memory of that special day rose in Kauffman's mind. They had spent their honeymoon in a private cabin on a train that took them back across the United States to California. For a week and a half, the two were inseparable, constantly by each other's sides and holding hands. After only ten days of marriage, Kauffman reported for duty aboard the *Meredith* in San Diego. Before stepping on board, he kissed and hugged his wife good-bye, promising her that he would one day come back to her.

"Saying good-bye to you is the hardest thing I've ever done," Kauffman told his new bride as they embraced for the last time.

On the *Meredith*, Kauffman often lost himself in those memories, especially during the quiet, early morning hours when he'd watch the red sun slink into the sky over the South Pacific. After seeing the horizon light up on October 15, 1942, Kauffman, an ensign, chatted with several of the sailors. The men on the *Meredith*, whose crew of 260 mostly came from the New England states, were uneasy. Their mission to Guadalcanal, which sits in the Solomon Islands about twelve hundred miles northeast of Australia, was significant: Henderson Field, the U.S.-controlled airbase on Guadalcanal, had only three hours of aviation gasoline left in reserve, which forced all the American planes based on Guadalcanal to be grounded. Ever since August 1942 when a division of marines had landed on Guadalcanal and seized the airfield that the Japanese were building, intense fighting had ensued on the over-two-thousand-square-mile island. The Japanese had reacted violently to the unexpected attack on their airbase—it was the first major American offensive in the Pacific—and both sides poured reinforcements into the area.

The Japanese, operating from their massive bases at Rabaul and Truk, made repeated, aggressive attempts to cut up American supply convoys that motored for the island. The jungle airstrip on Guadalcanal was vital to both sides; it was one of the few useable airfields on the islands of the South Pacific. And now it was one of the most fiercely fought-after pieces of land in the world. Admiral Chester Nimitz had recently said of the situation on Guadalcanal, "It now appears that we are unable to control the sea in the Guadalcanal area. Resupplying the positions [on Guadalcanal] will only be done at great expense to us."

The captain of the *Meredith*, Harry E. Hubbard, had warned his crew that they were headed into dangerous waters. On the morning of October 15, Hubbard had been informed that five Japanese transport ships had landed on Guadalcanal and deployed several thousand new troops west of Lunga Point. Hubbard figured that the American forces on Guadalcanal would be doomed unless they were quickly reinforced and resupplied. Hubbard had also received intelligence that stated enemy ships were closing in on the *Meredith*'s advancing position. Explaining this dicey situation to the ship's officers—including Kauffman—Hubbard said they had no choice but to press forward and try to help the soldiers on Guadalcanal. The troop carriers in the convoy turned around, but the *Meredith* and the U.S.S. *Vireo*, the tug in the convoy that controlled one of the barges, maintained their original course, hoping to deliver their cargo of five hundred quarter-ton bombs and ten thousand gallons of aviation gasoline to the marines on Guadalcanal.

"We're in for a difficult time," Hubbard had told Kauffman and a few other officers. "We're going to be vulnerable."

The morning passed slowly. Kauffman stood on the bridge and, using binoculars, scanned in all directions, hoping not to spot anything. At first, he didn't. But then at 10:45 A.M., with the ship about 130 miles southeast of Guadalcanal, Kauffman zeroed in on a sight that made his heart pound: Two enemy carrier planes were flying low and slow through the golden morning light. Kauffman quickly relayed the sighting to Captain Hubbard. After consulting with other officers, Hubbard, who had graduated at the top of his class at the naval academy in 1925, ordered the crew aboard the *Vireo* to prepare to come aboard the *Meredith* because the *Vireo* lacked the firepower to defend herself. As Hubbard transmitted this message, a friendly plane, a PBY seaplane, approached the *Meredith* and flashed this simple message: TWO EMEMY CRUISERS 20 MILES WEST AND HEADING YOUR WAY AT HIGH SPEED.

At 11:40 A.M., radar aboard the *Meredith* came alive with pips, detecting a large group of unidentified planes forty-five miles north. The bogies appeared to be gunning for the *Meredith* and the *Vireo*, but they soon disappeared from the screen. It could only be assumed that they were going after the U.S.S. *Hornet*, an aircraft carrier, and her escorts; they were about two hundred miles away from the *Meredith* and heading away to the southeast. Captain Hubbard quickly moved the *Meredith* alongside the tug and asked the *Vireo* crew if they wanted to come on board. The tugboat skipper was hesitant to leave his ship and his command, but the protection that the destroyer offered was far superior to any defense the tug could mount should the Japanese appear, so he reluctantly ordered his men aboard the *Meredith*.

As soon as the *Meredith* had safely picked up the *Vireo* crew, Captain Hubbard reversed course and ordered full speed ahead, hoping to get closer to air support. As it stood, the *Meredith* was naked: They had no air cover and the U.S.S. *Hornet* and the other ships were too far away to provide any assistance should the Japanese attack. "We need to be ready for anything," the captain told a few of his officers. "We're on our own."

The *Meredith* increased her speed. Kauffman moved from the bridge to the gun director deck, which was located above the pilothouse, still holding binoculars. He glanced at his watch. It read 12:15 P.M. Then he heard a noise directly above him; he titled his neck. Diving down out of the bright sunshine, Kauffman saw the silvery wings of two Japanese bombers, barreling straight toward the ship. "Holy fucking shit!" Kauffman yelled, as enemy aircraft approached. The dive-bombers had flown at an altitude that was too high for the *Meredith*'s radar, which was only a surface search-unit, to detect. Then, in the distance, more Japanese planes appeared. They were low-level bombers, torpedo planes and fighters that had skimmed along the wave tops, just underneath the *Meredith*'s range of detection. Within seconds, a total of thirty-eight planes, which had taken off from the Japanese carrier *Zuikaku*, swarmed the *Meredith*. The Captain urgently ordered, "Battle stations prepare for surface action."

Kauffman knew what would come next. When the Japanese attacked like this—dozens of planes flying low and high—it meant they were on a hunt to kill. The *Meredith* made for a delicious target. Without any aerial support, she would have to defend herself against the enemy planes that kept appearing, one after the next.

The *Meredith*'s 5 inch guns opened fire on the lead bomber, but the pilot still bore down on the ship, the sound of the plane's engine growing louder and louder. Only seconds had passed since Kauffman first spotted the plane diving out of the sun, and suddenly it was only five hundred feet away and closing in. Kauffman immediately sprinted toward the bridge to speak with the captain. When he looked up again he saw the plane release a bomb. It looked like the pilot would slam into the ship's superstructure, but he pulled up just in time.

Kauffman could tell right away that this first bomb was going to be a direct hit. It landed on the bridge, passed through the spot where the helmsman had been standing moments earlier and penetrated to the next deck below. Kauffman hit the ground. The bomb exploded. Deck plates and gratings flew in all directions. The blast threw Kauffman fifteen feet in the air. He landed on his hands and knees almost where he'd been standing before, dazed. He looked around and saw several of his shipmates also lying on the deck, badly burned. Kauffman struggled to find his breath—the wind had been knocked out of him—then staggered to his feet. As smoke cleared, he realized that dozens had been killed by the initial blast, including everyone on the bridge deck except Captain Hubbard, who was severely burned, the ship's doctor, and a few enlisted men.

The bomb severely disabled the ship. All telephone communications, the ship's gun controls, and steering controls were destroyed. The fuel tanks had also been blown open, scattering heavy fuel over the decks and surrounding water. Many of the men were now covered in fuel as everyone tried to maintain their composure and get to their battle stations.

Moments later, another bomb fell out of the bright sunshine, striking the port side of the ship a few feet in front of the bridge. The explosion rocked the ship, nearly breaking it in two. The blast sent dozens of men overboard. Kauffman was knocked down when the second-bomb erupted, but he got back on his feet. Dozens of planes were still overhead, buzzing in the sky. A torpedoman, John Hunter, yelled to Kauffman, "Come on, Mr. Kauffman, let's get us a machine gun and shoot those bastards down!" As soon as the word "down" flew from Hunter's lips, a torpedo struck the *Meredith*, throwing both Kauffman and Hunter into the air, hurtling them overboard. In the water, Kauffman lost consciousness.

Chaos broke out on the ship. Men were running in all directions, panicked. The torpedo had exploded near the ammunition ready locker. The blast ignited star shells and flares, which set the oil on the water's surface on fire. Down in the engine room, men made frantic, desperate efforts to restore power. Up on the decks, gunners scrambled to get to their weapons. A few fired their .50 caliber machine guns, but they were no match for the Japanese onslaught. These Japanese fighters had failed to locate any carriers in the region, so they focused all their firepower and ferocity on the *Meredith*.

The assault continued. Only three minutes had passed since Kauffman saw the first plane in the sky, but the *Meredith* was already sinking. Bombs and torpedoes kept hitting; each explosion slightly lifted the *Meredith* out of the water and tipped her to the side. Near misses threw the flaming oil that was on the water all over the ship, which burned many of the men. The air was now heavy with the smell of flames, sizzling steel, and salt water.

Captain Hubbard, lying on the bridge with severe burns on his face, neck and arms, still tried to shout out orders. He implored the machine gunners to keep shooting, and told his men to maintain order. The gunners did knock seven of the enemy fighters out of the sky, but this was a one-sided fight. In less than 5 minutes of coordinated bombing, thirty-eight Japanese fighter planes made hits with an estimated fourteen bombs and seven torpedoes, ripping the ship apart.

Things were happening so fast that the men on the *Meredith* didn't have time to even consider what their lives had meant, to review who they'd loved, to consider the fate that threatened them. Oil fires burned on the inside and there were gaping holes in the *Meredith*'s sides and decks. On the bridge Captain Hubbard, despite being injured, stayed calm. He called out, "Send a message: '*Meredith* sinking,'" but the radio room had been destroyed. Finally Hubbard, as torpedo planes strafed the bridge, gave the order for his crew to abandon ship. Ten minutes had passed since the first bomb had struck.

For those inside the engine room, raging floods made it nearly impossible to get out. Up on deck, as soon as the call to abandon ship had been made, lifeboats were launched. The two motorized whaleboats had been damaged in the attack and could not be released from their cradles, which meant that the crew had to share the small non-motorized lifeboats— rafts, basically—that could hold ten to fifteen people. With Japanese zooming over the *Meredith* and spraying her with machine gun fire, Botswain Kevin Singletary cut the lashings to the lifeboats. The lifeboats slid overboard and into waters that were being stirred by a suddenly strong wind. The *Meredith* continued to sink. Thirteen minutes had passed since the first attack. Now those who were still alive had only one chance for survival: They had to swim to their rafts.

In the water, Kauffman opened his eyes. He'd blacked out, but now, wearing a life jacket and floating face up, he was twenty feet from the ship. Crewmates were all around him, many floating face down, others burned so badly that Kauffman couldn't recognize them. Still in a daze, Kauffman couldn't detect any sounds; the loud explosions had momentarily dulled his hearing. He looked back at the ship, saw that it had begun to roll over. He turned his head and in the distance there was a liferaft. He started swimming in its direction. As he pushed through the water, Kauffman again looked back at the ship, just to make sure it really was sinking, that he wasn't hallucinating. The *Meredith*'s propellers were lifted in the air, still spinning. Kauffman saw that the men in the engine room were still trying to perform their jobs even as they were descending to their graves.

At just past one in the afternoon, as Kauffman continued to swim for his life, the *Meredith* slid down bow-first into the whitecaps. The last man seen on the ship was Joe Oban. He was firing a 20 mm gun into the sky at planes overhead. He was still strapped in the harness, which kept him from being kicked off the gun each time it fired, when the *Meredith* disappeared into the water. Oban had once made a statement that he'd never leave his gun until he shot down a plane. Now he honored that statement to his death, firing his gun at the Japanese planes that were strafing his helpless shipmates in the water.

"Godamn, Japs," Kauffman said to himself as he swam. "I'll kill every one of them if I get a chance." Many of Kauffman's shipmates—including a few of his good friends on board—were clinging to pieces of floating wreckage. Kauffman would never see them again.

As Kauffman and other survivors swam for the rafts, several Japanese planes dove, heading right for them. "Look out!" Kauffman heard someone yell. As he looked up, a few planes came bearing down on him, machine guns ablaze. The planes buzzed just above the water, spraying the area with bullets, deliberately shooting survivors even after the ship was gone. Kauffman had never seen this kind of evil. The United States Navy had a policy that outlawed such cruelty as shooting defenseless enemy soldiers. Kauffman had never hated anything in his life—at his core, he was a softie who enjoyed nothing more than singing a tune—but now enmity filled his heart. Kauffman dove into the water as the planes whizzed overhead and unloaded their machine guns. When Kauffman came to the surface, several of the men who had been swimming right next to him had been shot, blood gurgling out of their mouths. Kauffman checked on a few of the wounded, but there wasn't much he could do. Most were dead within minutes.

In the distance, Kauffman could see four rafts tied together, about seventy-five yards away. He wasn't sure what to do. If the Japanese planes returned—they had just flown out of view—Kauffman figured they would concentrate their machine gun fire on those rafts. But then Kauffman saw several men swimming toward the rafts. Thinking that it was better to be with his shipmates than alone, Kauffman started kicking his way toward the rafts. When he passed over the spot where the ship had gone down, an explosion reverberated up through the water; a powerful jolt hit his feet and buttocks, slightly lifting him up. The explosion was probably a depth-charge on the ship that had detonated at its set depth. Once again, Kauffman wasn't injured.

Six rafts had floated off the *Meredith* and into the water. The first raft quickly filled up with six men. The men on this raft made a snap decision: They'd try to make it to the tug *Vireo*, which had been damaged by the Japanese but was still adrift a mile away. The men started paddling with their arms and one wooden paddle.

Near the spot where the *Meredith* went down, four rafts were tied together, while a fifth drifted away. Each of the *Meredith*'s life rafts had rations lashed to the plywood grating that formed the bottom of the raft. The rations included cans of meat, malted milk tablets, two canteens of fresh water, first aid supplies, maps, signal flags, and flares. A total of 141 crewmen had survived the initial attack—a little more than half of those on board. Six were on the raft that was making a run to *Vireo;* thirty-four were struggling to stay close to the raft that had drifted away; and the remainder were near the four rafts that were tied together.

In this last group there wasn't enough room on the rafts for all the men, so most of the sailors who weren't wounded—including Kauffman— remained in the water, clinging to the rafts' lifelines. Everyone was covered in oil; the whites of everyone's eyes sticking out like those of a hobgoblin. Most were naked; their clothes had been either blown or burned off.

After drifting together on the four rafts for about 30 minutes, Ensign Dan Haible told Kauffman and a few other officers that he was going to swim to *Vireo*, which was more than a mile away. Haible explained that he would board the *Vireo* and bring back the ship's motorized whaleboat and search for more survivors. Kauffman asked Haible if he thought he could make it, and Haible replied with an emphatic, "Yes, Sir!" Haible, a former star swimmer at the University of Colorado, then unbuttoned his life jacket, tossed it aside, and started swimming the breast stroke. Six hours later, around 7:00 P.M., Haible was helped on board the tug by the five men on the first raft who had reached the *Vireo*. Once he was pulled up on the ship, Haible collapsed, so weak that he couldn't even walk for about 30 minutes.

Despite his life-threatening injuries, Captain Hubbard made it to a raft. He was lying in one of the four rafts that was tied together when Kauffman first saw him. The captain was in bad shape. His face and arms were swollen from burns, and he couldn't see. The men regarded their captain the same way Catholics regard the Pope, and so his condition was terrifyingly upsetting to the crew. "I'm badly burned," Hubbard told the ship's doctor, Michael Bowers, who was on the raft with Kauffman and the captain. "You sure were right about those flash burns." Days earlier the doctor and the captain had talked about the dangers of flash burns—a burn due to brief exposure to intense radiant heat—and now they were slowly killing the captain.

As the doctor tried to comfort Hubbard, someone yelled, "There's a flying fort!" Kauffman looked up and, there in the mid-afternoon light, was a B-17 flying overhead at about twelve thousand feet. The men screamed wildly, hoping to catch the pilot's attention. But the B-17 gave no signal that it had seen any of the life rafts, and the plane soon melted into the horizon. An hour later—some two hours after the *Meredith* had been sunk—the survivors heard another roar in the distance. They all looked up into the sky again, but this time they saw several Japanese planes, seemingly headed right at them. Some men ducked, others jumped into the water, afraid that the rafts would be strafed. But just as some men were swimming away, the planes peeled off in another direction.

The officers in the water knew that a U.S. carrier and other surface ships, which were greatly outnumbered in the region, had been directed to the southeast of their present position in order to avoid a confrontation with the superior Japanese forces. This meant that the *Meredith* and the *Vireo* were the only U.S. ships in the area, and that a rescue might not happen for quite some time. Realizing this, Kauffman, the doctor and a few other able officers, began to take charge. One of the first navigational decisions made aboard the life rafts was to stay in the oil slick that the *Meredith* had left behind. Instead of trying to paddle to the *Vireo*, which the other raft had done, the men on the four rafts that were tied together opted to hold their ground, afraid that the Japanese would return and sink the defenseless *Vireo*. Meanwhile, aboard the *Vireo*, ensign Haible and his five shipmates suffered a devastating blow: While lowering the motorized whaleboat by hand, it slipped and the bottom was punctured. The boat could be fixed, but the six shipmates figured it would take about five hours. They just hoped that the sailors floating in the oil slick could hold on that long. Many had burns that required immediate care.

While in the oil slick, Doctor Bowers calmly told everyone who was suffering from a burn that they should apply the heavy, emulsified oil to their wounds. Though it would initially sting, the doctor said, it would also protect the skin from the sun, which on this October afternoon in 1942 shone brightly. Eventually, Doctor Bowers also convinced those with deep wounds to pack their cuts and gashes with fuel oil. The men screamed in agony when they did this, but the act slowed the loss of blood and helped save their lives—at least momentarily.

As Kauffman hung onto a lifeline while floating in the water, he looked into the raft and couldn't even recognize a few of his shipmates. With their crushed features and charred bodies, Kauffman was surprised that they had lasted this long. Late in the afternoon, the ship's chief storekeeper, a sailor that everyone simply called "Silva," started to have difficulty breathing. Burns and blood covered most of his body and, after about 10 minutes of taking labored breaths, he stopped breathing altogether. The doctor moved over and examined Silva; he could feel no pulse or heartbeat. A few of the stronger shipmates who were in the water—including Kauffman—pulled Silva to the side of the raft, removed his identification tag, cut off his life jacket, dragged him out of the raft, then swam him out a short distance before letting him go. Kauffman wanted to say something profound as Silva dropped into the blue ocean, but no words came to him.

After Silva died, Kauffman returned to a spot beside the rafts. The sun was beginning to go down—it was about 6:00 P.M.—and Kauffman thought many of the men wouldn't survive the coming night. Some men were burned so severely that the hair on their heads was gone. Others suffered broken legs, arms, and ribs. The groans of the dying and the steady lapping of the waves against the four rafts—*plooop, plooop, plooop*—were the only sounds that rose though the humid, heavy air. Though the men reeked of oil and sweat, the aroma of burnt flesh hovered over the men like a cloud. Even the uninjured sailors were growing tired. The healthy men had been in the water and hanging onto the rafts for several hours, and it was a grueling activity. The arms of even the strongest survivors were becoming weak, their legs cramping. There were about one hundred sailors on or near the four rafts. Each raft could hold about ten men before it started to take on water, which meant that about sixty men were in the water the entire time.

Realizing that a routine needed to be set up, Kauffman and a few other officers organized a "waterbuddy" system: Each man would have a waterbuddy with whom he could switch places between the raft and the water. The badly wounded would stay inside a raft at all times; everyone else was assigned a waterbuddy and would trade places every few hours. In the raft, the men were to try to sleep. "We might be out here for days," Kauffman warned the men, "so we need to rest whenever we can."

A mile away from the four rafts, the men aboard the *Vireo* finished repairing the punctured whaleboat around 10:00 P.M. Instead of launching the motorized boat in the darkness, the sailors decided to stay on the tug until dawn. At that point they'd hunt for survivors.

Throughout the night, the minutes continued to pass slowly for the men on the four rafts that were clustered together. A quarter moon glowed in the clear sky like a giant comma, radiating a faint, milky light that fell on the ocean. Stars dotted the black roof of the universe; occasionally, one would shoot across the sky, leaving a luminous streak in its wake that would disappear a heartbeat later. The men rarely talked, but every so often Kauffman would hear cries for help in the dark distance. These desperate pleas came from the voices of men who had been on the outside of the raft and had lost their strength—or had fallen asleep—and floated away in the current. None of the able-bodied men dared to go after these drifters because it would have been virtually impossible to locate them in the darkness. After a few minutes, the cries that shot across the oil-covered water would fall eerily silent.

Later in the night one man jumped off the raft and began to swim, believing he could see land. Kauffman and other healthy crewman tried to save him, but the addled sailor was adamant that an island was just twenty yards away. He was never seen again. Another deranged sailor stood up in the night and announced that he was going to "go below decks." Before anyone could stop him, he dove head-first into the water—he also was never seen again.

When Kauffman switched places with his water buddy in the middle of the night, he saw that the captain was shaking uncontrollably. The doctor huddled over him and wrapped his arms around the captain trying to keep him warm, but Kauffman didn't think the captain would last much longer. It hurt just to look at the captain, whose face was now black with burns. A few men remarked on the captain's deteriorating condition, but other than that, all conversations were centered on one topic: When would the rescue ships pick them up?

The most valued possessions this night were the five-gallon water casks that had been stored on each raft. When the wounded got very thirsty, they were given a sip of water. Kauffman and the other officers didn't know how long they'd be drifting at sea, so they were careful to ration the water. Yet some men, not wanting to appear weak, refused their water and asked that their portion be given to the wounded. Others tried to drink saltwater. They'd take a mouthful, hold it in their mouths for a few seconds, then spit it out, hoping that they would absorb some drips of moisture. A few men tried an old Boy Scout trick of placing a shirt button under their tongues in the hope of inducing salivation. But their bodies were beyond parched, so this rarely worked. For food, a few of the men on this first night tried to eat the oil-covered cookies and malted milk wafers that they had in their provisions. Those who did eat two or three cookies vomited them up in minutes, unable to digest the oil.

Late in the night the men heard a loud rumbling sound. As it grew closer, a few claimed that it was an advancing ship. "We're rescued!" one sailor shouted. He then jumped into the water and started swimming furiously toward the noise. But it wasn't a ship; a sudden thunderstorm was blowing in. The men on the rafts yelled to the sailor who was now swimming toward the squall, but it was too late; the sailor disappeared in the distance. Once the storm was over the rafts, the men lay on their backs with their mouths agape, trying to catch the fresh water.

Over the next several hours many more men died from their burns. Kauffman, realizing that he was as healthy as anyone, put himself in charge of disposing the dead. He'd remove their life jackets, tow them out a few yards from the raft, then let them go. Then he'd tell one of the men in the water to take the spot in the raft that was open. During the small hours of the night, several died on the rafts. The deaths started to become so routine that the men stopped saying anything once somebody died. Kauffman would simply remove the body in silence, and the dead sailor's spot would be taken by another man.

When the sky began to lighten early the next morning, the captain was struggling to breathe. Around 8:00 A.M.—about twenty hours after the attack—the captain died from burns and blood loss. The doctor cut off his tags and life jacket and Kauffman led him away from the raft. When he was let go, a gunnery officer said, "We are giving them a good man this time." After that no one said a word. They just looked in silence as their captain floated away on his back, his face and hands burned black.

At daybreak on the second morning the six men who had reached the *Vireo* the night before and repaired the whaleboat began the search for their shipmates. First, one of the sailors climbed up to the tug's top deck and scanned the horizon for signs of life. No rafts were visible. The six men tried to pinpoint their starting point before drifting, but that was as specific as they could get.

They hopped in the whaleboat, turned on the motor, and pushed away from the tug. The men looked in all directions as they darted through the water, but the first five hours turned up nothing. At noon they heard a noise in the sky; a Japanese scout plane was crisscrossing the area. They assumed that the plane was looking for the pilots that gunners on the *Meredith* had shot down. Not wanting to be seen, the men quickly guided the whaleboat behind the *Vireo* to stay out of the scout plane's field of view. Then they boarded the tug and loaded as much food, water, and gasoline onto the whaleboat as it could hold. They also took the ship's compass and navigation chart. At this point they believed that they were the only survivors of the *Meredith*, and once the scout plane had disappeared, they boarded the whaleboat and prepared to make a run for Espiritu Santo Island, which they figured about four hundred miles to the south.

As the sun grew hotter on Day 2—the date was October 16—the men on the four clustered rafts smeared more oil on their faces, necks, and arms to prevent sunburn. Even though they had just endured a horrific night in which many men had gone delirious and died, there was a sense of optimism among the survivors. During the daylight hours a rescue plane or ship would find them—they were certain of that—and that they wouldn't have to face another night alone floating in oblivion.

Indeed, for the first few hours of the morning, the men appeared relatively upbeat to Kauffman. A few talked of the first thing they would do when they were rescued—the consensus was to drink a gallon of water—while others spoke about how they would tell everyone how brave their captain had been. A handful of men even felt so good that they went for a playful swim just to cool down. At noon, however, the mood changed when one word was shouted. A sailor floating fifteen feet from the rafts spotted several large dorsal fins circling around him in the water. He screamed, "Sharks!" and then frantically kicked back to the raft. But halfway to safety, a six-foot tiger shark attacked, chomping several bites out of his legs. "A shark's eating me!" the sailor yelled. Two men in the rafts jumped into the water and pulled the wounded sailor onto the raft. The sailor, missing part of one leg, was in shock. Blood spurted out of his legs like soda out of a shaken can as he screamed in agony. He'd be dead within hours.

To most of the young men in the water and on the four rafts, sharks were the stuff of myths. In fact, many of the men had never given sharks a second thought until now. Navy lore was full of stories of what one should do when a shark attacks, but only a few on these rafts had really paid attention to those hypothetical situations. Some had learned in their training that they should kick their legs as furiously as possible to deter the "hyenas of the sea," as sharks were often called by the sailors, but most of the men had no clue how to repel the aggressive, blood-thirsty predators.

The group of tiger sharks, which numbered in the fifties, now circled the rafts. They had likely been following the U.S.S. *Meredith* even before she was sunk. Sharks frequently track ships and feed on the refuse that is hurled overboard. Made of steel, the *Meredith* also emitted low-grade electrical currents that could have attracted the sharks. Tiger sharks, which typically range ten to fourteen feet long and weigh 850 to 1,400 pounds, have a very good sense of smell and keen eyesight, which meant that the sailors at the greatest risk were those who were naked or only partially clothed. The tigers likely focused on color contrasts, such as that between a white-skinned body and a dark blue sea.

Swimming at an average speed of 2.4 mph but able to burst up to 43 mph over very short distances, the shark has dark, tiger-like stripes on its back. It has a large, thick body with a blunt snout. The tiger's teeth are serrated and razor-sharp. Most biologist aren't sure why tiger sharks attack humans, but the fish also eats turtles, seagulls, other sharks and, at various times, have been found to ingest tin cans, goats, sheep, snakes, reindeer, and monkeys. They often attack using what is known as "bump and bite" maneuvers. First they'll bump their victims to disorient them, then they'll rip away chunks of flesh with their teeth. This was the attack of choice for many of the sharks on this horrifying afternoon.

Kauffman tried to calm the men. As soon as the first dorsal fin appeared, panic spread like a poisonous gas among the sailors. Kauffman had learned almost everything there was to know about tiger sharks when he was a midshipman, and he knew that these were menacing creatures. From his spot in the water—he was holding onto a lifeline—he told the sailors that they needed to be brave. He boldly shouted to the men, Either fight or die.

This was the moment that Kauffman had spent much of his young life preparing for. Ever since he had plucked that drowning boy out of the Merced River seven years earlier, Kauffman had never been afraid of water. He was an excellent swimmer and still as fit as he was when he played football. He didn't allow himself to be scared, because he didn't want the men to see fear in his eyes. "I've got to be strong," Kauffman told himself. "I'm going to get these guys through this."

The tiger sharks were as big as men, and Kauffman told the sailors— especially those who were still in the water with him—to think of the sharks as if they had two arms and two feet. "You *know* you can kill another man," Kauffman yelled, "together we will overcome this." Kauffman instructed the men to keep their legs tucked tightly underneath them as they floated in the water.

Kauffman then reached for his belt—he was wearing a white T-shirt that had been stained black by the oil, a life jacket, khaki pants, underwear, and a belt—and unsnapped a six-inch hunting knife. A few months earlier a group of Boy Scouts had sent the crew of the *Meredith* hunting knives. Many carried them on their belts at all times, and now Kauffman's knife became an essential weapon. "These sharks don't like to be cut up," Kauffman told the crew. "You've got to send them a message that you're going to fight back if they come after you."

After the first attack, the school of tiger sharks circled the four rafts at a range of ten to fifty yards out, stalking their prey. The men in the water all gripped their lifelines tight, staying as close to the rafts as possible. They all wanted to climb into the rafts to safety, but they knew the rafts would sink if they did this. Holding his knife in his right hand and his lifeline in his left, Kauffman prepared to lunge—knife first—if a shark got close. It was now 2:00 P.M. on Day 2.

Just as Kauffman began to think that the sharks might not attack, a sailor five feet away screamed in agony. The yell was cut short as the shark pulled the sailor under water. A few men dove trying to save the sailor, but they couldn't locate him or the shark in the dark water. Within minutes, the sailor's blood floated up to the surface, coloring the water red. The sailor was never seen again. Kauffman again urged the men to stay calm. "Let's keep our cool and work through this together," Kauffman said. "We have no other choice."

Later in the afternoon, the sharks grew more aggressive. One sailor who was sitting on the edge of a raft had his buttocks torn off. Another let out a blood-curdling scream and then held up the stump of his arm, which had been bitten off at the elbow. When a shark closed in on Kauffman, he did exactly what he told his shipmates to do: He fought. Kauffman jumped at the beast and stabbed him in the eyes with his knife. "Take that you son of a bitch!" Kauffman yelled as he drove the knife into the shark's skin. The shark retreated, hemorrhaging blood. A few shipmates hollered in approval. "Let's kill all of 'em!" one sailor shouted in Kauffman's direction.

By late afternoon, the sharks began targeting the weakest of the men who were in the water, the ones who offered the least resistance. Kauffman saw five of his shipmates get pulled under—all of them were either so tired or weak that they didn't even say anything as they were dragged to their death. The sharks, attracted to the scent of blood, also started going after the men with open wounds. The sailors had tried to pack their wounds with oil to stem the loss of blood, but if just a little bit of blood seeped out of the wound, a shark would track it.

By this time Kauffman and a few other officers had devised a plan to ward off the sharks: Two men in the water were to put their backs to the raft and, with their arms interlocked, they'd stick their arms and legs outward. When the sharks approached, the men kicked and splashed the water in unison, which usually succeeding in scaring the sharks off.

Later in the afternoon, just as the flaming yellow sun was starting to fall out of the sky, Kauffman changed places with his waterbuddy and took a seat in the raft. He shut his eyes and let his mind go electric with visions. He daydreamed of his new wife, of how she had smiled up at him and batted her blue eyes as they stood at the altar. His mind rewound to his carefree days at the naval academy, how he enjoyed nothing more than strapping on his leather helmet and practicing with the guys on the football team. He went back to that November afternoon in Philadelphia in '41—it wasn't even a year ago—and he could still hear the hum of the

crowd as they watched Navy play Army. He remembered running onto the
field and giving his buddy, Bill Busik, a big hug after Busik had made the
game-saving interception. He recalled how he and Bill celebrated until
dawn, having the time of their lives. He thought about . . .

"Holy Shit!" a sailor screamed.

Stirred from his reverie, Kauffman opened his eyes and was shocked
at what lay two feet in front of him in the middle of the raft: A seven-foot
shark, his mouth open. It had leapt into the raft moments before. A few
of Kauffman's crewmates had opened a canister of dry food, which evi-
dently attracted the shark. Before anyone knew what was going on, the
shark took a bite out of the thigh of a lieutenant. Without hesitating,
Kauffman jumped on the shark, driving his knife into its back. Kauffman
then grabbed the shark by the tail and flung him about five feet overboard. "Get the hell out of here!" Kauffman screamed as he tossed the
shark back into the water. He then looked at the lieutenant. Blood spilled
out of his thigh. Kauffman took his shirt off and tried to put a tourniquet
on the lieutenant's leg, but it was too late. The lieutenant soon became
delirious and died four hours later.

After the sun went down, the condition of many men on the four rafts
continued to deteriorate rapidly. The majority suffered from sharp abdom-
inal cramps. Everyone was nauseous and most were vomiting regularly.
When the men would fall into a light sleep, they would have fantastic
dreams, usually about a rescue ship. When a few men woke up from these
dreams they were so despondent that they leapt overboard and tried to swim
to an imaginary boat. Mentally stable men were usually successful in catching a delusional crewmate and pulling him back on the raft, but not always.

Late in Night 2, with a rescue seeming as if it would never happen, a
few men lost their grip on reality. Some started eating the raft's wood
crating. One young man, who was badly burned and whose flesh was
peeling off, thought he was back home on his farm in the west. He
wanted everyone to get off the raft. When he started taking swings at the
crewmates, they had no choice but to beat him unconscious. Later a lieutenant commander stood up and said to his shipmates, "I think I will go
get some cigarettes." He then jumped out of the raft and never returned.

By midafternoon on Day 3 the group of four rafts had split into two
groups of two, which were several hundred yards away from each other.
Another single raft that had been alone ever since the *Meredith* went
down had drifted a considerable distance from the other two groups.

In Kauffman's group, there had been little dissension. The rations were shared equally among the healthy men and a greater proportion of water was given to the weakest. The men still honored the water-buddy system and everyone generally looked after each other like family. Late in the day a wounded man in the group feared that he was being a burden on his shipmates. So, using all the energy he had, he crawled out of the raft and swam silently away from the group, giving up his life so that the shipmates would have a better chance at surviving. Kauffman tried to coax him back, telling him that he would help him get through this ordeal, but the sailor didn't return.

The sharks continued to circle the rafts all day, but they didn't attack until twilight. First a shark jumped up and bit off the finger of a sailor who was sitting on the edge of the raft. The shark came back a few minutes later and ripped a chunk out of his thigh. The sailor fell into the water, and a moment later the shark returned a third time and snatched his entire body. After witnessing this gruesome event, a few of the men started to babble and cry uncontrollably. Two men jumped into the water, while others sat as still as mannequins, comatose with fear.

The third night was a more vivid nightmare than the first two. Hallucinations were as rampant as the sharks. Some men, thinking that an enemy sub was approaching, dove into the water to try to fight it. Others jumped into the ocean thinking their bunks were beneath their raft. Still others believed that a scuttlebutt—a drinking fountain—was also located just beneath the life raft. The mentally stable men were often able to retrieve those who believed something existed underneath the raft, but again, not always.

Even men who were relatively uninjured were beginning to see things and lose grasp of reality. Some believed that they were smoking cigarettes and they asked their shipmates for a light; others thought they were back in their houses in the United States and wondered why their moms weren't home.

Kauffman was still perfectly sane, and his mind was preoccupied with one topic: water. The men were running out of drinking water. Sailors who at first declined to take a drink were now accepting every time a sip was offered. As Kauffman eyed the men in the raft as they laid in the moonlight in their ripped, oil-stained clothes, most were so weak that they couldn't stand. Kauffman figured that maybe the strongest could survive another 48 hours, but not much longer. The weakest? They could go at any minute. Most of the sailors had given up hope, and they had quit talking about being rescued. Some even appeared happily resigned to the fact that their fate was to perish on a raft in the South Pacific. The men were tired of fighting the sharks and tired of just fighting to survive. They had seen would-be rescuers come and go throughout the third day—a few U.S. planes had flown over the rafts, but they were too high to see them floating in the middle of the ocean—and most of them believed that the navy had forgotten about the U.S.S. *Meredith*.

During this chilly third night, men who hadn't prayed since childhood were now reciting psalms and scriptures that they had learned years ago in Sunday Bible study. One of the most frequently uttered was Psalm 23:

> *"Though I walk through the valley*
> *of the shadow of death*
> *I will fear no evil*
> *For Thou art with me . . ."*

Reciting these lines of scripture steadied the men. Saying the words in a cool, soft voice made them momentarily forget the hopelessness of their situation. But Kauffman never could forget it. He dreaded the coming morning. He didn't want to count how many familiar faces had disappeared during the night.

Kauffman tried to shut his eyes and lose consciousness, but sleeping was hard. Even though he was as fatigued as he'd ever been, he could only sleep in two minute spurts, then he would jolt awake, fear rushing through his body like a electrical shock.

When the sun rose over eastern waters to mark Day 4, Kauffman was wide-awake, his swollen eyes alert. He anxiously scanned the sky—unlike most of the men, Kauffman still held a flicker of hope of being rescued— for an American plane. At first, as usual, he saw nothing, just blue sky and a few white puffs of clouds. But then it appeared like an answered prayer: a U.S. PBY Catalina seaplane cruising through the bronze morning light at five thousand feet.

Upon seeing the plane, the spirits of the men on the rafts rose all the way to heaven. The plane was on a reconnaissance mission in search of information on the whereabouts of the Japanese fleet. Once the plane's crew spotted the oil slick, they dropped to an altitude of fifty feet to investigate. The crew was shocked to see, there in the patches of oil, men on life rafts frantically waving their arms. Because the men were covered in oil, the crew at first couldn't discern if they were Americans or Japanese. On their next trip over the men, the crew determined that the flailing men were, in fact, star-spangled soldiers. Just then, for the first time in about 48 hours, the sharks dispersed and dove to deeper water, scared off by the noise that the plane and the *Meredith* crew were making.

The PBY circled back again. It flashed its lights and rocked its wings, signaling that a rescue ship would be coming shortly. The plane deployed smoke floats to mark the position of the survivors; it also dropped emergency life rafts equipped with supplies. The plane turned and flew away from the men. Just before it sank over the horizon, the men on the raft saw the plane drop a lifejacket into the water. Below the plane, a few miles away from Kauffman's raft, was Chief Lamont Norwood, who had swum off alone after he thought he saw land. A school of sharks, their fins sticking out of the water, trailed Norwood by ten yards—and were closing in on him. The plane crew considered shooting the sharks, but were afraid they'd accidentally hit Norwood. With no way to help Norwood, the plane cruised out of the survivor's field of sight, leaving Norwood to fight off the sharks by himself.

The U.S.S. *Grayson*, *Gwin*, and *Seminole* were about thirty miles away from the survivors. Using an Aldis Lamp, the PBY signaled to the ships, "Follow my course, men in water." An hour later, the *Grayson* and the *Gwin* had reached the survivors. The *Gwin* launched small motorized boats into the water that were driven by rescue personnel. The rescuers had expected to find men with open wounds and broken bones. But, much to their surprise, no such men existed on the life rafts. Anyone injured was already dead—or had been eaten by sharks.

As the *Grayson* approached Kauffman's group, sailors on board threw cargo nets and rope ladders over the ship's sides. Yet most of the men in Kauffman's group were too weak to climb—some couldn't even stand. On Kauffman's raft a few drops of water still remained in one of the water kegs. Before leaving the raft, one survivor held up the remaining water keg. Most of the survivors were now on the deck of the *Grayson*, looking down at the last man in the raft. As the sailor looked at the water keg, he glanced up at the men, smiled, then proudly dumped its remnants into the sea, as if to say, "We won." Seeing this, Kauffman started chanting in a weak, trembling voice, "*Meredith—Meredith—Meredith.*" His shipmates soon joined in. Then they all started to softly cry.

• • •

After the survivors were aboard the three ships, a sailor on the *Grayson* saw through his telescope a man swimming toward the ship. It was Norwood, the lone swimmer, and he was the last of the eighty-seven survivors to be hauled aboard and rescued. Four days ago there had been 260 men aboard the *Meredith*.

Once safely aboard the *Grayson*, Kauffman was handed a shot-glass full of scotch whiskey, which he promptly vomited. He then walked to the shower and scrubbed the oil off his skin. He put on a T-shirt and shorts and ate a bowl of chicken noodle soup. He then ambled to a bunk, and plopped down. He lay flat on his back, shut his eyes, and then didn't move for 15 hours except to breathe slow and steady.

Of all the survivors, Kauffman was the only one able to bathe himself, eat for himself, and walk himself to a bunk. In the last four days he never had felt the cold finger of death tapping on his shoulder. Now, as he laid still throughout the night, he dreamed of better days.

The next day a doctor examined the survivors. In each case, the doctor reached the same conclusion: This man should be dead. All had suffered significant weight loss, in many cases up to twenty pounds. Their ear drums had been pierced with hundreds of tiny holes. Fillings in their teeth had been jarred loose or lost. White water-blisters covered them. Many burns and puncture wounds had become gangrenous. Nonmalignant growths often appeared around nerve centers. Most men suffered from rasping coughs and upper respiratory infections. They had oil forced into body openings as a result of the explosions. Several had developed sties in their eyes. And everyone had lower back pain.

As soon as they were strong enough, the survivors who were on the U.S.S. *Grayson* started talking to each other about their experience. They congratulated one another on surviving, but many also felt profound guilt for still being alive while so many of their shipmates had been lost in the battle. Over the next few days, as the survivors struggled to make sense of it all, hundreds of stories were exchanged about their fallen friends.

For many of the men, the worst was yet to come. Three days after the rescue, the captain of the *Grayson*, which had taken on sixty-three of the eighty-seven survivors (three more would die aboard the rescue ships), spotted a Japanese bomber and opened fire. Though the Japanese plane got away, when the general alarm sounded and the guns started blasting, the ship shook—an agonizing experience for the survivors. They were below deck and locked in watertight compartments. When they heard the guns firing, many leapt out of their beds and became delirious with shock. Six men fainted and about a dozen became hysterical. Many had to be physically restrained.

A few days later, the *Grayson* stopped at a secured port on a South Pacific island to drop off several of the survivors at a base hospital. Many had infections from shrapnel and required immediate attention. While there, Kauffman noticed that the U.S.S. *Shaw* was also moored in the port. Wearing sandals that he'd fashioned out of rope and rubber and dressed in some tattered clothes that a sailor aboard the *Grayson* had given him, Kauffman boarded the Shaw. There he knocked on the cabin door of one of his best friends from the naval academy.

"You look awful," Bill Busik told Kauffman when he saw him. "What the heck happened?"

13

1942

ON THE SAME OCTOBER AFTERNOON that the *Meredith* plunged
into the blue darkness of the South Pacific, some eye-grabbing sports
news leaked out of Washington: President Roosevelt decided that the
Army-Navy game of 1942 would not be played in Philadelphia. An Associated Press report on October 15 stated that the President ruled out the
City of Brotherly Love as the host site for the game because it would re-
quire too much travel for both of the schools. There was a nationwide ban
on all nonessential travel in the States to conserve gas, and the President
decreed that the Army-Navy game would have to be played with that re-
striction in mind—if the game would be played at all.

The last time the United States had been engaged in a world war, the
Army-Navy matchups were called off in 1917 and '18. In the fall of '42 a
handful of officials at both academies argued strongly that the game
should be canceled again, believing the contest would divide military men
who were stationed overseas. In pubs and on street corners up and down
the Eastern Seaboard—indeed, in spots all around the country—the de-
bate raged: Should the service boys play? Many considered this game the

gold standard of American sport. In some ways it was even bigger than war, and those who wanted the game to go on thought that canceling it would send a signal of weakness overseas. Others were adamant that the game should be called off, saying that it was just a distraction and a waste of resources.

Finally, on October 22—the same day that Kauffman detailed his chilling experience to Busik aboard the U.S.S. *Shaw*—the White House reached its decision: The game would go on, and it would be held at the navel academy's Thompson Stadium. The next day the announcement was splashed on front pages of newspapers across the nation, one of the few times during the war that a sports story crept onto the lead page of the country's top papers. Even the Old Gray Lady, the *New York Times*, gave the story a prominent position.

> *"Since no railroad facilities afford the means of transportation to Annapolis on regularly operated lines and since there is a compelling need to save gasoline and rubber, tickets will be issued only to residents of Annapolis—not to outsiders," the White House announced in a statement. "Only the members of the Army team and such other officials whose presence is needed for the actual playing of the game will go from West Point to Annapolis. Every precaution will be taken to prevent persons living outside of Annapolis—in Washington or Baltimore or other nearby places—from securing tickets to the game. . . . The fact that the game was scheduled before the war was declared and its cancellation at this late date undoubtedly would cause great disappointment throughout the armed forces, in and out of the United States, was discussed at length before the decision was reached to permit the holding of the game this year."*

In Annapolis, midshipmen and locals alike were ecstatic that the game would be played on their home turf. For one autumn afternoon, the town would be the center of the sports universe. One Annapolis resident, Virginia Russell, a legal secretary, couldn't contain her enthusiasm, telling a local paper, "Just imagine how exclusive we're going to be, and how the rest of the country will envy us." At West Point, the news arrived like an early Christmas present. Olds and Romanek still had one season of football left before they marched off to war—they were a class behind Busik and Kauffman—and both craved a second chance to beat the Middies. They didn't care where they played Navy or even if anybody watched. They just wanted a chance to prove to themselves that they had the talent to topple the Midshipmen.

The game also presented the Army players an opportunity to salvage their season, which had been a disappointment. Though Army won its first four games in '42 by an average of nineteen points, the team slumped in midseason, losing two straight to Penn and Notre Dame. Nonetheless, in the days leading up to the '42 Army-Navy showdown, the Cadets were listed as a two-touchdown favorite over the Middies, whose record heading into the game was 4–4.

The '42 game would be unlike any other in Army-Navy history. To purchase a ticket, which cost $4.40, citizens had to travel to the naval academy and sign an application swearing that they lived within a ten-mile radius of the State House in Annapolis. The only exemptions were granted to naval academy employees, to girlfriends of midshipmen who planned on attending the academy dance the night before the game, and to the 210 newspaper reporters, radio announcers, photographers, and telegraph operators who were covering the game. Even Navy's football players had to apply for admission to the stadium. The First Lady, Eleanor Roosevelt, a regular at the Army-Navy games, wasn't allowed to attend because she lived outside the ten-mile boundary.

About a week before kickoff, Army and Navy officials made a controversial decision: The Corp of Cadets would not be allowed to make the trip down from West Point to attend the game. Subsequently, the superintendent of the naval academy ordered all third and fourth class midshipmen to sit behind the Army bench and to cheer for the Cadets. These were going to be the fill-in fans for Army. Though they wouldn't be forced to wear West Point colors and wave Army flags, these young midshipmen were told that they had to yell and clap just as loudly for the boys from West Point as they would their own team. Many midshipmen snickered when they were first given this order, but they had no choice but to follow it.

To learn the Army cheers and fight song, Navy sent two of its cheerleaders up to West Point a few days before the game, where they were taught a crash course in Army cheering. The Cadets' cheerleaders went over the proper cadence of the cheers and songs and gave the two midshipmen several hundred copies of a "Song Book" that listed all the cheers and songs. On the back page of the Song Book, which was distributed to all the third and fourth class midshipmen, was a note from the Corps of Cadets. "The Corps of Cadets desires to express its appreciation to the

Regiment of Midshipmen for its good sportsmanship in furnishing a cheering section to support the Army team. This demonstration of good will and cooperation will do much to cement the feeling of *friendly rivalry* that must always exist when Army and Navy teams meet."

Two days before kickoff, Olds, Romanek, and the rest of the Cadet football team boarded a steam-powered riverboat on a Thursday morning and traveled down the Hudson. Instead of riding a train to Annapolis, the Army team was ordered by Washington to travel by boat so that the rails could be kept open to transport war-related resources. The change in plans suited the players just fine, because as the riverboat floated down the Hudson and under the George Washington Bridge, past the towering buildings of midtown Manhattan, past the Statue of Liberty, and then out into the Atlantic for a trip down the coast, Olds, Romanek and the rest of the Cadets were able to relax. Wearing their long gray coats, they ate box lunches of roast-beef sandwiches and enjoyed the scenery, talking of how they were going to make the most of this last opportunity to beat Navy.

"We've been waiting for this game ever since we got to West Point," Olds told a few of his teammates on the river boat. "It's our turn to win one of these dadgum games."

For Olds, it had been a whirlwind few months. A few weeks after the '41 Army-Navy game he had decided, once and for all, that he would become a pilot like his father, so he joined the Army Air Corp. In the fall of '42, during the heart of football season, Olds spent about a third of his time at Stewart Airfield, located just north of the Academy, where he studied and trained. In a typical two-day period, Olds would have a class at the Point in the morning, then board a bus and travel seventeen miles to the air base and fly that afternoon. He'd spend the night at Stewart and fly again the next morning. After that he'd hop back on a bus and return to the academy, where he'd have classes all afternoon and, later on, football practice. The next morning the schedule started over again with morning classes at the academy. With his life overflowing with responsibilities, Olds often couldn't find time to study during the day. So many nights, after the lights went out at 9:30, Olds would sneak into a bathroom and, sitting on a toilet while holding a flashlight, he'd read his textbooks and take notes until two or three in the morning.

A month into the football season, Olds' schedule grew even more compacted when he started practicing night flying. He'd spend up to three hours each night flying up and down the Hudson River Valley, zooming through the darkness, dogfighting an imaginary enemy. The drone of these planes was so loud it often kept Coach Blaik up at night in his West Point quarters, where he'd lie in bed and worry about whether or not his players who flew would be alive for the next afternoon's practice.

Blaik had reason to worry. Five of Olds' classmates perished while training at Stewart, which was roughly an L-shaped airfield. Olds saw one classmate die when he slammed into a mountain. Two others were killed in spin-related accidents, while two more lost their lives in landing accidents. Olds, considered by the instructors as one of the top pilots of his class, tried not to think of the scary odds whenever he witnessed a classmate crash in a ball of flames. Like most great aviators, Olds didn't lack confidence. He talked and acted as if he was the best young pilot at the academy, and when a classmate got in an accident he didn't brood over it. He simply believed that the reason a classmate had crashed was because he'd made a mistake. "If you make just one dumb move, you won't be around very long," Olds told a friend.

On the riverboat, Olds peered out at the New Jersey shore. Because of the trip to Annapolis, he was given four days off from pilot training, and now he tried to forget about combat. Like all the cadets, the war usually dominated Olds' thoughts. Almost every week a new story of a recent graduate being wounded or killed in combat circulated through West Point. Olds had wanted to join the fight overseas ever since he was in prep school, and that day was rapidly approaching. Though he was still as tough and resilient as anyone who'd ever stepped onto the academy grounds—his teammates all believed that—Olds no longer boasted the reckless, devil-may-care attitude that he brought to the Point. Two-and-half years of academy training had infused him with discipline and responsibility. He knew that other pilots would soon be trusting him with their lives, and this grave realization made Olds more circumspect in all areas of his life. In the classroom, on the football field, and up in the air, Olds didn't take as many chances as he used to—his way of preparing for war.

Romanek also was girding for combat. His mother had sent him dozens of letters relaying the hardships that people in Poland—including Romanek's relatives—were enduring at the hands of Hitler. With the arrival of every new letter, Romanek grew more determined to fight. Ever since he was a junior in high school, Romanek had been refining his soldiering and leadership skills. Now, as graduation approached, he felt prepared to assume command of other men. Romanek had originally wanted to join the Army Air Corps, but failed the eye exam. So, like many of the top students at West Point—Romanek would graduate near the top of his class—he entered the Corps of Engineers. "That's where all the smart guys are," he joked to Olds. "Besides, it'll be safer on the ground than in the air."

Romanek didn't really believe that. He knew that the engineers were often on the front lines in major assaults, clearing areas of mines and other obstacles, building roads, and performing other essential duties in the initial phases of a ground attack. His time at the academy had taught Romanek that one of the keys to leadership was to always exude an air of confidence—and now he did. You could almost see his self-assuredness when he walked into a room, his posture as straight as an ironing board, his chest pushed out. It wasn't cockiness or arrogance that Romanek radiated, just a belief in himself that he'd accomplish—somehow, some way—whatever needed to be done. He had to, if he wanted to stay alive. With graduation seven months away, Romanek, like many of his classmates, bore the earmarks of an outstanding officer.

The morning of November 28, 1942 broke clear and cold in Annapolis. A whisper of wind blew from the north. Because of the wartime restrictions, only 11,700 people made the pilgrimage to Thompson Stadium—the smallest crowd to attend in Army-Navy game since 1893, the last time Army and Navy played in Annapolis, when a crowd of about six thousand watched the players in knit caps slug it out. Most in the stands in '42 bought a game program, which included a note from President Roosevelt, who praised former Cadets and Midshipmen football players now fighting around the world. "On battlefields and on seas throughout the world," the President wrote of the former football players, "they are knitting still more firmly the ties of comradeship which they first formed on the playing fields of their homeland."

The Army team occupied the visitor's locker room, which had no heat or hot water. It was so frigid in the locker room that as the players dressed, they could see their breath, and many players wrapped blankets around their shoulders. Blaik, sensing that his players wanted to get out to the field to run around and warm up, was brief in his pregame speech. "We know what we have to do," Blaik told his players. "Execute, execute, execute. If we do that, we'll walk out of here with a win."

Just as Army was about to kick off, Bill Busik huddled close to his short-wave radio aboard the U.S.S. *Shaw*, which was motoring through choppy waters in the Guadalcanal area. More than a month had passed since his buddy Hal Kauffman had appeared on his ship, with his body gaunt, bruised, and cut up. Busik immediately gave Kauffman one of his extra uniforms to wear and they talked for hours not only about Kauffman's struggle to stay alive, but also about the good times they shared as team-mates. After a few hours, Busik relayed some good news: He'd met a girl and gotten married. "I got to know her only a few days before I reported to duty on the *Shaw*," Busik told Kauffman. "She's a vision."

A week after graduating from the naval academy, Busik sat in the officers' club in San Francisco chatting with friends when a waitress named Margaret Andrus asked for his order. Once Margaret's shift was done, she and Busik talked for hours. Even though Margaret wasn't a big football fan, she'd heard of Busik and knew that he'd played football for Navy. Three days later Busik boarded the U.S.S *Shaw*, but he wrote a letter to Margaret—he called her Midge—almost every day. After a few months at sea, Busik, still burning hard for Midge, asked her to marry him in a letter. She wrote him back and accepted his proposal, and they tied the knot at a chapel in San Francisco when Busik was there on a ten-day shore leave.

"She's the best thing that ever happened to me," Busik told Kauff-man. "I just want to get this war over with so I can get back to her."

A month after sharing the news of his nuptials with Kauffman, Busik prepared to listen to the '42 Army-Navy game. A war was going on all around him, but for the next two hours Busik, as he sat in his tiny quarters, would be transported halfway around the world, to a place where all that mattered was a game. To Busik, listening to this broadcast would be as sat-isfying as a home-cooked meal of fried chicken and apple pie served hot.

Navy received the opening kickoff, beginning their initial drive on their own 28-yard line. The tone of the game was set on the first play from scrimmage when the Midshipmen gained 8 yards on a sweep to the left side of the field. During the run, three Navy lineman had hit Army play-ers with either an elbow or fist to the face. The three Cadets tumbled to the ground. In the defensive huddle following the first play, the Army players felt that the Midshipmen had just pulled an orchestrated, low-down dirty trick. On the sideline Blaik was irate. After Navy quickly gained three first downs, Blaik called a timeout and motioned his defense over to the sideline. "Keep your heads in the game," Blaik said. "I'll let the officials know what's going on and the illegal tactics will stop."

After the timeout, Army's defense stiffened and forced a punt. The first quarter ended in a scoreless tie, and after 15 minutes of action it was clear to everyone in the stands that the game was quickly getting out of hand. Both sides were playing more aggressively than any Army-Navy game in recent memory. All the anxiousness that the players felt about what the coming months would be like, all the fear that the players tried to keep at bay, all the frustration that they felt because of the war-time restrictions—it all boiled over onto the field. The players channeled everything they felt into this game, and the result was a bloody fight.

When the second quarter began, Olds' temper was about to erupt. On several plays on defense he'd been smacked in the face or clipped from behind—which he interpreted as cheap shots. Five minutes into the second quarter, Olds fought back. As Navy's Hal Hamberg dropped back to pass, Olds beat his man at the point of attack and broke through the line of scrimmage. But just as he neared Hamberg, a Navy blocking back delivered a vicious forearm shiver to Olds' mouth. Olds fell to the ground, and as he lay writhing on the grass in pain, he raised his right hand to his mouth to rub his teeth. His mouth felt like it'd just been hit by a baseball bat, and he quickly realized that his two front teeth had been knocked out. Blood pouring from his mouth, Olds crawled around on the ground, searching for his teeth. Frank Marriet, an Army defensive lineman, kneeled down and asked Olds what he was doing.

"I think I lost some teeth," Olds said. "Help me find them."

"You need to get out of here, Robin," replied Marriet. "You're in really bad shape. You need a doctor right now."

"But I gotta find my teeth," Olds said.

"Why?" asked Marriet.

"I don't know, I just do," said Olds.

But after more prodding, Olds got up and, still bleeding like a man chewing on glass shards, was led off the field. He walked right past Romanek, who was standing on the sideline and strapping on his leather helmet. Romanek was serving as Olds' backup for this game and, after seeing what had happened to his friend, gusts of rage shook Romanek. "Play smart," Blaik instructed Romanek. "Don't do anything that will hurt the team. I'm telling you, play smart!"

Romanek didn't listen. He flew recklessly around the field. Over the next several plays, he hit players in the jaw, he clipped a few Midshipmen, and eventually he was flagged for a personal foul. As soon as that flag was thrown, Blaik pushed a substitute onto the field for Romanek. As Romanek jogged to the sideline, Blaik, screaming, demanded that Romanek stand right in front of him.

"What the hell was that?" Blaik asked Romanek. "If you ever do that again, you'll never play football for Army again."

Olds laid on a table in the locker room. In two separate places his teeth had stabbed through his upper lip, which was badly swollen. Captain Ollie Neiss, the team's doctor, worked for 10 minutes sewing up Olds, giving him 34 stitches. When Neiss was finally finished, Olds looked as if he'd been in a car accident. Cotton was jammed up his nose, and blood was splattered all over his face and uniform. Nonetheless, when Neiss was finished, Olds hopped off the table, grabbed his helmet, and ran back onto the field. He wanted payback.

A single crossbar made of heavy plastic had been affixed to his helmet, a device that served as a temporary facemask to protect his mouth. Olds ran directly to Coach Blaik, staring at his coach with intensity shining in his eyes. Using his hands and grunting like a cavemen, Olds motioned that he wanted to get back in the game. Blaik asked the team doctor for his opinion. "He'll be all right," replied Neiss, "if he can stand it." Olds signified that there wouldn't be a problem, that he was fit to play. "Okay, Robin, go get 'em," Blaik told Olds with a grin.

When Olds ran onto the field, he scanned the Navy huddle for the blocking back who had knocked out his teeth. Olds couldn't speak very well, but as soon as he saw the back he growled like a monster, spitting blood. The Midshipmen lined up and pitched the ball to a back on a sweep to the opposite side of Olds for a 4-yard gain. On Olds' second play, Navy ran directly at him. Shedding his initial block, Olds was suddenly face to face with the blocking back who'd hurt him. Olds shoved him to the ground, then jumped in the air and came down, right knee first, directly onto the player's rib cage. The blow knocked the wind out of the blocking back and broke two of his ribs. "How's that feel?" Olds grumbled as he stood on the player, who was eventually hauled off the field on a stretcher and wouldn't reenter the game.

At halftime, the score was tied 0–0. But five minutes into the second half Navy's Joe Sullivan, a running back, broke through the line of scrimmage and raced 40 yards for a touchdown. The extra point was good, and the underdog Midshipmen had a 7–0 lead. Blaik paced up and down the sideline, upset that his players were losing their cool. They were committing penalties and ignoring their assignments, more interested in trying to hurt a Midshipman than doing what it took to win the game.

As the clock counted down, Olds didn't miss a play on either offense or defense, and two more Navy players were helped off the field after absorbing a blow from Olds. Olds' valiant effort even impressed the Midshipmen in the stands who sat behind the Army bench—the Cadets performed the West Point cheers and sang the Army fight song just like they were taught—but Olds alone couldn't carry Army to victory. Navy won 14–0.

"Robin, I'm sorry about you losing your teeth," Blaik told Olds on the boat ride back to West Point.

"That's all right," Olds replied with a swollen smile. "I always wondered how I'd look without them."

Two decades later, Blaik would call the performance that Olds gave on that cold afternoon in November of 1942 the most courageous he'd ever seen on a football field, and later that year sportswriter Grantland Rice would name Olds to his 1942 All-America team. For the record: Olds never did find his teeth.

14

ARMY

THE PHONE CALL CAME EARLY on an April morning in 1943. Two months shy of his graduation from the Point—and five months after he had played in his final college football game—Robin Olds was walking across the Plain when a stone-faced administrator approached him. The words he spoke thundered in Olds' ears. "Robin, your dad is asking for you," the administrator told Olds. "He's not well."

Robert Olds, now a two-star general, lay dying in a Tucson, Arizona, hospital room from the sudden onset of periocardial disease, a hardening of the lining around the heart. Ever since he'd entered the Army Air Corps, Robin had thought often of his father, of how they used to watch the planes take off and land at Langley Airbase when Robin was a boy. And now, whenever Robin flew, he could feel his father's courage and spirit rising up in him every time he strapped himself into the cockpit.

One of Olds' instructors at West Point, Lieutenant John Hacker, recognized early on that Robin had the ideal makeup of a great fighter pilot. He possessed just the right ratio of brains, ego, and guts. One night, the lieutenant decided that he and his pupil should have some fun together, just the two of them. Taking off from Stewart Airfield, the two flew Beech AT-10s, twin-engine trainer planes of all-wood construction, and pretended they were in a nighttime dogfight. First they tore south through the darkness down the Hudson River to New York City. After zipping by the Statue of Liberty, whose torch lit up New York harbor, they made a U-turn and proceeded to fly north under the George Washington Bridge. Over the next hour they buzzed under every bridge on the Hudson River from New York City to Albany, laughing the entire way like kids sharing a secret joke. Hacker and Olds never told anyone at the academy what they had done, but that evening the instructor knew it was only a matter of time before his student would be able to teach him a few flying lessons.

But now Olds' heart grew heavy with the news that his father was gravely ill. He and his little brother Steven, who was a plebe at the academy, hopped on a B-17 that was already scheduled to fly to Tucson and hitched a ride. Because his father was a two-star general, Olds and his brother received special permission to leave the academy for a few days. Their father had fallen sick quickly, and when Olds arrived at the hospital the doctors told him that his father didn't have long to live and that it was time to say final prayers and good-bye. Kneeling at his father's bedside and cradling his hand, Olds told his father for the first time that he was going to become a fighter pilot. His father smiled and told his son, "I never went up in the air without learning something new, so never think you know it all."

A few hours later, with Robin still grasping his father's hand, Robert Olds died at age forty-seven. Both sons were devastated, especially Robin. He'd always viewed his father as a man made of iron, a man who could never melt away. Standing over his father, young Robin made a promise to himself: He would make this man proud of him as a pilot in the war.

On May 30, the day before graduation, the cadets who had successfully completed their air corp training assembled on Trophy Point. It was a splendid spring morning; a refreshing breeze blew up off the river. General Henry H. Arnold, the commanding general of the Army Air Force, addressed the 206 cadets. "How you boys perform in the next few weeks, the next few months, will be critically important to our country's safety," the General said. "Congratulations. Now make us all proud." The general then approached each cadet, shook the cadet's hand, and pinned on his wings. After the general moved past him, Olds couldn't stop himself from glancing down at the silver-plated wings every few seconds. Even when the ceremony was over and Olds was walking across the parade ground to the barracks, he still kept sneaking peeks at his shiny wings.

The next morning the commencement speaker was General Arnold, the architect of America's Air Force. A steady patter of rain fell on the Field House as the General delivered his remarks to the June Class of '43. A total of 514 Cadets—the largest class in West Point history—now sat in the Field House, minutes away from becoming officers. Because of the gasoline shortage, few visitors arrived by car. Instead, the majority of the girlfriends and parents came by train to West Point for the ceremony. The most determined visitor might have been Mrs. John W. Rhea, who had traveled from Waldo, Arkansas, to see her son graduate. Four days before commencement, she injured her hip when she fell while walking on the academy grounds. A frail woman, she was carried on a stretcher from the post hospital to the Field House for the graduation ceremony, where she saw the exercises from a balcony near the main platform. She figured it might be one of the last times she'd ever see her only boy, F. W. Rhea, who at age twenty was one of the youngest men ever to graduate from the Point.

In somber tones, General Arnold told the graduates that they would be "commanding and leading troop batteries, companies, or squadrons in actual combat within six months." He demanded that the men be tough, and characterized the Japanese as "uncivilized savages" who must be exterminated "like termites." "War is a ruthless business," the General said. "But I believe we are now ready for a decisive year."

At 3:00 P.M., some 5 hours after General Arnold concluded his remarks, Henry Romanek stood at the altar of the Catholic Chapel, watching his bride to be, Betsy Wells, stride down the aisle. They had met four years earlier when Romanek was in prep school in Washington, D.C. on a blind date. They went to a Saturday night dance at the Army-Navy Country Club in Arlington, Virginia, and Romanek was smitten within seconds. Betsy was a traffic-stopping blonde with hazel eyes, and right away, the air was electric between them. They had so much in common. Betsy's father was a major in the War Department in Washington, and she always respected men in uniform. During the three years Romanek attended West Point, the couple wrote letters to each other frequently. Romanek eventually invited Betsy up to West Point for Christmas vacation during his plebe year, and that's when he knew he wanted to marry the girl of his dreams.

The day after they married, Romanek and his new bride visited New York City, and then took a train south to Virginia Beach for their honeymoon. Like everyone else at the Point who had entered the Corp of Engineers, Romanek was given a month's leave—and he planned to get as much enjoyment out of the next thirty days as possible. At Virginia Beach, Romanek and his wife went on moonlight walks along the beach and danced at a local officers' club. One evening at the Navy Beach Club they bumped into Robin Olds, who was also enjoying some R&R before going to war. A bachelor who didn't mind an occasional belt of whiskey, Olds and his fly-boy buddies were quite a sight as they sat around a table and talked of killing Germans and Japanese. Olds even sneaked in a few dances with Romanek's wife, Betsy.

After a few days in Virginia Beach, Romanek shook Olds' hand, wished him luck, then boarded a train with Betsy. They spent the next few weeks at Romanek's home in New Jersey and with Betsy's parents in Washington. On July 1, Romanek reported to the base at Fort Pierce, Florida, where he was schooled in beach landings. Weeks later his engineering battalion was moved to a base outside of Norfolk, Virginia. In the Chesapeake Bay, they trained to be amphibious engineers, practicing loading and unloading landing ships with equipment. Romanek didn't know it, but his platoon was preparing for what would be the key moment of the world's second great war. They were training to storm the beach at Normandy.

15

BARNACLE BILL

ON A COOL JANUARY MORNING in 1944—six months after Robin Olds and Henry Romanek graduated from the Point—Margaret Busik sat down at the kitchen table in her San Francisco apartment to read the *San Francisco Chronicle*. Sipping hot coffee and nibbling buttered toast, she flipped through the paper, anxious to find out as much war news as possible. She and her husband Bill wrote almost every day, but often weeks went by before their letters reached each other's hands. She missed him desperately—she spent many late nights thumbing through their wedding pictures—and prayed each day for the war to end.

She opened the paper, hoping to find a mention of the U.S.S. *Shaw*, the ship her husband was on. She knew that the *Shaw* was somewhere in the South Pacific fighting the Japanese, but Bill wasn't allowed to mention any specific ship movements in his letters, so she wasn't aware of the precise location. Now she read about how actor Jimmy Stewart, one of the stars of *The Philadelphia Story*, had recently completed a daylight bombing mission on Ludwigshaven in Germany, flying with forty-seven other bombers of the 445th Group based in Norfolk, England.

She continued to scan the newsprint, smudging her fingers. She learned that British and American forces had broken through the Germans' winter defense line in Italy, as the Allies had recently taken the village of San Vittorio and now hoped to "romp to Rome." In the Pacific theater, the U.S. 6th Army had recently landed on New Guinea's north coast and taken Saidor, a Japanese supply depot. General Douglass MacArthur now seemed on his way to driving the Japanese off of New Guinea. Indeed, on this morning, the war seemed to be going reasonably well.

Margaret flipped another page, and a story about a former Navy football star leapt out at her like a burglar from the bushes: Bill Busik, the paper reported, had gone overboard on the U.S.S. *Shaw*. He was now missing—and presumed dead.

Three weeks before Margaret had read those heart-wrenching words, her husband was up in the gun director of the *Shaw*, standing about fifty feet above the water. Holding binoculars to his eyes, he scanned the cloudy horizon, looking for enemy aircraft. The date was December 26, 1943, and the *Shaw* was patrolling at ten knots about six miles to the northeast of Cape Gloucester, located at the western end of New Britain, a tiny island in the Solomon Sea off the coast of New Guinea. The *Shaw* had been providing support for the troop landings at Hollandia, a town on the north coast of New Guinea. The *Shaw*'s guns provided cover for the advancing Allied soldiers and bombarded the enemy on the shore. The previous few days had been relatively uneventful for the boys on the *Shaw*. Enemy planes occasionally showed up on radar, but the destroyer never took any hits.

On the afternoon of December 26, the sea was calm. Up in the director, Busik was still laughing about a request he'd received from an officer sitting next to him at breakfast: Could Busik tell the table a Navy football story? It was a familiar question, because everyone aboard the ship, from the lowest-ranking enlisted man to the captain, knew Busik's biography. Just a month ago, they had all listened to the '43 Army-Navy game together—for the fifth straight year, the Middies beat Army, this time 13–0 at West Point's Michie Stadium. Many of the sailors and officers on the destroyer had also tuned in to the radio broadcast of the '41 Army-Navy game, when Busik had thrilled them all with his running, passing, and defense.

In fact, when Busik reported to the *Shaw* on July 1, 1942, for active duty, he was treated differently than the other officers. He had star power, and it burned brightly in everyone's imagination. Busik's shipmates frequently asked for his autograph and there always seemed to be someone begging him to tell a football tale. Busik obliged every time, and he was so good at spinning yarns that he made his listeners feel as if they were with him in the huddle and on the field, surrounded by one hundred thousand fans.

Busik's past endowed him with a special power, and the first time he used it was three months after he graduated. He'd been on the *Shaw* for about sixty days when she was in the battle of the Santa Cruz Islands, Busik's first interaction with an enemy. The battle, which took place on October 26, 1942, would be the last of the carrier battles around Guadalcanal. The *Shaw* was one of fourteen U.S. destroyers involved in the engagement. Her mission was to provide cover for one of the two U.S. carriers in the area. Busik, at the time, was a damage control officer, and his battle station was the forward battery, meaning he was in charge of the forward guns. Using binoculars, he'd tell the men on the guns when and where to fire. On the morning of October 26, Busik was in the forward battery, scanning the horizon, looking for dots in the sky. For the first few hours of the day, there was nothing out there, just blue sky and a few clouds.

The ship next to the *Shaw* in the screen around the carrier was the U.S.S. *Porter*. At 10:55 A.M., Busik, while sipping on a cup of coffee, again scanned the horizon for enemy aircraft. Suddenly it appeared: A Japanese plane was dropping out of the sky, having approached the Task Force at a high altitude. Within seconds of spotting the plane, Busik telephoned his captain, requesting permission to fire. Before he heard back, Busik saw the plane drop a torpedo in the water. Busik again telephoned the Captain, this time telling him that a torpedo was in the water. Busik could see the wake of the torpedo several hundred yards away and heading in their direction. The captain ordered the engine room to back down on the power. The torpedo would have intercepted the ship had the *Shaw* not slowed down. Seconds later, the torpedo whizzed in front of the bow of the ship—and headed directly into the belly of the U.S.S. *Porter*, which had stopped to pick up a downed U.S. pilot. The torpedo exploded midship into the *Porter*'s port side, flooding its fire rooms. The *Shaw* then dodged another torpedo—this one missed the disabled *Porter*—and circled the *Porter* to inspect her. At 11:30 the commander of the Task Force ordered the *Shaw* to rescue the crew of three hundred people aboard the disabled *Porter*.

As Busik helped the crew of the *Porter* come on board, he was terrified to see the condition of the survivors. This was the first time in the war he'd seen men injured, and these poor boys were tough to look at. Many were covered in blood. Others were so burned that their faces had seemed to melt like ice cream, while still more suffered from life-threatening shrapnel wounds. In the months that he'd been on the *Shaw* Busik often felt as if he'd been fighting a phantom enemy that never materialized. But now the awful reality of the enemy's firepower was spread before Busik's eyes.

Busik's stateroom was located next to the wardroom, which sailors aboard the *Shaw* quickly converted into an emergency medical room. As soon as this medical room filled up, Busik began escorting the wounded to officers' bunks, including his own. The *Shaw* only had one doctor and one hospital corpsmen aboard ship, and there was little they could do for the men other than give them shots of morphine. When all the wounded had been moved, Busik tried to comfort the men.

"I wish there was more I could do for you, sailor," Busik told one boy who was seriously burned.

"Tell me a story," the sailor replied. "You're Bill Busik from the Navy football team, right?" the sailor asked.

"Correct," replied Busik.

"Tell me something about it,"

Busik began talking, detailing all that he could remember from his big Army-Navy showdowns. The Navy football legend tried to get their thoughts focused on football rather than pain. He told these dying boys about the crowd at the '41 Army-Navy game, about what it was like to have thousands of eyes locked on your every move, about how even Army fans had cheered for the Navy players. He told them everything he could remember about those bright days of being a Midshipman football player, trying to mentally transport the wounded away from the place they were in now, and the sailors were held spellbound by his stories. Some of the boys even smiled through their suffering.

One boy was in particularly bad shape. He was young, maybe nineteen years old, and he was lying in Busik's bunk, shaking uncontrollably. Burns covered his head and chest; he was in shock. Busik called for the doctor, and he soon appeared with a syringe of morphine. The doctor asked Busik to hold the boy down so he could stick the needle in his arm. Busik cradled the boy's face with his hands, trying to comfort him, telling him in a voice that was as soothing as a prayer that everything was going to be fine, that he was safe now. The doctor gave him the shot. As Busik lifted his hands away, the boys' ears stuck to Busik's hands. They'd peeled right off his head. Less than an hour later the boy was dead.

Like all the men aboard, Busik was proud to serve on the *Shaw*. Among the ships in the Pacific Fleet, the *Shaw* was symbolically significant. She had been in dry dock at Pearl Harbor when the Japanese dropped three bombs on the front section of the ship, causing a fire that exploded her ammunition magazines and practically demolished her from the mast forward. When the magazines exploded the entire fore section of the *Shaw* was lifted high into the air, and it shattered into several pieces. A photograph of the explosion was published throughout the world; it became *the* picture of the attack.

After December 7 the *Shaw* was considered a total loss, as were her sister ships, the U.S.S. *Cassin* and the U.S.S. *Downs*. The Japanese even announced that the *Shaw* had been sunk. For ten days following the attack no one knew what exactly to do with the twisted, blackened destroyer. The *Shaw*'s skipper, commander W. G. Jones, said he "wouldn't have given a nickel for it." To Jones's surprise, on December 18, 1941, he received an order to "take the *Shaw* back to mainland United States and get her cleaned up." For the next three weeks, working day and night, civilians from Hawaii and members of the *Shaw* crew repaired the ship. A temporary bridge was built. A sturdy blunt bow—basically, a metal nose to the ship—was installed. And then, under her own power and with the same engines it had before the attack, the *Shaw* sailed away from Hawaii to the Navy Yard on Mare Island near San Francisco.

The journey wasn't easy. The ship was stiff and light. When she ran into stormy weather, waves engulfed the vessel. She tossed and turned and, at one point, nearly capsized. The men slept little, and after ten days the slow voyage was completed. Once in San Francisco, the *Shaw* underwent six more months of repairs. Busik joined the ship a few days before she once again set sail on July 4, 1942. "We're better than ever," said Commander Jones as the *Shaw*—the ship with nine lives (or at least two)—rolled back into the sea.

Eighteen months after being rechristened, the *Shaw* patrolled the waters off of New Guinea. Up in the gun director's deck, which was about sixty feet above the water, Busik held binoculars to his eyes, scanning the clouds. It was precisely 4:38 in the afternoon of December 26, 1943. It had been a quiet day, but then Busik spotted several dark specks circling high in the sky. Immediately recognizing the specks as Japanese fighters, Busik telephoned the ship's captain, asking him for permission to give the order to fire. Busik wanted to spray the sky with bullets before the planes started peeling off and diving down. But the captain was delayed in responding to Busik. Without hearing back from the captain, Busik gave the order to shoot anyway. "We're going to get these guys before they get us," Busik said.

Just as the *Shaw*'s guns began blazing, the first plane dove, heading at the *Shaw* in a fifty-degree dive. When the dive-bomber got within about one thousand feet of the *Shaw*, the plane burst into flames, hit by the *Shaw*'s gunfire, and went out of control. The plane crashed into the sea about fifteen hundred yards to the port side without dropping any bombs near the vessel. Busik felt vindicated. In his training at the naval academy he was schooled in all the nuances of when to engage the enemy, and he was taught to pepper enemy aircraft with fire as soon as he thought they were about to attack the ship. Sure, he didn't have the authorization of the captain, but he went with his own instincts. It was a split-second decision, and it proved to be the right one: Moments after the ship's gunfire had knocked it down, the plane started sinking into the ocean.

Then a second plane dove. Busik again gave the order to fire. Seconds later, shells hit the plane at about fifteen hundred feet, and smoke spewed out as the plane descended toward the *Shaw*. But this time, the Japanese pilot didn't lose control. At about one thousand feet in the air, the aircraft released one five-hundred-pound bomb. A fraction of a second later, it released two smaller one-hundred-pound bombs. From Busik's position in the director, it looked like the bombs were heading directly at him; he could even see the circular nose of the five-hundred-pounder bearing down on the spot where he stood. He thought he was a dead man. He braced himself against the railing of the gun director's deck, expecting to get blown into past tense. He took a deep breath and closed his eyes, ready for heaven.

The five hundred-pound bomb struck the water about ten feet off the starboard side and about fifteen feet forward of the bridge. The two smaller bombs smacked the water on the port side, about ninety feet from the ship. All three bombs then burst. Shrapnel and water flew everywhere. More than 110 holes were instantly cut into the port side of the ship, three feet of water had been thrown onto the ship, and dozens of men were killed instantly.

When the concussions of the blasts reached Busik up in the gun director's deck, it produced a whiplike effect. Busik, already some sixty feet above the ship, was sent flying into the air. Sailors watching the drama unfold from nearby ships shouted and signaled man overboard—but in fact Busik's leg got caught in an antenna and mast guide wire. The wire wrapped around his right calf, and it left him dangling—unconscious— high above the ship. After a few moments he woke up, confused, upside down, amazed to still have breath in his lungs.

Dangling forty feet above the ship like a fish caught on a line, Busik thought of his wife. As he swayed through the air, he knew that if he fell he'd never see her again. "I gotta hold on," Busik said to himself. "I'm not letting go." Busik recalled all the football stories he had shared with the wounded soldiers just weeks ago, and he wondered what his life would be like if this war hadn't erupted and he'd been able to try out for Curly Lambeau's Packers. "I surely wouldn't be in this predicament now," he thought to himself.

After a few minutes, Busik took a personal inventory: Shrapnel had hit his ribs and legs, but other than that, he felt fine. Then he noticed that his naval academy class ring was no longer on his finger. It was snug on his left ring finger minutes ago—and all ten fingers were present and accounted for—but now his ring was gone.

Ten minutes after he was blasted into the air, a few shipmates reached Busik, untangling him and reeling him to safety. He was escorted below the deck where the ship doctor attended his wounds. "I guess the Japs are paying us back all that scrap iron we gave them before the war," Busik joked with the doctor. "By the way, doc, have you seen my ring?"

"Sorry, sir, I haven't," replied the doctor.

Some 5 hours later, two decks below the bridge, a sailor was emptying a garbage can when he noticed something shiny on the bottom. It was a naval academy ring from the Class of '43. On the top of the ring was a sapphire stone and engraved on the inside of it were the words: William S. Busik. The sailor walked to Busik's stateroom and knocked on his door.

"Sir, did you lose this?" the sailor asked.

"Good heavens," replied Busik. "It blew off my finger when the bombs went off. No matter what, I'm never taking this thing off again. I'm in your debt, sailor. Thank you."

Moments after Margaret Busik read that her husband was missing in action, she bolted from her seat at the kitchen table. She ran into her bedroom, fumbling to find a letter that she had received just days ago from her husband. She hastily yanked it out of the envelope and, with her hands trembling, looked for the date. There it was: January 2, 1944. Bill had sent it a week after he had reportedly gone overboard. Margaret then reached for the telephone, asking the operator to connect her to the *San Francisco Chronicle*.

"My husband is not missing," Margaret told an editor at the paper. "I got a letter from him just the other day that's dated after you said he was missing. This is going to upset a lot of people. Please run a retraction."

When Margaret wrote her husband and explained the mix-up, he laughed so hard it filled up the wardroom.

"I guess I'm on my second life," Busik joked to a few friends. "Who knows? If I'm lucky, maybe I've got a couple more in me."

16

EARLY JUNE 1944

WILLIAM LEAHY STOOD AS straight and still as a two-by-four, at full attention, as Dwight D. Eisenhower boarded the battleship U.S.S. *Texas* on May 19, 1944. Six months had passed since Leahy's friend and former teammate, Bill Busik, was nearly killed aboard the U.S.S. *Shaw*, and now Leahy stared into the blue eyes of the Supreme Commander of the Allied Forces with D-day just seventeen days away.

Eisenhower looked like an athlete. He had a powerful gait, his arms swaying confidently as he walked on board, and there was a bounce to his step. He had wide shoulders and a thick chest—a farmer's chest—and as Leahy looked at him he imagined that Eisenhower could still play football. Back in the fall of 1912, while at the military academy, Eisenhower was one of Army's top backs. After leading the Cadets to a victory over Rutgers, the *New York Times* called Eisenhower "one of the most promising backs in Eastern football." A few weeks later, however, Eisenhower severely injured his knee when he leapt off the back of a galloping horse. He never played football again.

But, at age fifty-three, he still possessed the graceful stride of a power player in his prime as he walked onto the *Texas*. Eisenhower had secretly flown to Belfast, Ireland, to inspect the gunfire support ships of the Western Naval Task Force that were anchored in Belfast Lough, near the city of Bangor. The U.S.S. *Texas* was the flagship of Battleship Division Five, and this was where Eisenhower came to deliver a message to the vast armada of Allied Ships amassed in the Lough. By most estimates, the total number of officers and sailors on these ships was probably around thirty thousand. One officer and one sailor from every ship in the fleet was on the *Texas* to hear the supreme commander speak; afterward they would return to their respective ships and report to their crews what Eisenhower had said.

A cool drizzle fell from a gray sky as Eisenhower prepared to make his remarks. The carpenters aboard the *Texas* had built a speaker's platform on the quarterdeck and Eisenhower's words were piped into the ship's loudspeaker system. Leahy, anxious like many young officers, leaned forward ever so slightly as the commander began speaking. "In the next battle we will have the greatest air coverage that has ever accompanied you and your forces in history," he said. "[Your superiors] provide for taking care of you when you are wounded, they see that you are disposed properly, that your guns are trained on the right targets, but, my God, men, you do the fighting! No general or other person in high capacity really fires that shot that knocks out enemy batteries and sinks ships. You are the people who do it. You are the men handling the guns and the turrets, the men handling the firing of the weapons, torpedoes, everything. You are the men who are winning the war."

As Eisenhower continued, his words stoked a fire inside Leahy. Ever since he learned of the attack on Pearl Harbor while he was sitting in Washington, D.C.'s Griffith Stadium on December 7, 1941, and watching the Washington Redskins play the Philadelphia Eagles, Leahy had been looking forward to combat. Though he never imagined he'd be stricken with it, he had caught war fever. He'd already lost many of his friends, former classmates, and former teammates. Just recently he'd heard that Bill Chewning, one of Navy's top tackles on the '41 team, had been aboard the submarine U.S.S. *Corvina* when it had been sunk on November 16, 1943, by a Japanese submarine near the Gilbert Islands. Leahy remembered that Chewning always seemed to be in the middle of the action. In the giddy aftermath of Navy's 14–6 win over Army in '41, it was Chewning in his smeared, bloody uniform, who had presented the game ball to coach Larson. That had been one of the best moments of Chewning's life. But now, like so many whom Leahy knew well, Chewning was gone forever.

As a first-division gunner officer aboard the *Texas*, Leahy, who had been stationed on the *Texas* since graduating from the naval academy, was assigned to what was called "Spot 1," located in the crow's nest 110 feet in the air. His job was to control the firing and aiming of the turrets. Looking through a large telescope, he'd determine if the shells were reaching their intended targets. After they had been fired, for example, Leahy might say "up one hundred." A shipmate standing next to Leahy would then relay the information via phone to the crew in charge of the turrets. As soon as they'd make the adjustment, they'd phone the crow's nest and then Leahy would give the order to fire. A lover of numbers, Leahy thought of his job as a problem-solving exercise. And now he knew he might soon be forced to give an order to fire that could kill hundreds of enemy soldiers with one command. "It's us or them," he thought to himself whenever he pondered this subject. "I have a job to do—and I intend to do it as best I can."

After Eisenhower finished his formal remarks on the *Texas*, he asked if there were any questions. A sailor, who Leahy thought couldn't have been older than eighteen, raised his hand and, in a cracking voice, asked, "I hear that in the upcoming invasion that we are going to land British troops and that the British Navy is going to land American troops. Is this true?"

Eisenhower smiled. "First of all, that is not true," he said calmly. "You're going to land the American troops. You're going to land your brothers, you're going to land your fathers, and you're going to land your sisters' boyfriends. And I will tell you right now that if we get to land I, by God, will keep us there. We are going to win this war!"

The answer caused the troops to clap and yell in approval. These were stirring words, and as Leahy listened, he knew he'd never forget them.

Twelve days later, on May 31, the ships were sealed; no more leave was granted. The sailors and officers were then told by their superiors that over five thousand vessels would participate in D-day. Now the wait began.

Robin Olds also was waiting. He'd arrived in England on a transport three weeks earlier, as primed as anyone to fight. After graduation from West Point he had joined the 434th Fighter Squadron of the 479th Fighter Group at Lomita, California, where he logged about 650 hours of flying time—far more than the average young pilot heading into combat for the first time. He also had spent some 250 hours in the P-38, the aircraft he'd be flying during the war. Called the Lightning, the P-38 had a top speed of 414 mph, making it a faster plane than any Olds would confront in combat. The Lightning handled well, but at low altitudes it sometimes wasn't as maneuverable as other aircraft.

Olds' first few weeks in the war were relatively quiet. His squadron mostly bombed bridges and railroads in France. Olds never encountered any enemy fighters during these runs, but one of his good friends from the Army football team, John Buckner, wasn't as fortunate. In mid-May of '44, Buckner, who had graduated fifth in his class in January of 1943, went on an early morning dive-bombing mission in northern France. His order was to take out a bridge. After crossing the English Channel Buckner spotted the bridge. Buckner dove down, released his bombs, and saw the bridge fall into the river it covered.

As Buckner climbed back into the sky, he felt satisfied, as if he'd just completed a five-course meal. Thinking all was clear, he allowed himself to relax as he guided his plane north toward the channel. But just as he started to think about what he was going to do when he got back to his base in England, enemy shells started exploding all around him. He continued to climb, gaining as much altitude as he could. But then a shell hit his engine. Before he could react, the engine stalled.

Buckner was now gliding at twelve thousand feet. He knew that if he attempted a belly landing—which he'd practiced many times—he could be taken prisoner, so instead he turned north and began gliding across the channel. When his plane dropped to one thousand feet, he knew it was time to bail. He could see the coast of England in the distance. Not thinking clearly, Buckner undid his parachute straps that were wrapped around his legs. Every time Buckner had gotten out of the plane, he always undid these straps. It was his routine. But now as he prepared to jump—this would be the first time he'd ever bailed—he paused just before leaping into the air. In the nick of time, he remembered a crucial bit of information: He needed his parachute now!

"Wait a minute, this is dumb," Buckner said to himself.

He then refastened his straps and jumped out of the plane and into the air, praying these would not be the last moments of his life. He was now at about eight hundred feet. Moments after his chute opened, he saw his plane plunge into the channel, crashing in a big splash. A strong breeze blew from the south, pushing Buckner closer and closer to the coast. After dropping from the sky for a few more minutes, Buckner landed safely on the beach. Knowing that the coast was heavily mined, he then sat in the sand and waited for someone to pick him up. Several hours later a few British soldiers arrived in a jeep and guided Buckner around the mines on the beach. Buckner had lost his plane, but not his life.

On June 5, 1944, a chilly midafternoon in southern England, Olds' commander called all the pilots in the squadron together for a briefing. "Our next mission is to escort some ships that are in southern England that will be heading south," the commander said. "Gentlemen, the invasion is on."

Finally it's here, Olds thought to himself. The moment he'd been training for since he arrived at the Point.

Henry Romanek was busy laying a live mine outside of Payton, England, when one of the forty-five men who was under his command finally spoke up. "Lieutenant, you're the bright one. Tell us where we're going."

Romanek wasn't surprised by the question. It was one that he'd been contemplating for weeks. Romanek had graduated number two in his class at West Point in military history. He knew the annals of strategy and tactics well, and after studying maps that depicted the shoreline of France, he knew exactly where the invasion was headed.

"We're going right here," Romanek told his soldier. He had grabbed a map and was pointing his finger to an exact location. A few soldiers leaned in close and read the words where his finger was resting: A beach the Allies called Omaha.

After the U.S.S. *Texas* had been locked down, the captain of the ship spoke to his crew. "The great events for which all of you have been working and preparing will shortly be launched," he said. "It also means that every possible effort must be made to prevent any leakage whatsoever of information from incoming operations, by whatever means—mail, personal contact, or signals. I consider that you are now at battle efficiency and the time has come to polish up all our weapons. From now until D-day only such drills as are necessary to maintain your present state will be conducted. But remember, the enemy we are going up against will tax our readiness to the utmost."

Leahy, like everyone else on the *Texas*, had been handed an order of the day when he filed onto the ship for the last time before D-day. It was from General Eisenhower, and Leahy read it with a high tide of pride in his heart.

> *Soldiers, Sailors, and Airmen of the Allied Expeditionary Force:*
>
>   *You are about to embark on the Great Crusade, toward which we have striven these many months. The eyes of the world are upon you. The hopes and prayers of liberty-loving people everywhere march with you. . . . Your task will not be an easy one. Your enemy is well trained, well equipped and battle-hardened. He will fight savagely. But this is the year 1944! . . . The tide has turned! The free men of the world are marching together to victory! I have full confidence in your courage, devotion to duty and skill in battle. We will accept nothing less than full victory!*
>
>   *Good luck! And let us all beseech the blessing of Almighty God upon this great and noble undertaking.*

After reading these words, Leahy had to take a deep breath. A seminal moment in history was rapidly approaching, he certainly understood that. Let the battle begin, Leahy thought to himself, as he folded the order carefully and put it in his pocket.

Hours after the *Texas* had been sealed, Leahy was handed the invasion battle plan. The *Texas*'s mission was to provide support of the troop landings on Omaha Beach. To prepare for the task, Leahy studied a detailed map of the area where the *Texas* would be providing cover to the invading troops. Analyzing the topography of Omaha Beach and the area behind it, Leahy noticed a church spire that rose about forty feet above the ground. The church sat on top of the cliffs that overlooked the beach. After examining the map for a few minutes, Leahy decided that he'd use the spire as his main marker. When he was up in the crow's nest and trying to figure out what directions he needed to give to his gunnery personnel, he'd locate the spire. From there, he would memorize how far all the main targets were located. "I just hope the Germans don't figure out what I'm doing and decide to take out that spire," Leahy told a friend on the ship. "It's a risk, but the spire is the best marker I can find."

On an early June afternoon in 1944, the *Texas* motored out of Belfast and began making her way toward the task force rendezvous point. The weather was poor, overcast with rain squalls, and there was a strong southwesterly wind. That evening, holed up in his quarters, Leahy studied the pictures and maps of Normandy with all the intensity he could muster. He laid all the material on the floor by his bunk and shined the yellow light of his gooseneck lamp onto the ground. He stayed up most of the night, imprinting every detail of the map into his memory. "I've got to know this better than I know my childhood neighborhood," Leahy told a few sailors on the *Texas*. "I'm not going to let anyone down."

The *Texas* and the column of ships from Belfast Lough were near the southwest corner of England when the postponement order was given. The invasion had been scheduled for June 5, but when Eisenhower received information that the weather forecast for the Normandy area called for overcast skies and a chance for thunderstorms, he decided to delay it. The only way the invasion would be a success, Eisenhower believed, was if it was performed under better conditions. Eisenhower hoped for clearer skies on June 6.

Leahy considered the delay a lucky break. It gave him more time to prepare.

A month earlier Romanek and his platoon moved out of the Payton area in England to meet the 29th Division in Dorchester. Leaving wasn't easy. For six months Romanek had lived in the St. Ann's Hotel in Payton, a place he'd grown to adore. Most of the local men were all off fighting in the war, and the women who were left behind showed open-armed hospitality to Romanek and all of his boys. Many of the soldiers in Romanek's platoon were quartered in the houses of locals, and Romanek would frequently stop in to see how everything was going. There, he'd play with kids and often was treated to a home-cooked meal. When Romanek and his platoon gathered up their gear for the last time and prepared to board a transport ship for Dorchester, the entire town of Payton turned out to say good-bye. For Romanek, it was like leaving family all over again.

Once Romanek and his platoon arrived in Dorchester, they drove on trucks into a massive camp that was enclosed with barbed wire. Soon after, the camp was locked down. On June 3, Romanek was summoned into a large tent. In it, a few sand tables were set up. On these tables every detail of the invasion was plotted. After being briefed on the invasion by superiors, Romanek called his men into the tent and explained exactly what they were going to do.

In the early morning of June 5, Romanek and his platoon were riding on the U.S.S. *Garfield*, an assault transport ship, when they were told that the invasion had been postponed. They were just hours away from going over the side of the ship and onto their landing craft, but now they were told to stand down for 24 hours. Romanek, like most of the young men he was with, enjoyed this extra day of peace. But this momentary reprieve also brought one hazard: it meant more time for reflection, more time to think about how June 5 might be his last full day of life.

Eisenhower awoke at about 3:30 in the morning on June 6. He drove from his trailer to Southwick House, located outside of Portsmouth on the south coast of England. This was the naval headquarters and Eisenhower first made his way to the mess hall. He was given a hot cup of coffee, but it did little to warm his spirits. Southwick House was shaking because of the stormy conditions outside. Eisenhower paced the room. Then Captain J. M. Stagg arrived with an updated weather forecast for Normandy. "I'll give you some good news," Stagg said. He then went on to tell the Supreme Commander that he was confident that the storm would break before dawn. All indications pointed to that, Stagg explained. For nearly a minute, Eisenhower silently considered the news as he paced around the room. Then he looked up and said quietly but firmly, "Okay, let's go."

17

OMAHA BEACH

HER BATTLE FLAGS FLAPPING in the wind, the U.S.S. *Texas* plowed through the rough seas, one of five thousand vessels motoring from England to the coast of France, pushing toward their date with destiny. The ships were ten lanes wide, stretching twenty miles across. Among these vessels were six battleships—three American, three British. The invasion planners expected to lose one or two of these battlewagons in the hours ahead, maybe more. The battleships would not only spray the beach with shells, but they would also draw the Germans' heavy firepower to them and away from the soldiers approaching the beach. Along with the U.S.S. *Arkansas*, the *Texas* was to unload her 14 inch guns about 10 miles off the shore of Omaha. The *Texas* was to fire on both Point du Hoc—where several German coastal batteries were located—and on enemy strong points defending the beach exits.

Now William Leahy stood on the deck of the *Texas*, a creaky ship that navy men called the Old Lady. Commissioned in 1914, the *Texas* was the oldest battleship in the U.S. fleet. Leahy started to walk along the deck and could see, splashing in the moonlight, the white tops of the waves smashing against the other ships as they pushed southward across the English Channel. As Leahy continued to walk, his mind raced. The ship boasted ten 14 inch guns, and Lehey, from his position in the crow's nest, would help direct the shore bombardment. Silently, he reviewed his orders: The *Texas* was not supposed to fire until 5:50 A.M. unless fired on. The first wave of infantry was scheduled to hit Omaha at 6:30. Just before that, the *Texas* would raise her guns and aim at targets farther inland.

Time ticked on. As the armada closed in on the coast of France, men on every ship wrote last-minute letters, frantically telling their loved ones how much they cared for them. Others played cards and tried to keep the mood light. Some huddled with chaplains, praying for strength and safety. The men who loved to read now tried to lose themselves in paperbacks that they carried in their back pocket. And many men just talked, confiding with each other. In many cases men who had just met began telling each other their most intimate secrets. But more than anything, all the men just waited . . . and waited . . . and waited for dawn.

Time continued to move. The *Texas* and the other ships came to a halt around two in the morning, about 10 miles off the five beaches of Normandy. Now the vessels bristled with activity. Chains clanked and rattled in the davits as assault boats were lowered into the water. Small patrol boats, their engines droning, zipped around from landing craft to landing craft. Announcements blared over the ships' PA systems: "Fight to get your troops ashore," one message roared. "Fight to save your ships and, if you've got any strength left, fight to save yourself!"

As men like Henry Romanek—who was aboard the U.S.S. *Garfield*— waited to climb down the nets and into the landing crafts that bobbed in the rolling sea, many exchanged home phone numbers and addresses, promising that they would contact each other's loved ones if they didn't survive the day. "Just in case," many of the men would say as they handed over a piece of paper with their information. Officers on every ship gave their final pep talks, imploring their men to be brave, telling them that the eyes of history were now focused on their every move.

Leahy climbed to his position in the U.S.S. *Texas*'s crow's nest, a perch about 150 feet above the ship's deck. As he looked down on all the action, it seemed as if an entire city was afloat in his field of view, humming with movement and bouncing up and down in the undulating waves. Leahy carefully watched the men load into their landing crafts, not knowing if he'd see any of them again.

The hands of the clock kept moving. At just after 5:20 in the morning, with the first waves of LCMs now headed for the beach, light started to rise, ever so faintly, over the eastern horizon. Minutes later, through his binoculars, Leahy could see the misty shores of Normandy. The beach appeared peaceful and quiet in the gray light of dawn, a place—Leahy thought—that would be perfect to take his girl on a romantic stroll. But at 5:35, as Leahy continued to inspect the beach with his binoculars, he saw movement at several shore batteries. "They're getting ready to fire," yelled Leahy. Realizing that he was under strict order not to fire unless fired upon, Leahy quickly phoned the captain. He explained that the Germans were about to attack the *Texas*, which was at anchor for fear of hitting a mine in the area. Leahy insisted that the *Texas* should fire first—the very first shot of this bloody day. "Hold your fire," the Captain told Leahy. "Repeat, hold your fire."

Just then, Leahy saw two shells whizzing toward the *Texas* out of the mist. "Brace yourself," Leahy yelled. The shells fell short of the *Texas* and exploded in the sea, causing a geyser of water to shoot upward. In seconds, Leahy then issued what he thought were the coordinates of the shore battery that had just targeted the *Texas* and gave the order to fire. Through his binoculars, Leahy tracked the shells as they streaked through the early-morning light. They exploded into the cliffs of Omaha Beach, causing chunks of the cliff to fall into the sea. A few Germans flew into the air as the shells dug a crater into the cliff.

Ernest Hemingway, a correspondent for *Colliers* magazine, was riding in a landing craft toward the beach when the *Texas* opened fire. He later wrote that the shells from the *Texas* "sounded as though they were throwing whole railway trains across the sky." He added, "Those of our troops who were not wax gray with seasickness were watching the *Texas* with looks of surprise and happiness. Under the steel helmets [the troops] looked like pikemen of the Middle Ages to whose aid in battle had suddenly come some strange and unbelievable monster."

By 5:50 A.M., fifteen minutes after the great battle had begun, enough light filled the sky that spotter planes began relaying information to Leahy on the accuracy of the *Texas's* shelling. He was told that several of the pillboxes up on the cliffs had been hit, but were still operational. The shells had left indentations and pockmarks on the concrete pillboxes, exposing their steel reinforcing rods, but still the guns up on the hundred-foot high sheer cliffs thundered and continued to fire. The 14 inch shells weren't penetrating the pillboxes. They had rendered many of the Germans inside the pillboxes deaf, but they hadn't silenced the gunfire.

Every time the *Texas* was targeted, it appeared to Leahy and the other officers in the crow's nest that the enemy shells were headed directly at their perch. "Sir, we're going to take a hit any second now," one of the officers said to Leahy. "Sir, I, I, . . ."

"Don't worry," replied Leahy. "It's going to take an almost perfect shot to get us up here. And hey, it's better to be up here than down below. Down there it's a much wider target!"

Using the single spire of the church at Vierville as his main marker, Leahy continued to give the coordinates of where he thought the German machine gun fire was coming from. "I'm killing hundreds," Leahy thought to himself. "Better those bastards than us."

The guns of the *Texas* kept firing. Sailors watered down the hot barrels with hoses. Leahy stuffed cotton in his ears and shouted the command to fire over and over, hoping to take out as many shore batteries as possible and pave the way for the boys who were now closing in on the beach.

At 6:15 the Texas turned her 14 inch guns on the exit road D-1 on the western end of Omaha Beach. Fifteen minutes later, at H-hour (the hour the operation was to begin), the *Texas* lifted her guns and aimed at targets beyond the beach. The first wave of men from the free societies of the world was about to hit the beach. Minutes later, Leahy, still standing in the crow's nest, couldn't believe what he was seeing through his binoculars: The beach, which just moments earlier had seemed so tranquil, was now a slaughterhouse.

As the landing craft that Henry Romanek rode in started to slow about 50 yards off of Omaha Beach, German soldiers on the bluff pointed their machine guns in the LCM's direction. Bullets began clanking off the metal sides of craft—*ping, ping, ping*—as the square-faced ramp came down. Romanek stood in the back of the LCM with the rest of the engineers; the infantrymen were in front. When the ramp was lowered, men started to push forward, yelling, "Go, go, go." But the machine gunners on the bluff had drawn a bead on the LCM's exit ramp. Before the first American solider in the LCM even hit the water, dozens of men simply fell forward, instantly rendered limp and lifeless. Blood splattered and spit through the air. Suddenly, there was nowhere to hide.

Romanek kept pushing his men forward. He and his engineers were supposed to erect beach panel markers on Omaha exit D-3 that would act as guideposts for approach landing crafts. They had spent months training for these next few minutes, but now they couldn't even get off their landing craft. Romanek yelled to his men. "We gotta get outta here," he screamed. "Keep moving."

Soldiers in front of Romanek kept falling like tall blades of grass being mowed down. Still he told his men to storm the beach. "We're going to do this," he yelled. Finally Romanek reached the ramp exit. He handed a polelike casing that held a beach panel marker to one of men and then jumped into the water. Yet just as he splashed into the sea, a bullet sliced through his chest. As he floated in five feet of water, with his mind wandering back to those glorious days when he was a West Point football player, a medic on the beach saw him struggling to breath.

Wearing a Red Cross armband, the medic sprinted into the water and swam to Romanek. All the medics on Omaha were told that their main job was to pull the wounded to safety. In most cases once the medic reached the wounded he would conduct a brief examination, evaluate the wound, apply a tourniquet if necessary, clean the wound, sprinkle sulfa powder on the wound and bandage it. Then he would drag or carry the soldier out of harm's way.

The medic reached Romanek, pulled him out of the water, dragging him past bodies that washed back and forth in the surf, and moved him behind a metal beach obstacle that was the shape of an X. "I'm going to drag you on your back over the beach—help push with your feet," the media yelled to Romanek. Too weak to talk, Romanek nodded.

Keeping his head down, the corpsman grabbed Romanek by his right arm and dragged him from one beach obstacle to the next. When Romanek looked back at the water, he could see hulks from landing crafts now burning in the water. On the beach equipment was strewn everywhere. Radios, field telephones, helmets, canteens, gas masks, life preservers—they were washing up with the rising tide. In the distance Romanek could see tanks ablaze in the water, black smoke pouring out of them. And with every crashing wave, another bloody body seemed to turn up at the water line.

The corpsman kept pulling Romanek. He had no other choice, because staying on the beach meant signing your own death warrant. Romanek tried to push with his feet and move his body as the corpsman dragged him, but his strength was gone. When they reached the shingle—which was the first rise in the terrain on the beach and was about five feet high—they joined about twenty other men, most of whom were wounded, some on their last breath. Romanek tried to stay alert and keep his eyes open, but then everything went dark. His body started rattling as if he were suffering from an internal earthquake. He slipped into shock.

From the cockpit of his P-38, Robin Olds could see that American boys were pinned underneath the shingle. All morning long he expected to engage German fighter planes, but they never appeared. In the previous months British and American fighters had driven the German Luftwaffe out of France. Olds and everyone else in his squadron believed the Luftwaffe would try to repel the D-day invasion and add to the congestion of the beach, but it never showed. (Of the 5,409 Allied fighter planes that participated in the D-day invasion, not a single one was shot down by the Luftwaffe.) So Olds just flew at 500 feet back and forth over the beach in a grid pattern.

Some ten hours earlier, on the eve of the D-day invasion, Olds and the other pilots of the 434th Fighter Squadron of the 479th Fighter Group were summoned to a briefing room at their base in Suffolk, England. "The invasion is on," the commander told the pilots. The commander then went over their orders, stressing that they were not to fire at anything on the ground. After the commander was finished, Olds approached him and volunteered to fly on the first mission in the morning. When a few other pilots also volunteered, Olds offered to fight them for it fist to fist. "Nobody wants this more than me and we can settle it outside if you want," Olds told his flyboy buddies.

But now that he was above Omaha Beach, Olds' frustration grew by the minute, unable to help his brothers on the beach. When he looked down through the smoke and dust that billowed up from the battle, he could see men jumping out of their landing craft and splashing into the water. Many landing craft had been capsized; others exploded right before Olds' eyes. When the German batteries thundered from the coastline, the vibrations of the blasts sometimes caused the wings of his P-38 to vibrate. Olds desperately wanted to strafe the beach—when he looked down, he had no problem discerning the Germans from the Americans—but because the Americans didn't have any air-to-ground communication, the invasion planners had decided that the P-38s wouldn't target anything on the beach. Yet now Olds could see that the action on the beach wasn't going well. He figured that Romanek was down there somewhere; maybe he was even flying directly over him. Olds hoped to God that his buddy was okay.

Romanek opened his eyes. Everything was blurry, like he was underwater. The arms of the corpsman were wrapped tightly around him. The corpsman had warmed Romanek and now Romanek regained consciousness. Wiping his eyes, Romanek looked back at the beach. No, he hadn't been dreaming: Dead men littered the sand. The corpsman spoke to Romanek. "I'll give you some morphine and then I'll look at your wound," he said.

The corpsman carried a combat compressor. He peeled back Romanek's clothing and found a hole in his back. He cleaned the wound as best he could with water and sulfa powder, then put a compressor on both holes, temporarily stopping the bleeding.

The corpsman left and then returned moments later with a canteen full of water, which he handed to Romanek. He also gave Romanek twelve sulfa pills, which the corpsman hoped would stave off any infection. "Take one of these every four hours," the corpsman told Romanek.

"I don't know if I'm going to be around every four hours," replied Romanek. "Maybe I can fight off the infection if I take them all right now," which was what Romanek did.

Before the corpsman left to attend to other wounded men, Romanek asked, "Hey, what's your name?"

"Smitty," he replied.

"Where you from?"

"Raleigh."

"That's nice," replied Romanek. "My wife is from North Carolina and she . . ."

Before Romanek could finish, the corpsman was gone, headed back to the beach.

The tide continued to roll in. It was about 9:30 A.M. Fatigue washed over Romanek like a morning shower as he lay on the rough shingle rocks and looked back at the beach. The sight of the massacre, which was unfolding two hundred yards from Romanek's position, caused his heart to sink. As he watched soldiers drop and scream and cry for help, Romanek thought of General Omar Bradley, the head of the U.S. First Army, and the words he had delivered to the 29th Infantry Division a few days before D-day.

"You're going to go in there and this is what you're going to do," Bradley said firmly. "Nobody is going to surrender. If you're wounded and you have ammo, you will fight until you die. No one will need to surrender because you will not be deserted on the beach. I promise you, you will not be deserted on the beach."

As he looked out at the landing crafts continuing to roll ashore, Romanek realized that Bradley hadn't lied. Thousands were going to die, but Romanek knew he was not going to be deserted and forgotten on the beach.

In the moments when the Germans weren't firing from the positions up on the bluff, Romanek could often hear them talking. Their voices carried in the wind, traveling down the bluff to Romanek's ears. But then, just as quickly as the voices could be heard, they'd be drowned out by the noise of the battle. There was naval gunfire, artillery, small arms, mortor fire, aircraft overhead, the shouts and cries of the wounded—it was hard to think, there was so much noise.

For the rest of the morning and throughout the afternoon, Romanek watched the struggle to storm the beach through the smoke, dust, and mist that rose from the battlefield. Though he was as tired as he'd ever been and seriously injured, Romanek didn't allow himself to sleep. If he did, he figured he might not ever wake up. So he let his eyes focus on the destruction and devastation taking place just two hundred meters away. As he looked on with sadness, he guessed the life expectancy for most of the men hitting the beach was about two minutes.

When darkness started falling, the sounds of battle began to fade. Naval gunfire, tanks, and infantry had disabled most of the German pillboxes on the bluff. But many German snipers lurked on the cliffs, and nearly every time a shot rang out in the night a wounded man near Romanek would shriek in terror. As far as Romanek could tell, there were no able-bodied American soldiers in his vicinity. Many of the soldiers were despondent and babbling incoherently. Others sat in silence and smoked cigarettes, the red glow of the ash illuminating their tired faces, while others still talked bravely of how they were going to survive this bloody day and seek vengeance.

All around Romanek the beach was dotted with debris. Guns, canteens, helmets, packs, gas masks, packs of cigarettes, a guitar—they all rolled back and forth in the tide. And late in the evening, Romanek could once again hear German voices rising into the cool night air. He detected mess kits clanking as the Germans up on the bluff ate dinner. They were so close—too close.

Romanek didn't close his eyes for more than a few minutes during the night, still afraid that if he fell into a deep sleep he'd never wake up. And on this endless night, in the faint light of the rising moon, one boy after the next who lay near Romanek lost his life. Romanek dug into the sand as best he could and braced for the night.

Just after daybreak, the shingle became secure. Twenty-four hours had passed since Romanek had landed on the beach, and now, finally, it was under Allied control. Later in the morning Romanek's company commander was searching up and down the beach for his men when he found Romanek. "You're still alive," he told Romanek. "Excellent work, solider."

After being placed on a stretcher, Romanek was transported by jeep to an open beach area where landing craft were dropping off and loading troops. Romanek was taken out to an LST (Landing Ship Tank) that was unloading part of the 29th Infantry Division and an anti-tank company. As the soldiers exited the LST, they saw Romanek and hundreds of other half-living soldiers being hauled up the side onto the ship, which would carry the wounded back to England. As Romanek peered into the eyes of the men who were looking at his bloodied body, he saw that they were petrified. Yet Romanek didn't notice one man hesitate, even for a moment, to move forward with his mission. This was heroism, Romanek thought, because they knew exactly what kind of hell awaited them. Seeing these American boys brought tears to his eyes; after a few moments, his eyes started leaking like little waterfalls.

The next day, June 8, a navy medical corpsman named James C. Smith—serial number 08334787—was killed on Omaha Beach. The man who had saved so many unknown soldiers, including Romanek, could not be saved himself.

18

THE FIELD OF COMBAT

THE LINE OF AMBULANCES seemed to stretch for miles, deep into the drizzly English countryside. They were the first things Henry Romanek, through his groggy eyes, spotted late in the afternoon of June 7, 1944, when his transport ship reached the beach in England. When the ship's unloading ramp opened, Romanek, prone on a stretcher, noticed hundreds of ambulances preparing to ferry the wounded from Normandy to a train, which would carry the soldiers to a makeshift military hospital located outside Oxford in the fields of Cheltenham. Even in his sleep- and blood-deprived state, Romanek was stunned by the number of ambulances, all in a line that snaked for as far as he could see.

The trains to the hospital were full of mangled soldiers. They lay on stretchers, and the moaning and groaning of the wounded filled the cars. Men drifted in and out of sanity as quickly as a hiccup. Some boys thought they were back home with their buddies and sitting at the counter of a soda shop, while others believed that they were standing in the white light of heaven. It was a long train ride, over three hours, and midway through it Romanek was overcome with blinding pain. He quickly called for one of the white-uniformed nurses to come to his side. "Nurse, can you please give me some more morphine," he begged the nurse in his car. "I feel like I'm going to die."

"Of course," the nurse replied, as she left to get more medicine.

But that night, once Romanek had made it to the section of the hospital that housed those with head-and-chest wounds, the pain returned. It was unlike anything he'd ever experienced before, a sharp, stabbing pain. Though Romanek was an officer, he had been accidentally transported to an overcrowded enlisted ward and now his bed didn't even have a mattress. Instead, he laid on a covered box spring, and to Romanek it felt as if every spring was a knife being twisted into his back. "I'm dying," Romanek told a nurse in his hoarse voice. "Please give me some more morphine."

"You'll just have to grit your teeth, soldier," she replied. "If I give you any more morphine, you'll have the morphine habit."

The nurse then read Romanek's tags and realized that he had been placed in the wrong unit. He was transferred to an officers' ward and was given a bed that had a mattress. Romanek thought he had reached paradise. Later that night a doctor visited Romanek. His name was Major White.

"How long have you been in the Army, Doc?" Romanek asked.

"They drafted me in March," replied Major White. "Then they taught me to salute, gave me a uniform, put me on an airplane, and I got here in May."

"Where were you working before?" asked Romanek.

"In Boston General Hospital," he replied. "I was the chief chest surgeon there."

"Well, I guess I'm in good hands," said Romanek. "Go ahead and fix me up."

The bullet that hit Romanek didn't stay in his body; it had exited through his back, leaving a hole two-inches in diameter. "We're not going to operate," the doctor told Romanek. "We're going to patch you on your chest and back and we'll put a tube in your back to drain your lungs. You should be outta here in a few months."

It was the best news Romanek could have hoped for. Now he had to wait and heal. But as he convalesced, his mind wandered back to the battle. More than anything, he wanted to know if his boys were all right.

When the fighting was finally over on the shores of Normandy, William Leahy and several members of the U.S.S. *Texas* boarded small transports and went to inspect Omaha Beach on a clear mid-June morning. They wanted to determine how effective—and how accurate—their shelling had been during the invasion. But once Leahy hopped out of the transport and started walking on the sand, it was difficult to focus on anything other than the total destruction of the area. The beach and the bluff were still littered with dead Allied and German soldiers and with body parts that would never be matched to the soldier they belonged to. As Leahy walked around in the eerie quiet of the morning, with the soothing sound of waves crashing onto the shore, it was hard to fathom that so much death had taken place here, on this beautiful, once peaceful beach in France. Leahy couldn't even hazard a guess as to how many had died, or how many he had a hand in killing.

After two hours of examining the area, Leahy and his shipmates prepared to return to the U.S.S. *Texas*. They hadn't been as accurate with their shelling as they initially thought, but they all took solace in one simple fact: The invasion was over, and it was they—not the Germans—who had claimed this blood-stained beach.

19

THE UNFRIENDLY SKIES

THE VOICE BOOMED through the pilots' living quarters, imploring the men to wake up. Robin Olds popped his eyes open, suddenly awake and alert, his heart pounding. In the darkness he looked at his watch: 4:05 A.M. It was August 14, 1944. A little more than two months had passed since the landings at Normandy—the Allies were now marching toward Paris— and Olds was based in Suffolk, England with the 434th Fighter Squadron of the 479th Fighter Group. After wiping the sleep from his eyes, Olds dressed quickly and walked to the debriefing room, where he was promptly handed his order of the day: The 479th was to bomb a bridge at Chalons Sur Saons, in Eastern France. They were to leave immediately, even though the sun wouldn't be rising for two hours. "For Christ's sake," Olds said to a fellow pilot, "this'll be impossible to do in the dark."

Grabbing his flight gear, Olds walked out to his P-38 Lightning. As his plane sat in the moonlight, Olds couldn't help but marvel at it. The German Luftwaffe had taken to calling the P-38 the "Der Gabelschwanz Teufel," the Fork-Tailed Devil, the nickname stemming from the plane's twin-boom design. The Lightning represented a breakaway from con- ventional airframe design, power, and armament. The cockpit sat in the middle of the main wing. On each side of the cockpit were the engines in front of what looked like two missiles attached to the wing that were the booms. These were fixed together by the rudder in the rear. Not only did the plane have twice the power and almost twice the size of its predecessors, but it also had four .50 caliber machine guns plus a 20 mm cannon. The guns were concentrated in the central fuselage pod, which made it easier for the pilot to line up his targets. The concentration of firepower in the Lightning's nose was so effective that a one-second burst of shots could destroy an enemy plane.

Possessing droppable fuel tanks under its wings, the P-38 was used extensively as a long-range escort fighter. A versatile aircraft, the Lightning was also used for dive bombing, level bombing, ground strafing, and photo reconnaissance missions. It had a span of 52 feet, a length of 37 feet 10 inches, a height of 12 feet 10 inches, and a loaded weight of 17,500 pounds. Its maximum speed was 414 mph, its cruising speed was 275 mph, and it had a range of 1,100 miles. It was, to Olds, a beautiful aircraft, and as he climbed aboard in the still dark morning, he felt as comfortable in the Lightning as he did in his bed back home.

Olds eased into the cockpit and slipped on his aviator goggles. He taxied down the base runway, the last in line of the 434th to take off. As he waited for his turn, a pilot in another squadron, unable to see the runway clearly, had run off it and was stuck in mud. Only one full squadron and half of another—or about twenty-four planes—were airborne when Olds received word over the radio that his squadron was being called back, that they had been "scrubbed" from the mission. But Olds and his wingman were already taxiing down a different runway when this order came over the radio, and they decided to pretend that they didn't hear the directive to return to base. They made a split-second decision to go for it, to take off into the night and join the other P-38s already in the air.

Olds was desperate to see some action, and even though it appeared that this mission wouldn't involve any dogfights with the Germans, he still pressed forward, anxious to blow up the bridge. For weeks Olds had been studying intelligence maps that depicted key German targets. Olds was blessed with a photographic memory and these maps were etched into his mind so vividly that he felt he could find the target with his eyes closed. But now as he rolled down the runway, Olds noticed that another P-38 was disabled, this one about one thousand feet directly in front of him. Olds yelled over the radio to his wingman in another plane, "Pull up!" and they both did. Olds and his wingman cleared the P-38, but when

Olds had reached five hundred feet, he couldn't find his wingman anywhere. Olds quickly determined that he'd become disoriented in the darkness, and was hopelessly lost.

"To hell with it," thought Olds to himself. "I've got a couple five-hundred-pound bombs on me. I'm going for the damn bridge."

Without giving it a second thought, Olds set a course for his target. First he coasted out near Dover. Then on over Callais; then Soissons. Every so often Olds would hear chatter from the other squadron over his radio; they seemed confident that they knew exactly where they were going. But as Olds drew closer to the bridge, the tone of the chatter started to change. Eventually he heard one pilot utter, "Sir, we can't find the bridge"—a statement that Olds heard repeated several times. About 5 minutes before Olds thought he'd be over his target, he heard the pilots from the other squadron confess that they were lost. "Let's head back," Olds heard the pilots tell each other. Though he knew he'd be flying alone, Olds stayed the course, wanting to hit this bridge as much as Ahab wanted to bag Moby Dick.

Olds got closer. Dawn slowly began to break. There was just enough light in the sky that, down on the ground, Olds could see a river; it glistened silver-gold in the pale light. Seconds later, he could see the bridge clearly, sitting there like a cobweb waiting to be brushed aside. With a wicked smile on his face, Olds dove, his P-38 whistling through the air, and made his run over the bridge. He had a perfect view of the structure. "Could it really be *this* easy?" he thought to himself as he unleashed both of his five-hundred-pound bombs. Seconds later, he felt an explosion. Olds couldn't see it for himself, but the bridge had crumbled into the river. Mission accomplished.

As Olds cruised back across France, he enjoyed the sunrise. Purposely flying low at one hundred feet, Olds gazed down at the countryside. He saw poplar trees lining the dirt roads. He spotted old farmhouses that reminded him of a Van Gogh painting. And he noticed vineyards that were spread over rolling hills. It all seemed so peaceful, the scenery on this lazy flight home.

But then, suddenly, the tranquility of the moment was dashed. About a half mile in front of him, Olds noticed two specks, like flies on a windshield. His pulse quickened. "God, I hope they're Germans," Olds said to himself. Olds hadn't been engaged in any one-on-one combat yet, and the prospect of a fight excited him. He couldn't wait to test himself. He wanted to see for himself if all those hours that he spent flying up and down the Hudson River Valley would pay off.

The two German pilots didn't see Olds coming, so Olds was able to intercept them. When he got close enough to have a good look at the planes, he determined that they were a pair of German FW-190 fighters. When Olds jumped them from behind, he lined up the wingman in his sights, then pressed the trigger on the stick and fired his guns. As the bullets spit out of the P-38, Olds let out a primal roar, and the German wingman's plane burst into a ball of orange flames. Black smoke poured out of the engines. The pilot then bailed out, and Olds saw his parachute open in the blue morning sky as the pilot floated down into the countryside. He was still alive. "That's one," Olds said aloud.

The lead fighter, realizing that Olds was now hot on his tail, broke off. Minutes later, after some deft dogfight flying, Olds had a clean shot at the lead fighter. He plugged him as well, the shots causing a stream of smoke to shoot out from the German plane. His aircraft badly damaged, the Luftwaffe pilot bailed, and the plane crashed not more than 150 feet from the other downed plane.

After his second kill, Olds circled back over the area where the second plane had gone down. Flying slow at about one hundred feet, Olds could clearly see the smoldering wreckage in the distance as he approached. But as he neared the flaring fire of the crash, he spotted a surprising sight. The pilot had landed within two hundred yards of his aircraft in a ploughed field, and now was standing there looking up into the sky at Olds. Seeing Olds approaching, the pilot dove face down in the mud. Olds, with the slyest of grins on his face, pointed his P-38 in his direction. Just as he was about to pass over the pilot at an altitude of fifty feet, Olds pulled into a victory roll and wiggled his wings—his way of saying good-bye to his German counterpart; and serving him a dose of his dust.

Later that night at the base officers' club, as Cole Porter tunes floated up from the juke box, Olds told his flyboys about the morning's events. Knocking back a glass full of scotch, Olds' story held everyone's attention. Olds could always fill up a room just with his presence, and now his words captivated even the bartender. "This is just the beginning boys," Olds told his fellow pilots. "The biggest fights for us are yet to come."

Eleven days later, on the morning of August 25, Olds and his fighter group were once again summoned early in the morning and given their order of the day. For the first time, the 479th was told to perform a sweep to Berlin. This meant that they would sweep in front of Allied bombers. If any enemy planes got in their way, the 479th would take them out.

At the day's first light, Olds and his squadron took off from Suffolk, England, all the pilots excited at the possibility of an approaching dogfight. Once in the air, they assembled into a "spread" formation, meaning that the group covered more sky than usual. A captain now and a flight leader, Olds was flying in what was called Newcross Squadron, and he positioned his plane to the far left of the rest of the group and a thousand feet higher. For the first 30 minutes, the skies were clear. Then, a few miles south of Muritzee, Germany, Olds' number three man called him and said, "Bogies at the 10:30 level." Olds verified the enemy planes, flying at about 27,000 feet, with his own eyes and radioed Colonel Hub Zemke, the leader of the group, and said, "Highway (Zemke's call sign)—bogies, 1030, level. Headed north. Okay if I check them out?"

As Olds waited for a response, a few more enemy planes appeared in his field of view. They were headed for the bombers that the 479th was scheduled to pick up. Olds still couldn't see the Allied bombers in the distance, but he knew that they were out there, and that the Germans were going after them. Finally he heard back from Zemke.

"Newcross Blue Flight," Zemke called out to Olds. "Take it left, buster."

Olds didn't need to be told twice. He was already closing on the enemy gaggle. He and three other pilots poured the coal to their engines, pushing their throttles all the way down. But soon two of the planes experienced engine problems and had to break away. Olds' number one man, B. E. Hollister, sat on his wing, high to his right. They closed in on the enemy and soon they realized it was more than just a few bogies. Upon closer inspection, they counted fifty-five enemy aircraft, all heading for the bomber force. The bogies were several thousand feet higher than Olds and Hollister, and it appeared that not one of the Germans had spotted the Americans. In the distance, Olds could see the white contrails that streamed off the bombers' engines. Behind him he couldn't see any members of his Fighter Group; they had disappeared from eyeshot. It was two against fifty-five, but Olds and his number two man continued to close. Olds knew that the bombers wouldn't have a chance if he and Hollister retreated.

They got closer. Olds then remembered his droppable fuel tanks. To increase his speed, he released the two 165-gallon tanks that were located under his wings. As the tanks fell through the sky, Olds' P-38 leapt and accelerated. He rode up closer and closer behind the outside right member of the enemy V-formation. Olds and Hollister both prayed that the

Germans wouldn't look behind them under their bellies—they would have spotted the Americans clearly—as they prepared to fire. "Make the first shot count," Olds told Hollister, "because all hell will break loose right after that."

Olds lined up a bogie in his sight; he was so close that the wings of the enemy aircraft spanned the reticule. Olds began to squeeze the trigger on his right hand grip. But just as he did, both of his engines sputtered and quit. They coughed again, then quit a second time. "Holy shit," Olds yelled to himself. "I forgot to switch tanks!"

When Olds had jettisoned his drop tanks, he'd forgotten to switch the fuel line. Now his engines had run dry. He quickly switched the fuel line and, never taking his eye off his target, pulled the trigger and fired on the German Me 109 while in glide mode. The enemy plane quickly caught fire and dove off on his right wing. Olds saw the pilot bail.

Olds' plane was still gliding. In a matter of seconds, though, the engines started sputtering again, and caught. Olds and Hollister peeled back, unsure of how the other German 109s would react. But the Germans were at a disadvantage: They didn't know how many P-38s were attacking them or where they were coming from. This uncertainty caused them to break their formation and scuttle their plan of going after the Allied bombers.

But before the Germans turned back, several of the 109s spotted Olds and Hollister. After a few adept dives and twists and turns, Olds had another German plane lined up in his sights. He fired his 20 mm cannon and peppered the plane with .50 caliber bullets. The enemy fighter rolled, inverted, and with smoke pluming out of his cockpit, the pilot jumped just before the plane slammed into earth. It was kill number two for the day—and number four in Olds' brief World War II experience.

In the middle of this dogfight, which took place at about fifteen thousand feet, Olds had seen a German plane attacking an American P-51 Mustang thousands of feet below. The Mustang was chasing a German 109, but there was another German 109 right on his tail, firing on the American. After seeing the plane he'd just shot down crash to the ground, Olds rolled, inverted, and dove straight down to try to provide aid to the American Mustang as quickly as possible.

Seconds after Olds began to dive, however, he hit compressibility. His P-38 essentially became stuck in the dive. His controls locked and his plane shook so violently that his canopy blew off. A rush of frigid air hit Olds, taking his breath away. He was now at ten thousand feet. By five thousand feet he knew he couldn't bail out; he was going too fast. At twenty-five-hundred feet he pulled back on the control column as hard as he could, hoping that he could force the nose to come up. His plane was still shaking and the cold air continued to blast into his face. But still the nose didn't budge. Olds was plunging straight into the ground.

At one thousand feet, Olds could see that he was going to hit the ground near a farmhouse in the countryside. He continued to pull back on the throttle. At 750 feet a sign of hope: The wings began to creak. The nose slowly started to rise; the denser air was slowing the aircraft enough that it gave Olds a chance to perform a high-G pullout.

Olds was at five hundred feet, still hurtling toward the earth. He could clearly see the trees on the ground, and the leaves rustling in the wind. The nose, ever so slowly, continued to rise. Olds descended to four hundred feet. He could see, down on the ground, the field of wheat he was going to crash into. Still Olds kept pulling back on the controls, pulling so hard that he thought the controls might snap in two. At three hundred feet another sign of hope: The plane began to level off, but was it too late? Olds didn't know, but he kept pulling on the controls like he was trying to pull a lock off a safe. Finally, at an elevation of no more than fifty feet, the plane leveled, and Olds exhaled. He was lower than some of the treetops, but he was still alive.

"I could have been buried on that goddamn farm," Olds thought to himself as he made his way back to England.

With the wind blowing in his face, Olds set a course back to his air base, ready to call it a day. But minutes later, as he was still rehashing in his mind just how close he had come to crashing, gunfire flew over his right wing. "That dirty son of a bitch," Olds yelled. There was another German 109 behind him, his guns blazing. Olds immediately pulled up as hard as he could on his controls and broke left, causing his P-38 to stall, just as he'd hoped. The pilot in the Me 109 overshot Olds' plane. Olds then leveled his wings and fired, yelling as he squeezed the trigger. Almost instantly, the Me 109 burst into flames and rolled over. With black smoke spewing from its engine, the Me 109 hummed straight into the ground. And with that, Olds had five kills under his belt, officially making him an ace.

Olds still had some 450 miles to go to make it back to his base in England. The skies were now clear of Germans, and Olds, for the first time since he'd strapped himself into his cockpit this morning, let himself relax as he buzzed through the blue sky.

· · ·

On his flight home, after coming so close to crashing, Olds recalled some of the good times from his life before the war. He thought about his Army teammates, and wondered where they were now. Was Romanek still alive? How about Hank Mazur, their splendid tailback? Or Ray Murphy, the captain of the '41 squad? Olds hadn't heard if any of his teammates had lost their lives in combat, but he feared some of them had.

As Olds got closer to his base in Suffolk, still flying through clear skies, Olds let himself slip into a reverie. On the grainy film of memory, he replayed the Army-Navy games of '41 and '42, recalling how special those afternoons were. Olds looked forward to the Army-Navy game of '44. Though kickoff of that game was still three months away, Olds was already thinking about how he'd listen to the game over the Armed Forces Network. For those two and a half hours, Olds figured the war would stop—at least for him.

In November of 1944 Army was ranked Number 1 in all the national polls, Navy Number 2. Unlike in '42 and '43, the issue of whether the Army-Navy game should even take place during wartime wasn't debated in the halls of Congress. But House Minority Leader William Martin did have an idea about how the game could help the war effort. He suggested that the purchase of game tickets be tied to the sale of war bonds. Weeks before kickoff President Roosevelt green-lighted the plan, and on December 2, 1944, the two teams squared off at Baltimore's Municipal Stadium.

The ticket prices for the game were the most expensive in the history of football—both college and pro. The prices ranged from $25 to more than $1,000, an unheard of amount for a ticket to any sporting event in the '40s. Before a fan would be handed a ticket, he had to show a war bond purchase receipt for each seat he was buying. Fifteen private boxes on the 50-yard line sold for $1 million apiece. When the gate was eventually tallied, the game wound up raising $58 million to repay the war debt.

The cadets traveled to Baltimore on a steamer that was escorted by five Navy destroyers, who protected the ship from German U-boats that lurked up and down the Atlantic Seaboard. They boarded the navy transport ship *Uruguay* on a Thursday morning, and they cruised into rough waters. Within an hour of leaving land most of the 2,300 cadets on board were seasick, many losing their breakfasts as they leaned over the rails and vomited into the ocean. The Navy team, conversely, merely hopped on a bus in Annapolis and rode 30 minutes into Baltimore.

Never in the history of the Army-Navy game had the two service academies played each other with so much on the line. Army was 8–0; Navy was 6–2. The winner of the game would win the national championship. In three short years the war had helped transform the football teams at the academies into two of the nation's finest. The top high school players in the country were attracted to the academies for one of three reasons: They wanted to become commissioned officers before heading to war; they wanted to avoid the draft; or they just wanted to feel like they were playing for their country. As a result, Army and Navy were able to collect talent during the war as easily as little girls collected dolls. And by the time they faced off in 1944, it was like two all-star teams facing each other.

As in '43, Army was led by backs Felix "Doc" Blanchard and Glenn Davis, both of whom would win the Heisman Trophy (Davis in '44, Blanchard in '45) before their Army careers were done. Davis led the nation in scoring in '44 and had been on the cover of *Life*, *Time*, and *Look* magazines. With Mr. Outside and Mr. Inside paving the way, the Cadets steamrolled through their season, beating North Carolina, 46–0; Brown, 59–7; Pittsburgh, 69–7; and Villanova, 83–0. (Army lost so many footballs on extra-point kicks against Villanova that officials eventually forced the team to go for two-point conversions to conserve pigskins.)

Navy was almost as good. After starting the season slowly at 2–2, they rebounded to shut out three of four opponents and had risen to Number 2 in the AP poll. Two days before the game, Navy assistant coach Rip Miller—the man who had recruited Busik to come play for the Midshipmen five years prior—chatted with reporters as the Middies went through their final practice. "I wonder if people know what this game means to our ten million soldiers and sailors scattered all over the world," said Miller. "It means at least a short relief from the job of killing and being killed."

Indeed, as kickoff approached, soldiers and sailors all around the world huddled around shortwave radios to catch the Armed Forces Network broadcast. Busik and Kauffman, both aboard ships in the South Pacific, gathered with other officers and retold stories from their playing days. Olds was at his base in Suffolk, England, when he tuned in to the action from Baltimore. And Henry Romanek, who had recovered from his D-day injury, was preparing to kill Germans as he listened to the action in a farmhouse in France.

Before the game, wounded war veterans were escorted to seats at midfield. Many hobbled on crutches, some were pushed in wheelchairs. Ambulances filled with wounded soldiers drove along the stadium's cinder track. The ambulance would stop and then a half-dozen soldiers—some missing appendages—would struggle out and be escorted to their seats. Sitting not far from the wounded men was Anna Roosevelt, the daughter of the president, who munched on cold chicken and drank from a thermos filled with hot coffee. It was a cold, clear day in Baltimore—perfect football weather.

After the teams ran onto the field, Ted Gamble, national director of the War Finance Division of the Treasury Department, grabbed a microphone that was linked into the stadium's PA system. He first thanked everyone for coming and supporting the war effort, and then said, "Let's get on with the game—until the Navy goat and the Army mule march together into Tokyo and Berlin." The crowd screamed in approval.

On the other side of the Atlantic Ocean, sitting on a folding chair in the basement of a farmhouse in Normandy, Romanek gathered with a few other West Pointers around a short-wave radio. Five months after being shot on D-Day, Romanek was back in France. He had spent 90 days in a hospital in England recovering from his wound. Once he was healed and released, he rode into Omaha Beach in a landing craft—this time, not a single bullet was shot in his direction—and he assumed command of an engineering company in the 146th battalion. When he first walked on the sands of Omaha, Romanek still had trouble believing that so much horror had occurred right here, and that he had somehow managed to live through it. "I don't know if I'll understand why I'm still around in the world," Romanek told one of sergeants when he reached the beach. "I hope it's because God has something great in store for me."

Now sitting in a farmhouse just off the beach, Romanek regaled the other West Pointers with tales from his past, telling the men all he could remember from the '41 Army-Navy matchup. As kickoff of the '44 game neared, Romanek tuned the radio to the BBC, which was broadcasting the game in Europe. "Boy, if we had had Doc Blanchard on our team in '41, there's no way Navy would have beaten us," Romanek said to the men with excitement in his voice. "That kid is really something special." When the game kicked off, Romanek closed his eyes. He could see the action play out in his mind, in color, in three dimensions.

For the first 30 minutes of the '45 game, the action was back-and-forth. Though undermanned, Navy only trailed 7–0 at halftime. "This is a little too close for me," Romanek said as he and the other men in the farmhouse sipped on scotch as they listened to the game. "Anything can happen when the score is this tight." Just as Romanek settled in to listen to the second half, the BBC interrupted the broadcast. "Ladies and gentlemen, we have inadvertently scheduled the wrong program," a voice said. "We now bring you a piano concerto."

"You gotta be kidding me!" Romanek yelled. "This is crazy."

Romanek wouldn't find out the score for a few days, but the Cadets did pull away late, winning 23–7. The victory gave Army its first-ever national championship. When the final whistle blew, the Cadets stormed onto the field and ripped down the goalposts. Army had lost five straight games to Navy, but now all the pent-up frustration and disappointment was washed away in one glorious victory.

Hours after the game Blaik and the Army players received a telegram from MacArthur, who was engaged in a bloody battle in the Philippines. It read:

"THE GREATEST OF ALL ARMY TEAMS—STOP—WE HAVE STOPPED THE WAR TO CELEBRATE YOUR MAGNIFICENT SUCCESS." — MACARTHUR.

20

THE END

EVERY TIME HE ROSE from his bunk, Jake Laboon rolled through hatches of the submarine like a blown-up balloon from the Macy's Thanksgiving Day parade. Aboard the U.S.S. *Peto*, he was known as the gentle giant who could blot out the sun, and he was constantly ducking and crouching whenever he rumbled from space to space. At 6' 4" and 220 pounds, Laboon had been a star blocker on the 1941 and '42 Navy football team; he mowed through opposing players like a machete through a wheat field. Against Penn in 1941, Laboon had punched a player in the face after the player had taken out Bill Busik with a cheap shot, and the sense of loyalty that drove him to take the swing was still with Laboon. He'd do anything for his brothers—a group that included everyone in the U.S. Army, Navy, and Marine Corps.

After graduating from the naval academy in June of 1943, Laboon was assigned to the *Peto*. Commissioned on November 22, 1941, in Lake Michigan, the *Peto* was the first naval submarine ever constructed on inland waters. In July of 1945 the *Peto* was on her tenth war patrol. She was eight miles off the island of Honshu, on lifeguard patrol; its mission was to pick up any downed Allied pilots. The Japanese had shore batteries set up on the beaches of Honshu, and they filled the sky with gunfire, trying to knock Allied planes out of the air. The batteries also targeted ships and submarines that got too close to the island.

At 2:39 on the afternoon of July 24, the *Peto* received a report from air cover that a "chicken"—a pilot—had gone down four miles off a beach of Honshu. No one on the *Peto* was alarmed by the report. They'd already picked up dozens of pilots without incident.

At first, the routine was like all the others. The *Peto*, which was already surfaced, motored toward the coordinates of the pilot, spotted him, then reeled him in. The entire affair took only seven minutes. But once the pilot, whose name was Lieutenant Clair, climbed aboard the sub, he urgently asked to speak with Captain Caldwell—on the double. "My wingman had to ditch closer to the beach," Clair told the captain. "Can you go after him?"

"What's his position?" asked the captain.

"I can show you exactly," replied Clair.

Grabbing a chart of the area, Clair pointed to the position of his wingman. He was only two miles off the island's coast, meaning that the *Peto* would be an enticing target to the shore batteries if she advanced to the downed pilot's position. The captain, fearing that the *Peto* would draw enemy gunfire, ordered all nonessential topside personnel to get below. The *Peto* then headed for Clair's wingman at full speed.

"He's in pretty shallow water and if those shore guns open up on us we won't be able to dive," the captain told Clair. "But we'll do our best."

When the *Peto* got within five hundred yards of the pilot, the shore batteries started hammering the water that *Peto* was now advancing into. As the submarine crawled forward, the captain told Laboon, who was standing with him on the bridge, "We can't get any closer. We'll have to put a man over the side. We'll have to pick this one up on the fly. I can't risk coming to a dead stop and making the *Peto* a sitting duck. Who's the best swimmer on board, Jake?"

"You don't have to ask for a volunteer, sir," replied Laboon. "You've already got one. I can do it."

Laboon was a transcendent athlete. Though he was known throughout the navy as a former Midshipman football player—in 1942 he earned All Big East honors as a tackle—Laboon had also excelled at lacrosse while in Annapolis. In 1943, his second year on the lacrosse team, he was a starting defenseman on Navy's national championship team and earned second-team

All-America honors. Laboon also was a deeply religious young man. He played the organ every Sunday at a local Catholic Church in Annapolis, and he was the president of the Catholic Midshipmen Organization. His friends often said he was too good to be true.

Laboon didn't hesitate to volunteer. He'd always been a strong swimmer and he was easily the strongest man on the submarine. Being so big made life difficult for Laboon on the *Peto*, but he chose to go into subs after graduating from the naval academy because he wanted to enter the war as quickly as possible. He'd considered becoming a pilot—that's what many of his buddies on the football team had done—but flight school required much more extensive training than submarine service. Like many in the naval academy, Laboon was afraid the war might end before he got a chance to fight, so he picked submarines as his specialty.

Up on the deck of the *Peto*, Laboon grabbed a rope, tied one end around his waist, and handed the other end to a sailor, telling him to hang onto it as if Laboon's life depended on it—which it did. As the *Peto* slowed, the shore batteries continued to fire in her direction. Shells splashed into the water all around him, exploding in loud thuds and sending sprays of water high into the warm South Pacific air. Before Laboon jumped into the mine-infested water, he looked up in the distance and noticed that on the shore of the island a passenger train had stopped on a bridge to let the civilians on board get a glimpse of the unfolding drama. Laboon, with the enemy shells still hurtling in his direction, then dove into the water.

He swam as quickly as he could, performing the breaststroke as he knifed through the cold and choppy water, covering a distance of about two hundred yards. When a shell landed near Laboon, he could feel the explosion thump in his chest. Laboon looked up. In the distance he could see the pilot bobbing up and down in the ocean swells. He put his head back down, and continued to plow through the water. On the submarine, the captain anxiously watched Laboon through binoculars, then looked up at the island, hoping that the Japanese wouldn't hit the sub—or Laboon.

Laboon reached the pilot. He had minor burns and wore a life jacket. He was so fatigued he could barely keep his eyes open, much less swim. As Laboon put his arms around the pilot, telling him that everything would be okay, he thought the pilot looked familiar. There was something about his face, his eyes, that he recognized. But Laboon kept that to himself—there were too many other things to think about right now. He told the pilot to wrap his hands around his waist; Laboon was going to drag him to safety.

Then he swam, paddling through the waters as furiously as he could, back to the submarine. The sailors on the other end of the rope helped reel them in, pulling on the rope fist over fist. The shore batteries continued to fire, each round sending sprays of water into the air. The shelling caused Laboon's adrenaline to surge, to rush through his blood like a stimulant, and he continued to swim, holding the pilot with one hand and pushing forward with the other.

When they finally reached the sub, Laboon was so winded he had trouble breathing. Still, he helped lift the pilot on deck, where a group of sailors grabbed the pilot's arms and carried him to safety. Laboon followed. But just as he struggled up onto the deck, another shell from the shore flew over the *Peto*, whizzing about ten yards over everyone's head. They scrambled below the deck and the sub dove.

As the *Peto* descended, Laboon caught his breath. Sitting on a chair in the wardroom, he took another long look at the pilot, who was being treated for his injuries. Laboon's thoughts traveled back in time—somewhere in his mental Rolodex, that face existed. He remembered being a kid in Pittsburgh. One morning when he was about fourteen he came to the kitchen for breakfast and saw his dad talking on the phone; he was furious. During the night the Laboon family car—it was a '31 Ford—had disappeared from their garage. The police had no idea who took it, but Laboon's father quickly figured out that their paperboy, E. P. Donnelly, had taken the car for a joy ride.

Laboon looked closely at the pilot, studying him up and down. He examined the nametag on his uniform. Improbably, it read: E. P. Donnelly.

Two weeks later, on August 15, Captain Caldwell spoke into the *Peto*'s loudspeaker. "This is the Captain. We have just received official word: The war is over."

The crew let out a collective roar. Men hugged and cried with joy. Soon the men would be going home to daughters, sons, mothers, and fathers. *The war is over.* To everyone on board, these were the four sweetest words they'd ever heard: *The war is over.*

Later that day Laboon cornered Captain Caldwell, saying he had some important news to share. "What would you say, Captain, if I told you that as soon as we get back home I am going to resign from the Navy?"

"You're kidding," replied the Captain.

"You know I'm a Catholic, don't you, Captain?"

"What's being a Catholic have to do with this?"

"Quite a lot, Captain. This patrol has made me realize something. I love the navy, but I want to become a priest."

"Are you sure this isn't a sudden impulse?"

"No, sir."

"Well, I'll be proud to approve your request."

Laboon and the captain then shook hands. The war may have been history, but Laboon was just getting started in the business of saving lives.

The morning of September 2, 1945, dawned overcast and gray in Tokyo Bay. It had been three years, eight months, and twenty-five days since Pearl Harbor had gone up in flames, a stretch of time in which 400,000 Americans had been killed in the world's second great war. But it was all coming to an end now, and Hal Kauffman had a front-row seat at the ceremony that would officially mark the conclusion of this global conflict. Kauffman was a commander now—he had been promoted from ensign shortly after the *Meredith* had sunk. And because of the courage and valor he had displayed during the *Meredith* disaster, he was invited to the U.S.S. *Missouri* to witness this final act of the war.

Less than a month earlier Kauffman had been standing aboard a destroyer as she was making her way toward Tokyo when he saw an enormous mushroom cloud swell high into the sky over the city of Hiroshima. The cloud kept expanding and expanding, growing impossibly big. The sky had been bright and clear over Hiroshima on that August morning, and it was as if a sudden storm raged over the city. Everyone on the destroyer guessed that a great bomb had blown thousands of people straight into eternity. "I'm sure glad I'm not there," Kauffman told a shipmate as they stood on the bridge and watched the cloud expand. "That must have been the biggest bomb in the world."

Forty-eight hours later a second atomic bomb was dropped on the city of Nagasaki. Now, as Kauffman waited on the deck of the U.S.S. *Missouri* for the Japanese delegation to arrive for the surrender ceremony on September 2, rage flowed into him. He couldn't stop thinking about his helpless *Meredith* shipmates; after the ship had gone down, many of his shipmates were killed by Japanese pilots strafing the sea. Kauffman imagined leaping out of his seat and breaking the Japanese foreign minister's neck as soon as he stepped on board. Like all of his Navy football teammates, the war had changed Kauffman. The gruesome reality of conflict had hardened him, making him question the inherent goodness of man. When he was at the academy, Kauffman was a daydreamer; now he only dreamed of going home. "I'd kill every goddamn Jap if I could," Kauffman told a friend a few days before the ceremony. "I know I can't, but it sure would make me feel good to get that much revenge."

Anchored about six miles offshore from the city of Yokosuka, the *Missouri* was chosen by Admiral Chester W. Nimitz as the location for the ceremony, a choice no doubt inspired by the fact that President Truman, who on April 12, 1945 was elevated from Vice President after Roosevelt died, was a Missouri native. More than one hundred ships from the Third Fleet surrounded the *Missouri*, their flags fluttering in the warm breeze. To the west, clouds obscured Mount Fujiyama. On the *Missouri*'s veranda deck an ordinary mess table had been covered with a green baize cloth, and on it rested two sets of surrender documents—one in English, one in Japanese. Two chairs stood on opposite sides of the table. Above the table, hanging on the quarterdeck bulkhead and encased in a black frame, was a tattered American flag with thirty-one stars. This was the very same flag that flew on Commodore Perry's flagship, the *Powhatan*, when he first sailed into Tokyo Bay in 1853, opening up the West's door to Japan. The flag had been at the naval academy's museum—Kauffman had seen it there frequently—but Fleet Admiral William F. Halsey had it flown in to the *Missouri* for this occasion.

Visitors began arriving on the *Missouri* at 7:00 A.M. Within an hour, all the Allied representatives, including Kauffman, were on board. At 8:00 the ship's band played the "Star Spangled Banner" while an American flag, the same one that flew over the Capitol in Washington, D.C., on December 7, 1941, was raised. The ship's superstructure was now jampacked. More than 230 journalists from around the world were on board, and there was precious little space to stand.

At 8:43 General MacArthur arrived. Thirteen minutes later the Japanese delegation, led by Foreign Minister Mamoru Shigemitsu, walked up the gangway and was directed to the table. The ship grew silent. All eleven Japanese delegates squirmed in their uniforms and looked uncomfortable, a fact that pleased Kauffman as he watched the proceedings. Kauffman stood within a stone's throw of the Foreign Minister, so close that he could see the lines on his defeated face. Kauffman had come a long way to arrive at this moment. There was his train ride with Busik across the heart of the country when they were still teenagers. There were the football games, the grueling practices, the camaraderie of the team. It was his football experiences, Kauffman was sure, that had enabled him to survive the horrors of this war. The toughness he learned on the football field had made him a warrior on the battlefield.

At 8:59, MacArthur stepped up to several microphones a few feet from the table. One was hooked into the ship's loudspeaker system; another was piped into a worldwide radio network. MacArthur's voice was deep and serious. "It is my earnest hope, and, indeed, the hope of all mankind, that from this solemn occasion a better world shall emerge out of the blood and carnage of the past, a world dedicated to the dignity of man and the fulfillment of the most cherished wish—for freedom, tolerance, and justice."

MacArthur then motioned the Japanese delegates to step forward and sign the documents. Shigemitsu, fumbling with his silk hat, appeared confused, unsure where to sign. General Richard K. Sutherland then pointed to the appropriate line and, at 9:04, Shigemitsu signed the document and surrendered his country's sovereignty. After that MacArthur signed, carefully drawing out his signature, letter by letter, in a grand fashion. The sun was shining now, and in the bright morning light MacArthur said a few final words. "A way must now be found to preserve the peace, because science has given us war of utter destructiveness," he said. "We have had our last chance. If we do not devise some greater and more equitable system, Armageddon will be at our door."

That afternoon Kauffman went back to his ship. He was tired to the bone, and that night as he lay in his bunk he thought about his wife, of finally seeing her again. The madness was over; it was time to get back to normal life. If he was lucky, he'd make it back to the States in time to see a football game later in the fall, but not just any game: the 1945 Army-Navy clash. Maybe even some of his old buddies would be there—if they were still alive.

In his sleep that night, no ghosts rose to haunt Kauffman. On this night, for the first time in years, all of his ghosts were gone.

21

THE REUNION

THE PRESIDENT ROSE FROM his seat in his midfield box at Philadelphia's Municipal Stadium, and instantly thousands of cameras clicked and flashed to snap his photograph. He waved and smiled gloriously. It was halftime of the 1945 Army-Navy game, and President Harry S. Truman began to walk from the Army side of the stadium to Navy's. As he made his way down to the field, he shook the hands of service men and wounded war veterans who were seated along the sideline. Robin Olds and Henry Romanek were there, and they stretched out their hands like the rest. Olds and Romanek were back in the City of Brotherly Love for an Army-Navy game for the first time since November 29, 1941. It seemed like they were living in a dream, being here on this soft autumn afternoon, so far away from all the bloodshed they had witnessed in the last few years. It was like coming back to life again, being here on a football Saturday, back at this game, this town, this stadium.

On the other side of the field, also sitting on the sideline, was a smattering of navy officers, including Hal Kauffman. He was looking around for former teammates, and he realized that several were missing. Bill Busik hadn't come home yet. He was stationed on a ship just outside of

Sasebo, Japan, helping to clear the waters of mines. Busik listened to the first half of the game on the Armed Forces Network, and it made him think about his last Army-Navy game and all the guys he played with. Of the twenty-two players who started in the '41 Army-Navy game, three had been killed in war-related activities. Army's Tom Farrell, a tackle, was an infantryman who lost his life at Anzio, Italy, on February 25, 1944. One of Farrell's Cadet linemates that day in '41, guard Willard Wilson, was killed in an air training accident in Texas on July 29, 1943. And Navy tackle Bill Chewning still was listed as missing in action aboard the U.S.S. *Corvina*, a submarine that failed to return from patrol on November 30, 1943. He would never be found.

Swede Larson also was gone. Two months after the '41 Army-Navy game, Larson traveled to the Aleutians and led a regiment against the Japanese. He then stayed in the South Pacific and saw action at Tarawa, Kwajalein, and the Marshall Islands. While he was at sea, he wrote his two sons a letter. Dated May 17, 1943, the missive read, "On leaving home to join the Marines in 1917, Dad gave me the following written advice, which I have always carried with me. I pass it on to you as the best guide possible for your conduct and approach to a full life. Be cheerful. Be patient. Obey. Be a man. Trust in God and talk often."

In February of 1944 Larson was ordered to Marine Corps headquarters in Washington. He served there until the war was over. In early November of '45, after he'd already finalized his plans to attend the Army-Navy game in Philadelphia, Larson was watching a football game in Atlanta when he felt his chest tighten. He suffered a massive heart attack and died shortly after at the age of forty-six.

More than a dozen reserve players from that game in '41 also were gone—killed in action—and now, as Kauffman sat in his seat and watched the president slowly stroll toward him, he counted himself lucky that he wasn't listed among the dead. Kauffman felt that he couldn't be any further away from the war than he was at this moment. In front of him on the field a hundred police officers formed two lines, creating a lane of protection for the president as he walked across the field on this cool, sunny afternoon in Philadelphia. Army, the top-ranked team in the nation, led Navy 20–7 at halftime, but very few in the crowd of one hundred thousand cared a whit about the score. This game, more than any Army-Navy game before it, was a celebration of America. And more dignitaries turned out to see this athletic contest than any in the history of sport in the United States.

The stands were a virtual Who's Who of America. Nearly ever member of the president's cabinet was present. So were such giant figures as Generals George C. Marshall, Omar Bradley, Henry (Hap) Arnold, James Doolittle, Jacob L. Devers, and Carl Spaatz. From the Navy side in attendance were Admirals Chester W. Nimitz, William F. (Bull) Halsey, and Ernest J. King. British Air Chief Marshal Sir Arthur Tedder and Fleet Admiral Sir James F. Somerville also were in the stands, sitting in the same vicinity as hordes of senators, representatives, undersecretaries, governors, and even several mayors.

Television viewers in New York and Philadelphia were often shown shots of the dignitaries. For NBC, this was a historical game. For the first time ever, NBC televised a sporting event that took place in one city (Philadelphia) and broadcast it in another (New York). Also for the first time, NBC used its newly developed "image orthicon," a device that enabled NBC's cameras to provide viewers with close-up pictures. The cameras were frequently focused on the president, and viewers were shown several tight shots of the president's face, always caught in an ear-to-ear smile.

Though a biting wind blew around the old horseshoe stadium late in the game, very few left their seats. Led by backs Felix "Doc" Blanchard and Glenn Davis, Mr. Inside and Mr. Outside, Army won the game 32–13 to capture their second-straight national championship. Afterward Coach Blaik, with wet eyes, told reporters in the locker room, "This is the finest team we ever had at West Point, at least in my time. We've got a whale of a football team."

In five years since taking over the program, Blaik had built Army into the greatest football power in the country. The Cadets went 9–0 in '45. A few weeks after the Navy game, Doc Blanchard would win the Heisman Trophy.

Just how dominating were the Cadets? The Newspaper Enterprise Association named Army's entire starting eleven to its 1945 All-America team.

After the game, Olds and Romanek and hundreds of Army officers gathered at the Benjamin Franklin hotel for a party. Held in a ballroom that was decked out in the Army colors of black and gold, Olds and Romanek talked all night long, reliving their glory days as Cadet football players. Dressed in their sharp officer uniforms, they sipped scotch as they shared their stories. Though neither had reserved a room at the hotel, Olds and

Romanek stayed at the party until the sun rose over Philadelphia. They were just so happy to be here, and they didn't want the fun to end. For these men the Army-Navy game was a link to the old days, the prewar days, the last link that many of them had. Everyone in the room understood that today was a new day, and it was almost as if the rest of their lives began at this moment. "You know, I wouldn't have even really cared if we'd lost the game today," Romanek told Olds that night. "It just doesn't seem as important anymore."

That night a similar party was thrown for Navy officers at a ballroom in the Bellevue Stratford Hotel. There, Kauffman joined several former teammates and, like Olds and Romanek, they all reminisced about their time as Midshipmen football players. Late in the evening, after they had quit dancing the jitterbug and bebop and the music had stopped, the '41 game came alive in memory, its details rising again as the former players rehashed the events of November 29, 1941. That seemed so long ago, the teammates agreed. A war had come and gone since then, and the country had changed dramatically in those four years. But tonight, as the teammates toasted their memories and clinked their glasses, they didn't talk about the new America, or how the terrors of war had changed them. Right now all that mattered was that they were together again, safe, happy as schoolboys at recess, and able to do the one thing that each man loved almost as much as his country:

Talk about the game of their lives.

EPILOGUE

BILL BUSIK STEERED HIS CAR through the narrow streets of Annapolis, motoring closer to the spot where his college football career began. It was a brilliant Saturday afternoon in the spring of 2003, and Bill wanted to take me on a tour. We drove through the main gate at the Naval Academy, cruising past dozens of young Midshipmen dressed in their starched-white uniforms, and parked just outside of LeJeune Hall. "I think there's something inside of this building that will interest you," Bill said, winking.

Bill eased out of his car. At eighty-four years of age, his knees were aching, the result of all those hits he took years ago on the football field. He had out-lived his first wife and most of his contemporaries, but still Busik had a luminous, boyish smile. As we walked toward LeJeune Hall, he put one of his big hands on my shoulder and pointed into the distance with the other. "Right over here was where Thompson Stadium used to sit," said Bill. "They tore it down years ago. Boy, I sure had some great times there." Seeing the gleam in his eyes, I realized that Bill wasn't pointing at just any empty swath of land. This was his field of dreams.

We walked up a ramp and into LeJeune Hall. He picked up the pace.

"It's right over here," said Busik, excitedly. We stopped in front of a display case; inside was a black-and-white team photograph of the 1941 Navy squad. Bill examined the photograph like he'd just unearthed it from a time capsule, studying it closely, squinting his eyes. He told me a little bit about every young face captured in the photograph, about how this player had won a Purple Heart in World War II, how that one had died in Korea, how this one was living down the street from him in Annapolis. "This was an amazing group of guys," Bill said, his eyes moistening at all the memories. "They were some of the greatest men I ever knew."

After World War II, Busik served as Intelligence Officer on the Staff of the Commander Mine Force, Pacific Fleet, based at Sasebo, Japan, and took part in the minesweeping operations in the waters off Japan and China. In the summer of 1946 he returned to the Naval Academy to be an assistant football and basketball coach. He was then detached in February 1947 to serve as Executive Officer of the destroyer U.S.S. *Brinkley Bass*. Over the next fifteen years Busik would steadily climb the naval ranks. In June 1960 he assumed command of the U.S.S. *Mahan*. Two years later he was again called back to the Naval Academy, this time to be the school's Athletic Director, a position he held from July 1962 to August 1965. He retired from the Navy on April 1, 1971 after thirty years in the service. Today he lives with his wife in Annapolis, just a few miles from the Academy.

Over the course of several afternoons in 2003, Bill and I sat in his basement office and flipped through his old scrapbooks. The yellowed newspaper clippings would always light a fire in his mind, sparking long-forgotten tales from his time at the Academy. "You learn so many lessons in football that apply to war," said Busik as he sat in a chair with a dusty scrapbook splayed across his lap. "That's why I think everyone on my team and everyone on the Army team who played in that great game in 1941 all distinguished themselves in war. Not only were we the best athletes, which naturally makes you a good soldier, but we were also accustomed to facing adversity, accustomed to finding answers to problems that at first seem like they can't be solved.

"On the football field, you learn about hard work, perseverance, toughness, and so many other things that apply to your experience on the battlefield. We were officers in the war, but really, we were just kids in our early twenties. But most of us were put in charge of hundreds of soldiers. It's much easier to deal with that kind of responsibility once you've had the experience of playing football in front of 100,000 people. Now that's *real* pressure."

. . .

"YOU REALLY DON'T NEED TO COME HERE TODAY," said the gravelly voice over my cell phone in November 2002. "I'm nobody special. I was just a guy doing his job."

"I'll only take a few minutes of your time," I insisted. "Five minutes, Hal. That's all I need. I've driven from New York City."

"Okay, I'll buzz you through the gate when you get here," he wearily replied.

So began my introduction to Hal Kauffman in the autumn of 2002. Kauffman wasn't feeling well—he'd nearly died in a car accident a few years earlier—but he greeted me at the door of his Annapolis condominium with a friendly smile. Like Bill Busik, Hal was eighty-four years old now. His health was failing; he had trouble walking and his skin was sallow. After saying hello, we sat down in his living room. I turned on my tape recorder and nonchalantly asked, "So, what can you tell me about the war?" Five hours later, I asked my second question.

As Hal spoke, he leaned back in his chair, and, with a faraway look in his eyes, he gazed out a window at the fading afternoon light. The stories then spilled out of his mouth like water out of a hose, not in drips and drabs, but in a rapid, steady flow. The events he recalled—the cross-country train ride with Bill Busik in 1939, the Army-Navy game of 1941, the sinking of the U.S.S. *Meredith* in 1942—all happened over sixty years ago, but the most intricate details of each experience were still vividly lodged in his mind, as if it all happened five minutes ago.

When he talked about the horror of the *Meredith* sinking, his eyes began leaking tears. My heart sank. I suggested we take a break, but Kauffman kept talking through his tears, telling me how happy he was that somebody was finally asking him to tell the harrowing story of the *Meredith*. "We were helpless in the water and the Japanese still tried to kill us when they strafed the water," Hal told me as he grabbed my hand tightly and inched closer to me. "You don't ever forget something like that. Never. It's pure evil."

After the war Hal earned an advanced degree in electronic engineering at the Massachusetts Institute of Technology (MIT) in 1949. From 1954 to '58, he served in the Bureau of Ships at the Navy Department in Washington, D.C. There he was the Preliminary Design Assistant in charge of designing the U.S.S. *Enterprise*, the world's first nuclear-powered aircraft carrier. In June 1956, he was elevated to the Project Coordinator for the Contract Design work on the *Enterprise*. He retired from the Navy in

1969 and currently lives in Annapolis. His wife Lois—the girl he first saw in his 10th grade English class and was immediately enchanted by— died several years ago. Once in a while he'll see Busik, who lives just a few miles away, and they'll recall some of the good times they've spent to- gether. Their friendship is going on sixty-five years now, and both men swear that the other one is the bravest man on the planet.

"I wasn't the biggest or the fastest or the strongest guy on the Navy football team, but I always figured I was more determined than anyone on the field," Hal says as he looks at his Naval Academy yearbook from 1941. "I basically never played, but what coach Swede Larson and all the other coaches taught me really helped me survive the *Meredith* sinking. They always demanded that you be disciplined, smart, and strong. There was always this expectation that you'd get the job done. Soon, all of us started to believe that we would get the job done, no matter what the circumstances.

"It was the same thing with the *Meredith*. I wasn't going to die. I just wasn't. I didn't even let myself think of that. I expected to get through it. So even when the sharks were attacking and men were getting eaten, I told myself that these sharks can go to hell, that I wasn't going to let them take me. I fought with all I had, and that's why I survived. I never gave in. Some guys lost it mentally. But I stayed mentally and physically strong. I think that all went back to my experience of playing football at Navy."

THE DOOR TO HIS STEAMBOAT, COLORADO, home swung open, and suddenly there he was, still big enough to cast an intimidating shadow. Robin Olds led me up a flight of stairs and into his living room, passing framed photographs that collaged the walls and told the story of his military career. Near the entry was a photograph of Olds in 1945 standing in front of a P-38, his young face looking at the camera with the intensity of a man about to do battle. Upstairs was a picture from 1967. In that black-and-white print Olds, a colonel by then, has a walrus mustache and is dressed in a flight suit. He was serving in Vietnam, where he would ultimately down four enemy MiGs, including two on May 20, 1967.

I visited Olds in July of 2002. He was eighty years old and still looked as if he was as tough as the hulking twenty-year-old Army football player he once was. Though his aching knees gave a twenty-one-gun salute of pops and creaks every time he sat down, he was in fine health. "I've had an incredibly interesting life," said Olds as he sat in a recliner in his living room, reviewing in his mind all that he had seen in his eighty years. "I wouldn't change a thing—except maybe beating Navy back in 1941. That loss still rubs me the wrong way."

After World War II ended, Olds began flying P-80 jets at March Field in California in February 1946 with the first squadron equipped to do so. Two years later he participated in the U.S. Air Force and Royal Air Force exchange program and served as Commander of the No. 1 Fighter Squadron at RAF Tangmere. When he moved to England, Olds took his new wife with him, a famous Hollywood actress named Ella Raines. Best known for her role as the heroine in the 1943 film noir *Phantom Lady*, Raines fell hard for Olds when they met on a double blind date—though they weren't set up with each other. "Ella was a movie star, a big celebrity," recalls Olds, smiling like he was just laying his eyes on Ella for the first time. "She made about twenty films and she even starred opposite John Wayne in *Tall in the Saddle*. We had a ball together in our early years. She'd join me in England and then she'd have to fly back to Hollywood for a few months to do another movie. But we parted company in 1975. It just didn't work out."

Though Olds didn't see any combat in the Korean War—from 1955 to '65 he commanded two wings in Europe—in September 1966 he assumed command of the 8th Tactical Fighter Wing at Ubon, Thailand. He was a forty-four-year-old colonel by then, but still flew with the determination of a young pilot. By the time he returned to the United States in December 1967 to become Commandant of Cadets at the U.S. Air Force Academy, Olds was credited with four confirmed kills in Vietnam. (For his career, Olds had sixteen confirmed kills—twelve in World War II and four in Vietnam.)

Olds retired from the Air Force on June 1, 1973—exactly thirty-two years and eleven months after he first reported to West Point. "It's funny how all the lessons that Earl Blaik taught us on the practice field had a real application to fighting in war," says Olds, as he steps out of his kitchen after making two peanut-butter-and-jelly sandwiches. "If I had to build an Army, I would start by selecting football players from West Point. There's no one in the world that's more prepared to fight and lead men than an Army football player. I really believe that."

THE WORDS ARE WRITTEN in a delicate, deliberate scrawl. They are dated April 5, 2004, and they came to me in a letter from Henry Romanek.

"Death has always been tough on me," wrote Romanek at age eighty-two from his home in Honolulu, Hawaii. "I've seen hundreds of our young men cut down by enemy fire—rifles, machine guns, artillery. I've listened to their cries for help; they always cry for their mothers, never for their fathers. There are rare displays of bravado before battle, but usually there is just quietness, reflection and fear of what's to come. . . . Football games can and have been very intense for me. I've witnessed many injuries on the football field, but never the death and destruction that I have seen on the battlefield."

One day in the spring of 2003, I phoned Henry Romanek, having no idea what his World War II experience had been like. After speaking to Romanek for just five minutes, I realized that I had just stumbled upon an historical treasure of a man—and a true American hero.

The next day we spoke for eight hours over the phone—the first of many conversations we would have. He detailed his childhood, his days at West Point, his interactions with Coach Red Blaik, his experiences in the Army-Navy games, and then we talked about D-day. His words and descriptions of what happened on that civilization-altering day—rehashing it moment by moment, second by second—painted such a vivid description it was as if I could see it all unfold in my mind. He broke down a few times as he spoke, but like Hal Kauffman when he talked to me about the U.S.S. *Meredith* disaster, Romanek insisted on continuing. He had a story to tell, and he wouldn't stop speaking until he was finished—simple as that.

After the war Romanek attended Cornell University and earned a master's degree in Engineering. Romanek then steadily rose through the ranks. Romanek was first assigned to the N.C. State College in Raleigh, N.C., where for three years he created and implemented a corps of engineering ROTC program. (Many of the men he trained were ultimately sent to Korea.) In 1951 he became the officer in charge of the Inter-American Geodetic Survey Project in Cuba, a position he held for three years. From 1960 to '61, he was the Battalion Commander, 307th Engineering Battalion, of the 82nd Airborne Division based in Fort Bragg, North Carolina. He retired from the Army in August 1971. His wife Betsy, the girl of his dreams that he met while in prep school, died on July 2, 1996.

"It's hard for me to dig up these old memories and talk about them, but I want to honor everyone I served with, so it's something I don't mind doing," says Romanek, sitting in his home in Honolulu with a copy of Stephen Ambrose's *D-Day* resting on his lap. "Some of the best experiences of my life involved playing football at Army. There's nothing like running onto a field and having 100,000 fans scream and cheer. The one bad thing is that I still have nightmares about how I failed to score a touchdown after I recovered a fumble in the 1941 Army-Navy game. It's amazing, but I still think about that one play all the time.

"There's no doubt that playing football under Blaik helped prepare me to fight in the war. I think the world of the American soldier. I saw more bravery on D-Day than I thought possible. Men kept charging forward even though they knew they'd likely be shot and killed. It was incredible. To this day, it makes me proud to be an American, what all of us did on that day."

SHE WAS DECKED IN RED, white, and blue bunting, and her signal flags flapped in the warm spring breeze. It was March 18, 1995, and a guided missile destroyer was being commissioned at Pier 12 at the Naval Station in Norfolk, Virginia. The ship was christened the U.S.S. *Laboon* in honor of the late Captain John Francis Laboon, known as "Father Jake" throughout the Navy. Cardinal John O'Conner of New York, one of Laboon's closest friends, told a crowd when the U.S.S. *Laboon* was launched two years earlier at Maine's Bath Iron Works, "He was both Mr. Navy and Mr. Church," the cardinal said. "He treated a seaman as respectfully as he treated an admiral. May you of the *Laboon* be assured that if Father Jake has the influence in heaven that he had in the Navy, you will always be blessed with fair winds and following seas."

Laboon, who was awarded the Silver Star for rescuing that downed pilot and pulling him safely aboard the submarine U.S.S. *Peto* in July 1945, left the Navy at the end of war and became a Jesuit Priest. In 1958, Father Laboon returned to the Navy and over the next twenty-one years he served in almost every branch of the Navy and Marine Corps. He was the first chaplain assigned to a ballistic missile submarine squadron and eventually became the first chaplain for the Polaris Submarine Program. Later he was named the Senior Catholic Chaplain at the Naval Academy. Today the Academy's Chaplain's Center is named in Laboon's honor. He passed away in 1988.

ALAN SHAPLEY RECOVERED QUICKLY from nearly being killed on the morning that the Japanese rained death down on Pearl Habor. Two days after the surprise attack, Shapley sailed to San Diego to become personnel officer to the Amphibious Corps, Pacific Fleet. During the war,

Shapley was awarded two Legion of Merits with Combat "V" for outstanding service. He went on to have a decorated career in the Marines, retiring at the rank of lieutenant general in 1962. He died May 13, 1973.

Throughout the years, Shapley stayed in contact with Earl Nightengale, the sailor who Shapley saved from drowning at Pearl Harbor—an act that earned Shapley one of the first Silver Star Medals awarded in World War II. After the war, Nightengale landed a job at the radio station KTAR in Phoenix. A few years later Nightengale went to work for CBS radio in Chicago, and he quickly became one of the most famous voices of his day. He was perhaps best known as the voice of Sky King, a radio hero that kids all around the country would tune in and listen to during the mid-50s. In 1985 Nightengale was inducted into The Radio Hall of Fame. He died in 1989.

THEY GATHERED AT THE WEST POINT cemetery on a sunny September morning in 1999, standing around a marble tombstone in the shape of a football. To pay respect to the man who remains the most successful coach in the history of Army football, forty-one of Earl "Red" Blaik's former players from the 1940s visited their old coach's grave just hours before the field at Army's Michie Stadium was renamed "Blaik Field." "Blaik was the most challenging and demanding person I ever met," said Doug Kenna, the quarterback of the '44 team, to the crowd that day in 1999. "But he was also the most caring person I ever knew."

From 1941 to 1958, Blaik led Army to a 121-33-10 record. He won two national championships, coached three Heisman Trophy winners, and to this day is Army's winningest coach, boasting a .768 winning percentage. In 1986 President Ronald Reagan awarded Blaik the Presidential Medal of Freedom. Three years later, Blaik died at the age of ninety-two.

ACKNOWLEDGMENTS

DURING THE THREE YEARS that I worked on this book, I frequently spoke to my dad over the phone, telling him the stories that I was uncovering in the course of my reporting. He was riveted by all these tales, and he told me repeatedly that he couldn't wait to read the final product. Then, on April 13, 2003, my dad passed away, unexpectedly, at age sixty-four. He served for forty-three years in the U.S. Navy, retiring at the rank of commander JAGC, and he loved his country dearly. This book is dedicated to him and all the brave Americans who lay by his side at Arlington National Cemetery in Arlington, Virginia.

Dozens of people assisted me in completing this project, but no one lent a more helpful hand than Sara Anderson, my dream of a wife. An editor at *Southern Living* magazine and a veteran of *Redbook*, Sara pored over two versions of the manuscript and her graceful, line-by-line edits improved the book immeasurably. Thanks again, SP. I also bow my head to my mother-in-law, Pat Peterson, who preaches—and practices—the gospel of proper grammar. Her keen eye caught several mistakes.

Along with thanking Bill Busik, Hal Kauffman, Robin Olds, and Henry Romanek for all the time they spent with me, I want to express my gratitude to the following former Army and Navy players who dredged their memories at my insistence: George Seip, John Stahle, John Buckner, Raymond Murphy, George Maxon, Robert Pearce, Charles Sampson, Fred Schnurr, William Leahy, Robert Day, Richard Fedon, Arthur Knox, John Hill, and Alexander Zechella. I also want to acknowledge Swede Larson Jr., Lynn Chewning, and Father Joseph Laboon for speaking with me and providing old scrapbooks and pictures of their loved ones who have passed away.

My agent, Scott Waxman, once again proved to be invaluable. Not only was he a 50-50 partner in developing the idea for this book, but he's also become a good friend. Neal Bascomb, a gifted writer and author, also helped me at the very beginning, offering insightful suggestions on structure and pace.

The enthusiasm of my editor at St. Martin's, Marc Resnick, kept this project moving along. This is the second book that I've collaborated on with Marc, and his big-picture suggestions are always right on the money. He's also become a trusted friend.

My colleagues at *Sports Illustrated* were all supportive of this project. I especially want to thank David Bauer, Sandy Rosenbush, Larry Burke, Rich O'Brien, Hank Hersch, Mark Mravic, David Sabino, and Richard Deitsch for all they've done for me over the years. Pete McEntegart, a loyal friend and fellow *SI* writer, deftly edited the manuscript; Pete's fingerprints are all over what you now hold in your hands.

Others who helped or inspired along the way are Paul Stillwell, a historian who is an expert on the U.S.S. *Arizona*; Russ McCurdy, a U.S.S. *Arizona* survivor; Keith Shirk, a World War II veteran; Sandy Padwe, an instructor at the Columbia University Graduate School of Journalism; Samantha Anderson, my nifty niece; and three people who all died too young: Captain Ray Heese of Lincoln, Nebraska; University of Nebraska Professor Theodore B. Wright of Lincoln, Nebraska; and my good friend who was also my-father-in-law, Bruce Peterson, of Holdredge, Nebraska.

My final thanks go to my mother, Rosanne Anderson. If there were a team that featured the great moms of the world, she'd be the captain.

Lars Anderson
Birmingham, Alabama
Spring 2004

BIBLIOGRAPHY

WHILE I CONSULTED hundreds of books, reference volumes, magazines, and newspaper articles, what follows is a list of sources that were most valuable.

BOOKS

Ambrose, Stephen E. *D-Day, June 6, 1944: The Climactic Battle of World War II*. New York: Touchstone Books, 1995.

Ambrose, Stephen E. *Eisenhower, Soldier and President*. New York: Simon & Schuster, 1990.

Bass, Richard T. *The Brigades of Neptunes: U.S. Army Engineer Special Brigades in Normandy*. Exeter, England: Lee Publishing, 1994.

Bealle, Morris Allison. *Gangway for Navy: The Story of Football at the United States Naval Academy, 1879 to 1950*. Washington, DC: Columbia Publishing Co., 1951.

Becton, F. Julian. *The Ship That Would Not Die*. Englewood Cliffs, NJ: Prentice-Hall Inc., 1980.

Bladwin, Hanson W. *Battles Lost and Won: Great Campaigns of World War II*. New York: Harper & Row, 1966.

Blaik, Earl "Red." *The Red Blaik Story*. New Rochelle, NY: Arlington House, 1960.

Boyne, Walter J. *Aces in Command: Fighter Pilots as Combat Leaders*. Washington, DC: Brassey's, 2001.

———. *Clash of Wings: World War II in the Air*. New York: Simon & Schuster, 1994.

Clary, Jack. *Army Vs. Navy: Seventy Years of Football Rivalry*. New York: The Ronald Press Company, 1965.

DeGregorio, William A. *The Complete Book of U.S. Presidents*. New York: Gramercy Books, 2002.

Desmond, Flower and James Reeves. *The War: 1939–1945*. London: Da Capo Press, 1960.

Glenn, Tom. *P-47 Pilots: The Fighter Bomber Boys*. Osceola, WI: MBI Publishing, 1998.

Greunke, Lowell R. *Football Rankings: College Teams in the Associated Press Poll, 1936–1984*. Jefferson, NC: McFarland, 1984.

Keegan, Jack. *The Second World War*. New York: Penguin Books, 1989.

King, Larry. *Love Stories of World War II*. New York: Crown Publishers, 2001.

Layton, Edwin, with Roger Pineau and John Costello. *And I Was There: Pearl Harbor and Midway: Breaking the Secrets*. New York: William Morrow, 1985.

McWilliams, Bill. *A Return to Glory*. Lynchburg, VA: Warwick House Publishers, 2000.

Morison, Samuel Eliot. *The Two Ocean War: A Short History of the United States Navy in the Second World War*. Boston: Little Brown, 1963.

Natkiel, Richard. *Atlas of 20th Century Warfare*. New York: W.H. Smith, 1982.

Prance, Gordon W. *At Dawn We Slept: The Untold Story of Pearl Harbor*. New York: Penguin Books, 1991.

Ryan, Cornelius. *The Longest Day: June 6, 1944*. New York: Touchstone, 1959.

Robinson, Robert. *Shipmates Forever: The Life, Death, and Men of the U.S.S. Meredith*. Self Published, 1990.

Schoor, Gene. *100 Years of Army-Navy Football*. New York: Henry Holt and Company, 1989.

Silverstone, Paul. *U.S. Warships of World War II*. Garden City: Doubleday, 1964.

Springer, Victor G., and Joy P. Gold. *Sharks in Question: The Smithsonian*

Answer Book. Washington, DC: The Smithsonian Institutue Press, 1989.

Stillwell, Paul. *Battleship* Arizona: *An Illustrated History*. Annapolis, MD: Naval Institue Press, 1991.

Van der Vat, Dan. *D-Day: The Greatest Invasion—A People's History*. London: Bloomsbury, 2003.

Wilson, Ian. *From Belfast Lough to D-Day: The U.S.S.* Texas. Bangor, Ireland: North Down Borough Council, 1994.

PERSONAL COLLECTIONS, which include scrapbooks, correspondence, newspaper articles, yearbooks, military documents, and military records.

Bob Adrian, former Navy player.

John Buckner, former Army player.

Bill Busik, former Navy player.

Lynn Chewning, brother of former Navy player Bill Chewning.

Robert Day, former Navy player.

Robert Evans, former Army player.

Richard Fedon, former Navy player.

Hal Kauffman, former Navy player.

Art Knox, former Navy player.

Joe Laboon, brother of former Navy player Jake Laboon.

Swede Larson, Jr., son of former Navy coach Swede Larson.

William Leahy, former Navy player.

Joe Maloy, nephew of former Navy player Jake Laboon.

Rip Miller, deceased Navy assistant coach, courtesy Bill Busik.

Raymond P. Murphy, former Army player.

Robin Olds, former Army player.

Henry Romanek, former Army player.

Charles Sampson, former Army player.

John Stahle, former Army player.

Fred Schnurr, former Navy player.

George Seip, former Army player.

Vito Vittucci, former Navy player.

MISCELLANEOUS

Ewing, William H. "High Dive Off the Mainmast: When the *Arizona* Blew Up, It Flung Major Alan Shapley in a Wild Arc into the Harbor." *The Honolulu Star-Bulletin.* December 12, 1961.

Videotape of 1941 Army-Navy Game, courtesy Nimitz Library Archives, United States Navel Academy.

A Guide to the United States Naval Academy. New York: The Devin-Adair Company, 1941.

Bell, Frederick J. *Condition Red: Destroyer Action in the South Pacific*. New York: Longmans, Green and Co., 1943.

Robinson, Robert. *The Life and Death of the U.S.S.* Meredith: *A Tribute to Those Who Died and A Search for Those Who Survived*. The Tin Can Sailor, January 1990.

Telander, Rick. "A Very Singular Way to Play." *Sports Illustrated*, September 20, 1982.

Tucker, Ajax. *Coral Sea Episode*. Self-published memoir concerning the sinking of the U.S.S. *Meredith*.

Time magazine, "The Long Grey Line," June 11, 1945.

Army-Navy Game Program, 1939.

Army-Navy Game Program, 1940.

Army-Navy Game Program, 1941.

Army-Navy Game Program, 1942.

Army-Navy Game Program, 1991.

The Log, Football Issue. October 3, 1941, United States Naval Academy.

Walters, John. "The Offense That Refuses to Die: Disciples of the Single Wing Loudly Sing its Praises and Seek Converts." *Sports Illustrated*, October 5, 1998.

The Dreadnought: Newsletter of the Battleship *Texas* Foundation. Volume 3, Number 2, Fall 2000. Feature article. "The *Texas* Crew Returns."

AUTHOR'S NOTE

I'LL NEVER FORGET the day I first watched an Army-Navy football game. I was only seven years old, and my father had been telling me for weeks about how special this game between the academies was. So on game day we plopped down on the couch in front of the television in our Lincoln, Nebraska, home. My dad explained to me how these young men would soon be defending our country, how they were giving the next years of their lives to America. His eyes welled up at the end of the game when the Army and Navy players met at midfield and embraced. This, he told me, was sport at its finest. Twenty-six years later, those words still ring true. This is why I wanted to write this book.

When I started working on this project in the spring of 2001, I had no idea what direction it would go. All I had in my hands were two pieces of paper—one from the sports information office at West Point, one from the sports information office at Annapolis—that listed all the telephone numbers of the surviving members of the 1941 Army and Navy football squads. But when I tracked down Bill Busik, Hal Kauffman, Robin Olds, and Henry Romanek, I knew I had stumbled upon a special story.

More than sixty years have passed since the main events of this book occurred. In the course of researching this project, I consulted hundreds of published works, conducted hours of personal interviews, and examined dozens of personal materials such as diaries and scrapbooks provided by all the main characters. But still, discrepancies did emerge. In these cases, I analyzed all the relevant material and went with what I believed to be the most accurate information. Nonetheless, if there are any errors in this book, they are solely my responsibility.

A word about Bill Busik, Hal Kauffman, Robin Olds, and Henry Romanek: I owe a great debt to these four American heroes. They spent countless hours with me—both in person and over the phone—reliving the good as well as the terrible times from their youth. Their generosity was heart warming, as all four of these men treated me like I was a curious grandson. Without their assistance, this book would not have been possible. So thank you, Bill, Hal, Robin, and Henry. This is not my book; this is your book.